Language Change
in South American
Indian Languages

Edited by
Mary Ritchie Key

upp

University of Pennsylvania Press
Philadelphia

Copyright © 1991 by the University of Pennsylvania Press
"Southern Peruvian Quechua Consonant Lenition" copyright © 1991 by Bruce Mannheim
ALL RIGHTS RESERVED
Printed in the United States of America

Library of Congress Cataloging-in-Publication Data

Language change in South American Indian languages / edited by Mary Ritchie Key.
    p.   cm.
    Includes bibliographical references and index.
    ISBN 0-8122-3060-4
    1. Indians of South America—Languages—Classification.   2. Indians
of South America—Languages—Grammar.   3. Linguistic change.
4. Comparative linguistics.   I. Key, Mary Ritchie.
PM5008.L36   1991
498—dc20   90-26311
                                      CIP

Contents

Foreword

Historical and comparative work on South American indigenous languages is a great source of insight. No special plea ought to be needed to justify their study as phenomena in the physical and social world: if anything is worth analyzing and understanding it is human speech in its fabulous diversity—a diversity which has always existed but which in our days is exposed to radical diminution, not unlike the threat faced by living species.

In addition, linguists have commonly neglected South American languages, to the detriment of their craft. This is particularly true when it comes to classification and reconstruction and the ethnohistorical and archaeological interpretation which those two activities allow. An understanding of the difference between classification by resemblance or *type* ("comparative" in the ordinary sense) and by genesis or *filiation* ("comparative" in the special, professional sense) needs large geographical areas and great diversification to be feasible and convincing; and what better universe to explore than that immense region which is mercifully free of much of the intellectual folklore that must be first combatted in other parts of the world?

With regard, in particular, to the genealogical classification by filiation, we are offered an opportunity to satisfy a concrete, technical interest. Some thinkers of the past and present, including some of the most imposing and influential nineteenth-century comparativists, have thought that the methods for the reconstruction of Proto-Indo-European, much admired and indeed much worth admiring in their concreteness and coherence, could be special rather than general; that is, they might not be applicable to all languages. This is certainly not so, as has been shown (insofar as such a thing is possible) both deductively and empirically. But another question does arise: to what extent does the prevalence of given typological traits in given languages and language families in given areas yield more or fewer surprising, chronologically penetrating, and generally speaking, interpretable results?

No investigator can remain untouched by these thoughts, doubts, and hopes. This is why we profoundly and gratefully welcome the present undertaking.

Henry M. Hoenigswald
Franklin C. Southworth

Acknowledgments

The linguistic debt that the academic world owes is first of all to the native speakers of the languages that make up the data basic to our discipline. This volume and all useful linguistic work could not have been produced without the cooperation and dedication of the speakers of these beautiful and intriguing languages. In this volume, we recognize the expertise of Juana Cabral de Carripilón, Veneranda Cabral de Cabral, Marcelina Baigorrita, and Juana Carripí de Lima, speakers of Ranquel; Professor Francisco Tandioy J., José Chasoy Sijindioy, Miguel Cuatindioy C., Jacinto Garreta, Otilia Jamioy Y. de Peña, and Luis Manuel Tandioy T., speakers of Inga (Quechuan); Don Andrés Ramos, speaker of Atacama (= Cunza); among many others.

Comparative linguistic work is also indebted to the scholars who produced the descriptive works that make comparisons possible. Dictionaries and word lists are invaluable sources of data, without which comparative work would not be possible. The selected bibliography at the end of this volume lists only some of the scholars who have given us the foundation for our work.

I also express our appreciation to the many readers behind the scenes who have contributed to make this volume more accurate and valuable. In a more public way, the Instituto Caro y Cuervo, Bogotá, Colombia, deserves our thanks. The Director, Ignacio Chaves Cuevas, and Coordinator, María Luisa Rodríguez de Montes, conducted the 1988 seminar, "Estado Actual de la Clasificación de las Lenguas Indígenas Colombianas." They brought together scholars from about eight countries who summarized the knowledge of their respective families. These papers are also listed in the bibliography at the end of the volume. The impact of the seminar will long be felt.

My thanks to the authors who contributed to this volume, to Diane Enders of the linguistics office of the University of California at Irvine, and to all who offered help and encouragement along the way.

I

Introduction

Mary Ritchie Key

A Résumé of Comparative Studies in South American Indian Languages

Comparative studies of South American languages can contribute to our knowledge of language change that results from people distancing themselves in time and space from each other. This collection of articles by authorities on South American Indian languages treats some of the problems of change in sounds and grammar, aspects of change that are the indispensable background for understanding migrations and language classifications.

Background

Matters of similarities and differences have intrigued and baffled devotees of language probably since the first times that people gathered around philosophizing about themselves and their thoughts. Every intelligent speaker may observe that "they talk differently down around the bend of the river." The historical world as Westerners know it began recording these observations rather late in human history. Texts on the history of linguistics note that the Classicists remarked about language differences. The first several centuries of the Christian era in Europe give us very few glimpses of the intellectual world making statements about relationships between languages. Percival notes, for example, "It is thought that the first clear statement of the relationship between Hebrew and Arabic was made by Yehuda Ibn Quraysh of Tahort in North Africa, a Jewish physician who is usually assumed to have flourished at the end of the ninth century and the beginning of the tenth" (1987:30). A few centuries later, shortly after the New World was discovered again, this time by Columbus, observations about similarities and relatedness began in serious. What we know about languages in the early history of linguistics comes from people who were fascinated with languages. These observers were not trained linguists by any means, and it is to the credit of the remarkable human brain that some of this information displays a brilliance of insight. No matter that their occupations were varied: lawyers, statesmen, naturalists, physicians, and clergymen contributed, along with travelers and adventurers. It is of interest to note that even our more recent linguistics has been enriched by scholars and investigators such as Benjamin Whorf, with primary occupations other than linguistics.

Some early works appear to be just listings of languages: Gesner the naturalist organized *Mithridates* (1555) in much the same way that he organized his specimens. Still others grouped languages in classificatory style: Scaliger (1599) divided the languages of Europe into four major and seven minor classes. These earliest studies did not yet include American languages, though grammars were produced in the sixteenth century for some South American languages (Tovar and Tovar 1984).

It would be another century before data from native American languages would be seriously worked into scholarly studies. Then language classifications began to be used in order to answer such questions as "Where did the Indian come from?" (Greene 1960:511). A scholar of oriental languages, Adrian Reland (1708), examined various Indian languages: the Brazilian, the Peruvian, the Chilian, the Pocoman, the Carib, the Mexican, the Virginian, the Algonkin, and the Huron, and, to no one's surprise, concluded that if any relation is recognized between the languages of the two hemispheres, it must be sought after among the languages of Asia (Haven 1856:56). Remarkably, Reland's dissertation was written even before the Bering Strait was discovered. Other observers had other ideas, based on their own experiences and perspectives, respectively. The history of comparative linguistics, perhaps especially with regard to the enigmatic American Indian, shows that perspectives have more to do with the experiences and personalities of the observers than with actual facts. In particular, distortions and prejudices of the work often reflected simply the sociology of the times. Edward Brerewood, for example, wrote about the "diversity of languages" in 1614 and affirmed that "the Spanish, Italian, and French tongues are but the latine depraved, and corrupted by the inundation of the Gothes, and Vandals over the southerne partes of Europe" (Brerewood 1614, Preface).

Through the eighteenth century, comparisons of languages continued to be made—sometimes between two languages, sometimes among many, and sometimes between families of languages.

Catherine the Great embarked upon a comparison project in a grand style. She determined to compare all the known languages of the world and group them according to their similarities, thus producing the first comparative study on a global scale. She prepared a word list and sent copies around the world through diplomatic channels. As the lists were returned, she analyzed them and grouped the languages together by the inspection method. She commissioned Pallas to edit her research, which was published in 1786–89 under his name (Key 1977, 1980).

The next stage of comparative studies came into full bloom at the turn of the century. Sound correspondences had been noticed before, but the work of Rask, Grimm, Bopp, and others brought comparative linguistics into its glorious light. Scholars of American Indian languages now benefit from this heritage.

Early in the nineteenth century, investigators scurried for word lists of Indian languages, probably stimulated by Catherine's request to George Washington (see Key 1980). Peter Duponceau (1830:76) was proud that the languages he had studied ranged from "Greenland to Cape Horn," the southern extremity of South America. A collection of vocabularies from seventy-three languages is on file at the American Philosophical Society in Philadelphia, with South American languages included (Freeman 1962:537). Benjamin Barton's (1797) comparative list also included South American languages. Duponceau (1830:90–91) later announced that the United States government was preparing to publish a national work "on the model considerably improved of that of the empress Catherine," but I have not found any evidence of it. The matter of orthography immediately presented itself as a problem because of sounds in the New World languages that do not occur in Indo-European languages, so John Pickering wrote a detailed discussion of a "uniform orthography" (1821).

Duponceau indeed studied the Indian languages assiduously and influenced the recording and writing grammars of these heretofore unknown tongues, "confident that their development will contribute much to the improvement of the science of universal grammar" (1819:370). He was familiar with the writings of the celebrated mathematician Maupertuis (1750), who wrote on the origins of language and recommended studying the Indian languages "because we may chance to find some that are formed on new plans of ideas" (Duponceau 1819:370; Haven 1856:55–56). Duponceau had so steeped himself in the Indian languages that he recognized that the usual linguistic terminology could not suffice for describing the intricacies of the grammars; he is known for devising terms such as *polysyn-*

thetic to handle new constructions (Pickering 1831:599; Edgerton 1943:29). It is still true that the languages of the New World offer much to the Western world in the way of expressing nuances and representations of other world views. It is also true that orthographical problems still exist today and become even more formidable with the application of the computer to comparative studies. To illustrate, I use an example from the Mapuche language of Chile, which has historical documents dating back four hundred years. My files contain three recordings for the word 'ribbon, band' (*fajita*): *guton, nitrohue,* and *nguchrohue.* The letters g, n, and ng were used for the sound ŋ; u = i; t = chr = tʳ (the retroflexed stop); o = o; the verbal suffix *-n* is deleted when another suffix is added. In the recording of this morpheme, then, only one orthographic symbol is the same in all three recordings.

At about the same time as the advances of the first part of the nineteenth century, naturalist Alexander Humboldt was gathering information from the Amazon region to send to his brother Wilhelm in Germany, who pored over the linguistic data that changed theoretical discussions. Alexander candidly documented fieldwork difficulties—which even today hamper the flow of good linguistic material into the coffers of theoretical buildings—when he wrote that "it is impossible not to be constantly disturbed by the moschettoes, zancudoes, jejens, and tempraneroes, that . . . pierce the clothes with their long sucker . . . and, getting into the mouth and nostrils, set you coughing and sneezing" (McIntyre 1985:330).

One of the earliest comparative studies attempted in South America, concerning the Arawakan languages, was conducted by Felipe Salvador Gilij (1780–84). Gilij recognized sound correspondences among three of the languages—what he called "una coherencia mayor"—in the following examples (Gilij 1782:173):

Español	*maipure*	*güipunave*	*cávere*
tabaco	*yema*	*dema*	*shema*
monte	*yapa*	*dapa*	*shapa*

The significance of Gilij's work is apparent when one realizes that it predated the unfolding of comparative linguistics that was to occur in the following century. It was a time that marked the awakening of the scientific world, where rigorous methodology became requisite. It was also a time that saw the compilation of the first encyclopedias, wherein all the knowledge of the world was to be brought together.

Don Lorenzo Hervás y Panduro, for example, attempted to pack all that goes into the "Idea dell'universo" into six volumes, published in 1784–87. The languages of South America are discussed in his first volume. Hervás y Panduro's insights were remarkable. Though not without mistakes (which could only be recognized after the work of the nineteenth-century philologists), his discussion carries sound judgments and thoughtful advice. He commented about the possibilities of "chance" similarities between languages (Hervás y Panduro 1800:53); he emphasized the criterion of using both sound and meaning when choosing resemblances of vocabulary items (47); and he noted that these heretofore unwritten languages needed to have an alphabet of their own—the letters invented for Latin would not suffice for writing other languages (66). It is likely that his collection formed the major part of Wilhelm Humboldt's resources in American Indian languages.

Modern linguistics grew out of the comparative studies of the nineteenth century. That time of scholarly attempts to define races surely had its delimiting strictures on acceptance of observations of language resemblances. It is easy to look back over the two centuries of descriptive and classificatory work and find mistakes. Errors resulted of course from linguistic naiveté—after all, the discipline was struggling to be a proper science and to be a respected part of academia. But we also recognize today that errors of classification resulted from the mistaken beliefs about races that dominated the thinking of previous centuries. It is incumbent on us to recognize that such errors may form part of our inherited thinking processes; and that we take a fresh look at language data that give us a better picture of the history of South America, Indian migrations and settlements, and origins.

In the last generation we witnessed a surge of interest in native American languages, partly because governments have taken a new look at their human resources and partly because the rapid development of linguistics has invigorated a whole new group of young scholars in the countries of Latin America. The latter resource is all the more precious because many of these nationals are native speakers of the languages we have come to appreciate and value; thus they enrich the discipline of linguistics with vital information on complex systems (see, for example, Derbyshire and Pullum 1986; Key 1987; Klein and Stark 1985; and Rodríguez de Montes, in press).

History of Classifications

With the Age of Enlightenment came the realization that languages could be grouped into families only if there was comparable material on which to base the groupings. The word lists used through the centuries were products of their times; topological groupings of related words gave order to the universe, reflecting the thinking of those times. Thus, the proper order of the universe began with God and heaven; followed by father and mother (the family); then the body parts (from the head down); natural phenomena, plants, animals, and so on.

Comenius (1659), an early scholar who used the topological arrangement, organized his word list vocabulary according to what was "obvious to the senses." The list begins with God and the world, and then moves on to man and the condition of man, including body parts and the soul. Further, Comenius admonished that teaching should be true, full, clear, and solid (Preface). Both Gilij and Catherine the Great, whose works were published in the same decade, used a similar type of listing (Key 1980 : 76– 87). Such an optimal word list, however, was not practical for dealing with the many languages that had minimal linguistic data. Therefore, Balbi's atlas (1826) grouped languages according to a published word list of twenty-six items. Brinton used an almost identical word list for his classification of *The American Race* (1891). By the middle of this century, more linguistic material was available, and Swadesh returned to a larger number of lexical items to be compared, that is, a two-hundred-word list he compiled (Swadesh 1955).

With remarkable exceptions such as Gilij's work (1782), much of the grouping of languages in the early days was done on the basis of geography. Some of these connections, of course, were correct, because related languages may be spoken in contiguous areas, such as French and Spanish or Tacanan and Panoan (of Bolivia and Peru). The latter are geographically close across connected political boundaries as well as within the countries. Daniel Brinton (1892) proposed seventy-three groups; Paul Rivet (1924) followed with seventy-seven; but Wilhelm Schmidt (1926) held to a smaller number of thirty-six (see Gray 1939 : 412–17). Čestmir Loukotka, who spent a lifetime working with South American languages, projected his groupings at ninety-four in 1935 and 117 in 1968. Rivet and Loukotka presented 108 families in Meillet and Cohen's 1952 revision of the languages of the world. Many of the "groups" consisted of a single language, so these numbers cannot really be equated with Antonio Tovar's groups, set forth in his 1961 *Catálogo,* which listed single languages as unclassified. Norman McQuown's comprehensive listing in 1955 was a similar type of work. Joseph Greenberg (1956 [1960], 1987) and Morris Swadesh reduced the number into "revolutionary regroupings" (see Key 1979, Chapter 2). For his encyclopedia article, Jorge Suárez (1982) conservatively returned to a format that resembled the earlier proposals: he classified eighty-two groups—many of them single languages.

Holger Pedersen wrote a few short paragraphs about the American languages in 1924 (trans. 1931) and noted a "dizzying complexity": "It is incredible that there should be no kinship at all among some of these; but a peculiar course of linguistic development may make it difficult to discover what the original relationships were" (137). The difficulties of classifying range from relatively "easy" to complex. "Easy" (or at least well definable) questions have to do with such issues as multiple naming systems—one does not always know exactly which language is being referred to if the term used means something like "people of the north." More complicated difficulties have to do with different sources for material or with library data versus field notes (differences between written and spoken language). I have discussed these and other difficulties in "Methodology and Problems of Research" (1979:15–18).

To understand the wide range of proposals of classifications outlined in the preceding paragraphs, it is necessary to take into account varying perspectives, a concept that can be summed up in the useful cliché that differentiates *lumpers* from *splitters.* It is likely that people have always had an attraction to observing *similarities:* note the large numbers of people who choose mates who resemble themselves. But there is also a fascination with *differences:* it is not uncommon for a person to marry someone who complements—the attraction of opposites. The stances taken by the lumpers and the splitters, of course, are doomed to conflict, and this should be taken as a healthy measure of the situation of dealing with the languages of the Americas. Productive research needs differences of opinion and the unremitting testing of ideas. At times this results in conflicts—difficult to explain to the nonacademic members of the community, who might believe that seeking truth makes for agreement and harmony. On the contrary, too much agreement can be stultifying; it can preclude revision and development.

Whatever the total number of enumerated families of the continent of South America, there are still questions to be asked regarding the relatedness, if any, between the families. The symposium held in Colombia in

February 1988 at the Instituto Caro y Cuervo (Rodríguez de Montes, in press), set some of the questions in order. Investigators of language relationships began to see that the issues are so complicated that it is difficult even to articulate the problems. To some, it was an initiation into the complexities of evaluating one classification over another. I am sure that all serious scholars experience a similar phenomenon when they begin their work: the problem does not appear as complicated at first as it turns out to be. The more we learn about a particular topic we choose to research, the more complexities become evident. If students of native language problems of South America had thought that comparative linguistic analyses would answer the problems and come up with a quick and neat classification of the some 36 to 117 languages and families, they are now aware of some of the realities behind the controversies. Notwithstanding, at the Colombian conference some useful questions were asked that lead the way to bring order to the unclassified mosaic of some 600 languages in South America (Trillos Amaya 1988:42): What urgent tasks face us as we try to make a satisfactory classification of the Indian languages? What are the problems that hinder these tasks? What are the differences of methodology in analyzing "languages" and "dialects"? What criteria should one take into account when choosing a standard variety of language? What direction is comparative linguistics taking in South America?

History of Early Comparative Work

The classificatory work summarized in the previous section was the harbinger for work that was to be done after the methodology of comparative linguistics was developed. As is well known, the discipline of comparative linguistics involving sound correspondences was rigorously developed in the nineteenth century, and the systematic nature of sound correspondences was spottily commented on as far back as the seventeenth century (Metcalf 1972:97), but the methodology was not generally available until the twentieth. The bibliography at the end of this volume treats the stages of comparative work on South American languages, including preliminary remarks, word lists, and other bibliographies. As is to be expected of the early stages of theory application, the articles and books are of an uneven quality. This may be due to technique, but it also may be due to availability of material from particular languages that would be crucial to finding sound correspondences and their distributions.

Systematic comparative studies in South American languages did not, of course, begin full-blown. In the 1940s and 1950s there were many articles that noted some sound correspondences and made comments about genetic relationships (references in Loriot 1964; Hoijer, Hamp, and Bright 1965). These contributions fortified the base of the earlier proposals about relatedness among the languages.

The 1960s were important, in that comparative methodology began to be applied to systems as a whole, beginning with Shafer (1959, 1962) on Arawak and Aruakan; followed by Moore (1962) on the reconstruction of Colorado and Cayapa; Key (1963, published in 1968) on Tacanan; Matteson (1964) on Arawakan; Noble (1965) on Arawakan; Shell (1965) on Panoan; Davis (1966) on Jê; Orr and Longacre (1968) on Quechuan. The blossoming of comparative linguistics continued in the 1970s, and the 1980s began with great promise with Constenla's comparative Chibchan study (1981). Furthermore the conference in Colombia in 1988 stimulated the systematic reconstruction of the language families of South America (Rodríguez de Montes, in press).

As far as distant relationships between North and South America are concerned, we can note the pioneering study of Chipaya and Mayan by Olson (1964, 1965). With hindsight, I feel that it was premature to posit proto sounds, but this does not diminish the importance of the study, which, I predict, will be used again in the future for looking at widespread phenomena. A generation ago, it was felt that actual reconstruction was essential for establishing a relationship. Historical scholars will remember, however, that although Jakob Grimm had not reconstructed proto forms in his early studies that recognized relationships in the Germanic family, this did not detract from the importance of observing the regularities between series of sounds. As a matter of fact, use of the asterisk (*) with a hypothetical reconstructed form was introduced much later (see Hoenigswald 1973:69 for discussions), though the concept of a proto-language goes back much farther—at least as far as Leibniz. Proto forms are a convenience; they are not facts. More recently, I dealt with this question at length and pointed out that it was not the hypothetical form that had substance; rather, it was the regularity of sets of sounds that held the proof of comparisons (Key 1983). If there is great distance between the languages—as, for example, there would appear to be with Mayan and Chipaya—other languages would have come in between, and reconstruction of proto forms should not be attempted. The missing links should be sought; but it is also possible that that part of history is lost, in which case it may be impossible to reconstruct the lost languages. Nevertheless, if regularity has been seen, it is worthwhile to note it. It is even possible that the regularities have to do with borrowing, and especially if this is so, the reconstructions should not be attempted.

Here I also add a note of caution in using the term "cognate," which should be reserved for those sets of lexical items that are proved to be etymologically related by completion of the tedious and time-consuming labor of reconstruction (Key 1983). Before that proof is laid out, we can refer to lexical "similarities" or "resemblances." Statements about regularity remain important, however, in that there is a common history behind borrowings. A final observation on the bibliography at the end of this volume has to do with the use of glottochronology. Important pioneering studies experimenting with techniques and methodologies were done on the Tupi-Guaraní and Ge/Jê languages by Rodrigues (1958) and Wilbert (1962), respectively.

As noted in the previous section, there probably have always been those who are able to see differences as against those who are better able to note similarities. Problems in linguistic classifications and relationships deal with the interpretations of these opposing views. Recent publications on comparative matters bring an invigorating outlook from the point of view of biological systems that show traits parallel with linguistic systems. The term introduced to linguistics is "cladistics" (Hoenigswald and Wiener 1987). This approach distinguishes between characteristics which are more recently derived and those which are relatively earlier—to identify the pattern of branching in the development of a linguistic group.

The future is for those scholars who will take recent developments, along with the ideas of the last two centuries, to explore and experiment with the application and modification of our inherited ideas and discoveries to the growing abundance of linguistic data on the native languages of South America.

Present Contributions

The focus of this book is on language change, particularly as it is seen in comparative studies. Its contributors include scholars who have done fieldwork and are presently active in research in the native languages of South America. They are or have been in close contact with actual speakers of languages discussed here, and they represent seven countries and several major research centers of South America.

The first chapters deal with problems of classification. Languages may be classified for various purposes into historical and typological as well as genetic groupings. Monod-Becquelin brings a cross-disciplinary perspective to the study of groupings, with rich insights from the French schools of research. Past comparative studies of the Tupi-Guaraní language family, which is among the oldest documented language groups, have been based on reliable descriptive work, and thus form a firm foundation for the work of Soares and Leite, who take the problem of vowel shift and suggest a reformulation of the proto system. Villalón treats the Cariban languages with the modern techniques of multidimensional scaling and then matches the results with information of pre-Columbian trade routes and migrations. Her work is thus relevant to the networks and movements of the people, as well as to the genetic relationships of the languages involved.

The next section includes case studies of several language groups. Garay, from Argentina, describes a Mapuche dialect in that country and compares it with the Mapuche (= Araucanian) dialects of Chile. Of particular interest is the change in the fricative series; these are illustrated in an accompanying word list. The Quechuan languages/dialects are represented by Mannheim's article, which moves both horizontally and vertically through the dialects, bringing to light illustrations from ancient manuscripts.

Grammatical markers are the focus of the next section. The Quechuan and Mapuche languages are again investigated for their grammatical differences, by Levinsohn and Salas respectively. Native Quechua speakers have contributed by providing an analyzed text to illustrate the tense-aspect markers in the Quechua language of Colombia.

The next topic dealt with is ethnolinguistics, as represented by an extinct language, Atacama (= Cunza) spoken until recently by a group of mountain people in northern Chile. Rodríguez compares a ceremonial chant recorded in mid-century with a version of the chant he recorded and analyzed a generation later.

The final section in this collection moves across the American continents to project possible distant relationships. Granberry plots the dialect boundaries of Timucua in Florida (North America) and traces language resemblances to languages of the northern part of South America. Several word lists are presented, illustrating grammatical markers and lexical similarities. The last chapter is contributed by Wistrand-Robinson, who has spent considerable time with the Comanche (Uto-Aztecan) and Panoan languages. She presents an exemplary word list of one hundred items, with selected representations from the Uto-Aztecan and Panoan families. Investigators will be able to work efficiently with examples that are pertinent to the particular comparisons. I have advocated presenting the data in such a manner so that researchers may decide for themselves whether or not an example is useful. Interested scholars may also expand the lists according to their own experiences. Also, I have suggested that word lists such as these, at the brainstorming stage of exploring new possibilities, should not be thought of or labeled "cognate" lists, for the reasons I have given above; they are instead intended to stimulate research and to expand on other possibilities.

As with all new ideas and "discoveries," it is appropriate to approach the resemblances presented here (and elsewhere) with healthy skepticism. At the same time, one should not make snap judgments without saturating oneself in the data. Since the first recordings of American Indian languages in the sixteenth century, resemblances have been noted among them and other languages. There is sufficient descriptive material now, in addition to reliable comparative studies, so that establishing connections is an altogether viable possibility. There is plenty of work to be done in the future by both kinds of thinkers: those researchers who see "resemblances" and those who justify "differences." In whichever camp the contributors of this collection reside, they have one thing in common: the desire that comparative work will proceed with dispatch.

REFERENCES

Balbi, Adrien
    1826   *Atlas ethnographique du globe*. Paris.

Barton, Benjamin Smith
    1797   *New Views of the Origin of the Tribes and Nations of America*. Philadelphia: John Bioren. 83 pages.

Brerewood, Edward
    1614   *Enquiries Touching the Diversity of Languages, and Religions through the Chief Parts of the World*. London: Gresham College. 198 pages.

Brinton, Daniel Garrison
    1891   *The American Race*. New York: N. D. C. Hodges. Reprinted New
    [1970] York: Johnson Reprint Corporation.
    1892   "Studies in South American native languages." Philadelphia: McCalla. Reprinted from *Proceedings of the American Philosophical Society* 30.

Comenius, Jan [Johann] Amos
    1659   *Orbis sensualium pictus* (A World of Things Obvious to the Senses:
    [1970]   Drawn in pictures). Reprinted Menston, England: Scolar Press.
Constenla Umaña, Adolfo
    1981   Comparative Chibchan phonology. Ph.D. dissertation, University of
            Pennsylvania. University Microfilms 8207943.
Davis, Irvine
    1966   "Comparative Jê phonology." *Estudos Lingüísticos* 1.2 : 10–24.
Derbyshire, Desmond C., and Geoffrey K. Pullum, eds.
    1986   *Handbook of Amazonian Languages,* vol. I. Berlin: Mouton de Gruyter.
    1990   *Handbook of Amazonian Languages,* vol. 2. Berlin: Mouton de Gruyter.
Duponceau, Peter S.
    1819   "A correspondence between The Rev. John Heckewelder, of Bethle-
            hem, and Peter S. Duponceau, Esq." *Transactions of the Historical and
            Literary Committee of the American Philosophical Society* 1 : 351–448.
    1830   "The translator's preface." *Transactions of the American Philosophical
            Society* 3, n.s.: 65–96.
Edgerton, Franklin
    1943   "Notes on early American work in linguistics." *Proceedings of the
            American Philosophical Society* 87.1 (July): 25–34.
Freeman, John Finley
    1962   "Manuscript sources on Latin American Indians in the library of the
            American Philosophical Society." *Proceedings of the American Philo-
            sophical Society* 106 : 530–40.
    1966   *A Guide to Manuscripts Relating to the American Indian in the Library
            of the American Philosophical Society.* Philadelphia: American Philo-
            sophical Society.
Gesner, Conrad
    1555   *Mithridates.* Zurich.
Gilij, Felipe Salvador
    1782   *Ensayo de historia Americana.* Trans. Antonio Tovar. Biblioteca de la
    [1965]   Academia Nacional de la Historia, Caracas: Fuentes para la Historia
            Colonial de Venezuela. Vol. III.
Gray, Louis H.
    1939   "Antillean and South American." *Foundations of Language,* pp. 412–
            17. New York: Macmillan.
Greenberg, Joseph H.
    1956   "The general classification of Central and South American lan-
    [1960]   guages." In *Men and Cultures,* 5th International Congress of Anthro-
            pological and Ethnological Sciences, ed. Anthony F. C. Wallace,
            pp. 791–94. Philadelphia: University of Pennsylvania Press.
    1987   *Language in the Americas.* Stanford, Calif.: Stanford University Press.
Greene, John C.
    1960   "Early scientific interest in the American Indian: comparative linguis-
            tics." *Proceedings of the American Philosophical Society* 104.5 (October):
            511–17.

Haven, Samuel F.
   1856   "Archaeology of the United States; or sketches, historical and biblio-
           graphical, of the progress of information and opinion respecting ves-
           tiges of antiquity in the United States." *Smithsonian Contributions to
           Knowledge* 8. Washington, D.C.: Smithsonian Institution.
Hervás y Panduro, Don Lorenzo
   1784–87 *Idea dell'universo*. Vol. I: *Catalogo delle lingue conosciute e notizia
           della loro affinita, e diversita*. Cesena: 1784.
   1800   *Catálogo de las lenguas de las naciones conocidas*. Vol. I: *Lenguas y
           naciones Americanas*. Madrid: Administración del Real Arbitrio de
           Beneficencia.
Hoenigswald, Henry M.
   1973   "Linguistics." In *Dictionary of the History of Ideas,* ed. Philip P. Wie-
           ner, Vol. III, pp. 61–73. New York: Charles Scribner's Sons.
Hoenigswald, Henry M. and Linda F. Wiener, eds.
   1987   *Biological Metaphor and Cladistic Classification*. Philadelphia: Univer-
           sity of Pennsylvania Press.
Hoijer, Harry, Eric P. Hamp, and William Bright
   1965   "Contributions to a bibliography of comparative Amerindian." *Inter-
           national Journal of American Linguistics* 31.4 (October): 346–53.
Key, Mary Ritchie
   1968   *Comparative Tacanan Phonology: With Cavineña Phonology and Notes
           on Pano-Tacanan Relationship*. The Hague: Mouton.
   1976   "Lingüística comparativa y sincrónica: Método y perspectivas." *Es-
           tudios Filológicos* 11, pp. 103–12. Universidad Austral de Chile, Valdi-
           via, Chile.
   1977   "The Linguistic Discoveries of Catherine the Great." In *The Third
           LACUS Forum 1976,* ed. R. J. DiPietro and E. L. Blansitt, pp. 39–45.
           Columbia, S.C.: Hornbeam Press.
   1979   *The Grouping of South American Indian Languages*. Ars Linguistica,
           2. Tübingen: Gunter Narr.
   1980   *Catherine the Great's Linguistic Contribution*. Edmonton, Alberta,
           Canada: Linguistic Research, Inc.
   1983   "Comparative methodology for distant relationships in North and
           South American languages." *Language Sciences* 5.2 (October): 133–54.
———, ed.
   1987   *Comparative Linguistics of South American Indian Languages*. Special
           Issue, *Language Sciences* 9.1 (April): 1–117.
Klein, Harriet E. Manelis and Louisa R. Stark, eds.
   1985   *South American Indian Languages: Retrospect and Prospect*. Austin:
           University of Texas Press.
Loriot, James
   1964   "A selected bibliography of comparative American Indian linguis-
           tics." *International Journal of American Linguistics* 30.1 (January):
           62–80.

Loukotka, Čestmir
  1935   *Clasificación de las lenguas sudamericanas.* Prague: Josef Bartl.
  1968   *Classification of South American Indian Languages,* ed. Johannes Wilbert. Latin American Center Reference Series, vol. 7. Los Angeles: University of California.
McIntyre, Loren
  1985   "Pioneer of modern geography: Humboldt's way." *National Geographic* 168.3 (September): 318–51.
McQuown, Norman A.
  1955   "The indigenous languages of Latin America." *American Anthropologist* 57.3 (June): 501–70.
Matteson, Esther
  1964   "Algunas afiliaciones de la familia Arawak." In *XXXV Congreso Internacional de Americanistas, 1962,* vol. 2, pp. 519–23. México, D.F.
Maupertuis, Pierre Louis Maureau
  1750   *Reflections on the Origin of Language.*
Metcalf, George J.
  1972   "Philipp Clüver and his 'Lingva Celtica'." *Deutsche Beiträge zur geistigen Uberlieferung* 7:90–109.
Moore, Bruce R.
  1962   "Correspondences in South Barbacoan Chibcha." In *Studies in Ecuadorian Indian Languages I,* ed. Benjamin F. Elson, pp. 270–89. Norman, Okla.: Summer Institute of Linguistics.
Noble, G. Kingsley
  1965   "Proto-Arawakan and its descendants." *International Journal of American Linguistics* 31.3 (July), Part II: 1–129 (also pub. 38, Indiana University Research Center in Anthropology, Folklore, and Linguistics, Bloomington).
Olson, Ronald D.
  1964   "Mayan affinities with Chipaya of Bolivia 1: Correspondences." *International Journal of American Linguistics* 30.4 (October): 313–24.
  1965   "Mayan affinities with Chipaya of Bolivia 2: Cognates." *International Journal of American Linguistics* 31.1 (January): 29–38.
Orr, Carolyn and Robert E. Longacre
  1968   "Proto-Quechumaran." *Language* 44.3 (September): 528–55.
Pallas, Peter Simon
  1786–89 *Linguarum totius orbis vocabularia comparativa: Augustissimae cura collecta.* St. Petersburg.
Pedersen, Holger
  1924   *The Discovery of Language.* Bloomington: Indiana University Press.
  [1931]
Percival, W. Keith
  1987   "Biological analogy in the study of language before the advent of comparative grammar." In *Biological Metaphor and Cladistic Classification,* ed. Henry M. Hoenigswald and Linda F. Wiener, pp. 3–38. Philadelphia: University of Pennsylvania Press.

Pickering, John
  1821   "On the adoption of a uniform orthography for the Indian languages of North America." *American Academy of Arts and Sciences, Memoirs* 4.2:319–60.
  1831   "Indian languages of America." *Encyclopedia Americana* 6, pp. 581–600.
Reland [Reeland], Adrian
  1708   "Vocabularia variarum linguarum Americanarum." In *Dissertationum miscellanearum*. Utrecht.
Rivet, Paul and Čestmir Loukotka
  1952   "Langues de l'Amérique du Sud et des Antilles." In *Les langues du monde*, ed. A. Meillet and Marcel Cohen, pp. 1099–1160. Vol. 2. Paris: Champion.
Rodrigues, Aryon Dall'Igna
  1958   "Classification of Tupi-Guarani." *International Journal of American Linguistics* 24.3 (July): 231–34.
Rodríguez de Montes, María Luisa
  1988   "Estado actual de la clasificación de las lenguas indígenas Colombianas: seminario-taller reunido en Yerbabuena." *Thesaurus* 43, Boletin del Instituto Caro y Cuervo. Bogotá, pp. 173–81.
  In press   (ed.), *Memorias del seminario: estado actual de la clasificación de las lenguas indígenas Colombianas*. Bogotá: Instituto Caro y Cuervo.
Ruhlen, Merritt
  1987   *A Guide to the World's Languages. Vol 1: Classification*. Stanford, Calif.: Stanford University Press.
Scaliger, Joseph Justus
  1599   *Diatriba de Europaeorum linguis*.
Schmidt, Wilhelm
  1926   *Die Sprachfamilien und Sprachenkreise der Erde*. Heidelberg: Winter.
Shafer, Robert
  1959   "Algumas equações fonéticas em Arawakan." *Anthropos* 54.3–4: 542–62.
  1962   "Aruakan (not Arawakan)." *Anthropological Linguistics* 4.4:31–40.
Shell, Olive Alexandra
  1965   Pano reconstruction. Ph.D. dissertation, University of Pennsylvania. University Microfilms 66-4648.
Suárez, Jorge A.
  1982   "South American Indian languages." *Encyclopaedia Britannica*, Vol. 17, 15th edition, pp. 105–12.
Swadesh, Morris
  1955   "Towards greater accuracy in lexicostatistic dating." *International Journal of American Linguistics* 21.2 (April): 121–37.
  1959   *Mapas de clasificación lingüística de México y las Américas*. Cuadernos del Instituto de Historia, Serie Antropológica 8. México: Universidad Nacional Autónoma de México.

Tovar, Antonio
    1961   *Catálogo de las lenguas de América del Sur.* Buenos Aires: Editorial
           Sudamericana.
Tovar, Antonio and Consuelo Larrucea de Tovar
    1984   *Catálogo de las lenguas de América del Sur.* Madrid: Editorial Gredos.
Trillos Amaya, María
    1988   "Estado actual de la clasificación de las lenguas indígenas de Colombia." *Glotta* 3.1: 41–44.
Wilbert, Johannes
    1962   "A preliminary glottochronology of Ge." *Anthropological Linguistics*
           4.2: 17–25.

II

Classification and Typological Problems

Aurore Monod-Becquelin

How to Deal with Unclassified Languages: An Ethnolinguistic View of Comparative Linguistics

ABSTRACT

Cet article est une réflexion sur la classification possible des langues isolées, dans les cas où font défaut documents et descriptions antérieures et/ou lorsque les langues connexes ont disparu.

La question est la suivante: que peut-on substituer au classement génétique?

La méthode comparative relue à la lumière des développements récents de l'anthropologie linguistique ouvre des voies de recherche principalement exprimées dans l'oeuvre de Benveniste.

La grammaire comparée telle qu'il la pratique montre en effet que le sens et la forme de la grammaire d'une langue viennent du type de réponse qu'elle donne à un certain nombre de questions de nature intralinguistique.

En envisageant la langue comme une des réponses possibles à une structure conceptuelle déterminée de même qu'une expression culturelle n'est qu'une des formes possibles de la structure, on prend en compte le seul niveau auquel se conjoignent langue et culture, sans avoir recours aux catégories dites "universelles." [1]

One of the first things mentioned in the description of a language is its assignment to a family along with its relationship with the neighboring languages within the family. Most of the time nothing is made of the information afterward, except when the research deals with the subject of language comparison or glottochronological reconstruction. And yet all scholars are aware that it is quite a different thing to study a language related to a known family or a language with no established relationship.

Studying unrelated languages may be looked at in two ways.

It means, first of all, working on so-called "orphan" languages, lacking a definition that would establish them in the large classification of the world languages and in the history of human culture save by criteria considered minor (e.g., geographical criteria, which are used in the last resort).

But it also means trying to discover the unique manifestation of an original linguistic structure, a masterpiece of the human mind to be saved from oblivion. Unrelated Amerindian languages, for example, are often dying out—so studying them means preserving the dialect if not the idiolect, the language, and the family altogether.[2] As a matter of fact, for any researcher who has also worked on languages for which the family concept has been essential, one problem is quite clear. How should one approach the study of residual, dying-out, and unrelated languages? What should be included in the description so that this sample of natural language may eventually find its place in a different classification from the one used so far? Finally, is it possible to make up, at least in part, for the lack of the precious contribution brought by the comparison of a language with others of the same family or, if not, should unrelated languages be relegated with the curiosa?

My purpose is to take a new look at comparative studies in the light of more recent theories, such as anthropological linguistics or cognitive anthropology, and to present an approach to *language isolates* that makes up for the lack of related languages or of historical perspectives. My approach is not based on a new theory, but appeals to the methodological combination of two different research traditions.

We will consider the matter in two steps. First, we will briefly survey the method used in dealing with "lucky" languages, those that lend themselves to historical, archaeological, and even proto-historical investigations, those that have "true friends" among linguists: the philologists. Then we will review some of the new directions of anthropological linguistics.[3] The merging of the two points of view may suggest a few methodological principles so that unrelated languages may cease to be an unlabeled bric-a-brac just because they cannot be admitted into the museum of History.

In so doing, we will have brought to light the common concerns shared by these two theories, however remote from each other: a concern for cultures as well as languages, the emphasis on grammar, and the importance of meaning. Thanks to the clarification imposed by these guidelines, we will better appreciate the most convenient approach to use when dealing with an unclassified language.

*   *   *

Comparative-historical linguistics is supported by a gradually developed overall methodological system of such fecundity that, since the origin of Indo-European comparative studies at the end of the eighteenth century, it has continued to generate or foster a variety of objectives and, accordingly, various disciplines and schools depending on time, place, and people.[4]

Antoine Meillet, in 1924, described his own comparative study as a search for "historical clues" as opposed to one leading to the discovery of universal laws (Meillet 1924 [1984]: 1). Hence the diversity of themes in comparative linguistics: genetic classification, language evolution and change, dialectology, and reconstruction of common and proto languages, in addition to further in-depth study of such concepts as state of language, general characteristics of languages, specific features of individual languages, and classes of similar changes.

There are actually few themes beyond the scope of historical linguistics, broadly speaking, whether comparative, *stricto sensu* historical or positivistic, as with the neogrammarians. The concept of *structure,* for instance, or in any case the closely related one of *system,* arises: Meillet, a comparatist, but also a disciple of Saussure, emphasized that systems are to be confronted, leading through reconstruction to other systems— which he called structures—and obviously not to languages (Ducrot and Todorov 1972:23–24).

The philologists took fascinating trips upstream in time in a meticulous search for the accuracy of form and meaning—from *dieu* to **deiwos*— in order to reconstruct images blurred by the centuries yet probable and perhaps even faithful, since they were based on relations forming systems. "Once apprehended in their past and present, languages appear as systems covering both past and present, phonetics, grammar and signification, for they are systems of signs" (Kristeva 1981:211).

The importance of *grammatical correspondences* is also explicit and, although the place and the very notion of grammar may vary even to the point of being contradictory, grammatical elements, even when typology is not the main focus, remain a privileged material (Ducrot and Todorov 1972:24).

All research work, including that of phonetics, is concerned with *meaning,* if only in selecting or confirming the choice of the units to be compared. Besides, language is perceived as linked to society, and the history of languages is one aspect of the history of civilizations or cultures. Thus for Indo-European, the triumph of historical linguistics, an amazing fresco is drawn over nearly 4,000 years (since the first Hittite inscription, the first recorded token of Indo-European) by Germans, Danes, Italians, and many others, impregnated with the ideas of encyclopedists and romanticists, evolutionists and positivists, organicists and typologists.

What is, however, Proto Indo-European? It is a family of languages, and a civilization. "A common language implies a common civilization," Meillet asserted bluntly (Meillet 1924 [1984]: 17). It split up step by step into a multiplicity of common languages, generating Illyrian, Germanic, Celtic, Hittite, Indo-Iranian, Greek, Romance, Baltic, and Slavonic; these in turn continued to break up until modern times, when each country formed its own common language at the expense of local languages;[5] yet, beyond the amazing diversity of their cultural, historical, and sociological denotata, they maintained a share of their common significatum.

One of the tasks of comparative linguists is to relate, despite this split, a major common language with a type of civilization. It was the concern of Emile Benveniste, one of the greatest Indo-Europeanists, whose approach to the language/civilization question had much in common with that of the most modern anthropological linguistics. Orientations, or even directions, for the description of isolated Amerindian languages may thus be found among the subsidiary teachings of comparative linguists on the nature of the relationship between language and society. For this purpose, however, we will have to follow the path of anthropological linguistics and the lessons taught by this quite different theoretical system, which lays a stronger emphasis on the quest for signification.

*   *   *

In a lovely, unpretentious text, *La mentalité primitive et l'illusion des explorateurs,* Paulhan in 1926 does away, in just a few lines, with the "voyageur" ethnocentric prejudices. On the one hand he describes a pompous Westerner: "An English explorer, [the] Rev. A. L. Kitching, returning from a voyage in Africa, wrote about the Luganda tribes: 'Those savages have no notion of love.' The proof, he adds, is that 'many dialects do not have a specific word for *love;* in the most advanced dialect, loving God and preferring potatoes to meat are expressed by one and the same word, *ockwagala.*' Obviously, Kitching is ignorant of the French language and the fact that we too have only one word for loving beef and loving a woman" (Paulhan 1926 [1966]: 143). On the other hand, he quotes one of his Malagasy informants: "The French have a singularly concrete turn of mind. When we use a single word: *akoho,* they must distinguish between chick, chicken, hen or rooster" (151); or again: "Malagasy expresses things simply, whereas French is full of detours and details, and its first objective is to depict them" (148). Obviously, the author had meant to counter Lévy-Bruhl's idea that the primitive mind was incapable of abstraction. But his main purpose was to warn against holding as particularly representative of a language those features that are the most striking to the researcher. To avoid this, he recommends not to lose sight of one's own language, but to keep it at a distance and beware of illusion: "When the explorer takes for ideas the primitive's words, he is holding his own words as ideas and things" (153).

Structural linguistics is supposed to provide guidelines for resisting illusions of this type. Its brightest fruits—such as phonology, the analysis of genetic relations, or the study of taxonomy, to cite only the most famous—have fed the scientistic mirage of linguists and then of anthropologists. Structures are now apprehended beyond appearances and it has become possible to account for the pressures and consequent changes that affect them.

The preeminence of linguistics in the social sciences and the use made by anthropology of some of its methods contribute to reconciling two disciplines that had been separated according to the Cartesian principle. When America was first discovered, language and customs were perceived as recto and verso of one sheet both in the ideology applied to the Savages (Monod-Becquelin 1984:335) and in fieldwork practice (Monod-Becquelin 1984:339–40). Then, at the end of the eighteenth century, the scientific approach came to be applied to the study of peoples, leading to "diviser chacune des difficultés . . . en autant de parcelles qu'il se pourrait et qu'il serait requis pour les mieux résoudre" (Descartes 1637 [1949]). By a pendulum effect well known to epistemologists, Mauss's "phénomène social total," and the ethnological approach of fieldwork, along with the success of structural linguistics at the beginning of the twentieth century are leading back to an apprehension of things that was anticipated several centuries ago. Ethnographers are less and less working through interpreters, new formulations are proposed for the language/culture problem, structural linguistics is increasingly thought to provide cognitive organizations more abstract, and therefore more "comprehensive" and meaningful, and all this contributes to the reshuffling of the deck.[6]

During the second half of the twentieth century, titles are more and more explicit: *Façons de dire, façons de faire,* written by Y. Verdier, deals with oral tradition as well as anthropology; *The Social Use of Metaphor,* by David Sapir and Christopher Crocker, elucidates the common concern of a linguist and an anthropologist: "The anthropology of Rhetoric"; to say nothing of John Austin's *How To Do Things with Words,* which lays the foundations of Pragmatics and the Oxford Analytical School.[7] More recently, *L'homme de parole,* by Claude Hagège, substitutes for the speaker (abstract and deaf locutor facing an equally abstract and mute hearer) the "homme dialogal" (dialogical man). The same one is found, almost under the same name, by an American school, of which Dennis Tedlock is a good example. One of the chapters in his fine work *The Spoken Word and the Work of Interpretation* (1983) is entitled "Dialogical Anthropology." The statute of elicitation, the value of the quotation, and the concept of Speech are no longer taken for granted, but are open to inquiry.

The problem of meaning, which is now a common concern of anthropologists and linguists, can thus be considered from three different points of view:

1. The universalist point of view is illustrated by Lévi-Strauss, who, by a prodigious effort of abstraction, writes a topology of myths and narratives—and, whenever possible, a history as well—from the Bororo to the Comtesse de Ségur, which shows, over ranges of successive variations, the unicity of human preoccupations throughout time and space. It is in a way a work of philosophy. By an amusing effect of scholarly trends, the linguistic discipline that derived, as he did, from Jakobson, binarism, and formalism, and whose scope is, as Lévi-Strauss's, universalistic (i.e., generative grammar), is the least apt for dealing with anthropological problems, and is turning resolutely toward cognitive psychology.

2. To the particularist point of view may be ascribed most of the work of the past thirty years, which deals with the review and evaluation of indigenous taxonomies in order to establish as accurately as possible the categories and ways of thought that prevail in any given group. Componential analysis is one of its branches and has given some results (see Hymes, Tyler); it can be formalized (e.g., Lounsbury's studies on family relationships) and also claims to be of use in a comparative perspective.

3. The intermediate position deals with the system underlying action and speech patterns and considers the structure of a culture at a given time as the possible form of a more general, more abstract structure, of a cognitive type, from which the structure of the language also proceeds.

Since, for many reasons—differences in the evolution rate, in malleability and liability to interference and borrowing—language and culture changes do not always correspond, great disparities can be expected in the effects.[8] The process might therefore be figured as two large rhetorical developments from a common cognitive structure, in which each language state and cultural state of the society under study would be seen as one among many possibilities that could emerge. In a restrictive domain (poetry) but, suggesting a more general application, Ruwet (1975) has shown in the study of poetical figures that every trope is the final stage in a succession of forms: the poet may decide to terminate the process where he chooses, to create a metaphor or be content with the preceding metonymy. What is, in poetry, an individual choice, pertains to the collective and to the unconscious in society; historical events, contacts, and sudden shifts obviously alter both culture and language, each event having a different impact on words and actions.

✶   ✶   ✶

Let us now try to determine in what field items and relationships shared by culture and language may be apprehended.

These relationships do not pertain to universal grammar—where anthropological linguistics had nothing to say, being "mostly confined to the superficial aspects of language structure" (Chomsky 1970:114–15); as a matter of fact, universals as a whole "govern language properties that are simply beyond the reach of research in the limited scope that anthropological linguistics, mostly for very good reasons, calls its own."

On the other hand, such relationships are found by means of analyses, particularly grammatical, the results of which are applicable, at a very general level, to a whole "group" of languages. As an example, the nature and function of the ergative category existing in Kuikuru, a Carib language, and in several closely related languages, induce us to enquire by what means (whether morphonological, grammatical, or semantic) this category is replaced in the few Carib languages where it is not present. However, the grouping here may be somewhat different from the family proceeding from comparative studies, nor does it coincide with a typological class or an areal relationship. These points will be briefly reviewed later. The originality of this semantic grouping as opposed to the traditional modes of classifying will then appear clearly.

"Since comparative study is the only way to induce the history of languages, so long as a language is unrelated, it remains without history" (Meillet 1924 [1984]: 12). To this statement, Benveniste poses two kinds of arguments.

1. First of all, as illustrated in the above quotation, *genetic classification*

has limitations proportionate to its very strength: a language cannot be classified if the family has disappeared (as in the case of Sumerian), or if, in the absence of archaic remains, it is no longer possible to establish relationships with a previous language state, or if the languages under study are better defined, in terms of their mutual relationship, by degrees, than by relating them to a known older structure—"parenté par enchaîne-ment" (Benveniste 1966:105–6). Moreover, and this point will be further developed hereafter, there are other ways, perhaps just as satisfactory, of classifying languages, which have the advantage of allowing to deal with languages without history.

2. The *typological classification,* which does not coincide with the genetic classification—Benveniste shows that *Takelma* in Oregon should be counted as an Indo-European language (Benveniste 1966:115)—is tricky, since it rests partly on the linguist's insight and choices. Greenberg, even though he used it himself, underlines the drawbacks of the required cutting up into phonetic, phonological, grammatical, and semantic criteria as well as the arbitrary choice of any number of isoglosses (Greenberg 1968:127).

Structural resemblances may arise from what is called "groupement d'affinités" (affinity connections) whereby several languages of different origins, which are only related geographically, undergo identical develop-ments. The converging effect, added to borrowing and chance, may dis-guise the diversity of origin of languages forming, by a process as yet unelucidated, an "areal group" (Benveniste 1966:101).

The above classifications may support each other to some extent, but they all depend on the fact that "the analysis bears upon empirical forms and arrangements," that is, superficial features (Benveniste 1966:114).

> To overcome this basic difficulty, it must be recognized, first of all, that form is only a possibility of structure. . . . (115). The preliminary condition for a new classification of languages would be to give up the principle . . . that linguistics is concerned only with data, that language is entirely contained in its actual manifestations . . . linguistic facts are a result, and the question is: of what? . . . Every language has to solve a number of problems which con-verge on the central question of "signification." Grammatical forms convey the answers to these problems, with a symbolism typical of language; by studying these forms, their selection, their specific connections and organi-zations, we can induce the nature and the form of the intralinguistic problems they are answering. The whole process is essential, though unconscious and difficult to grasp. (1966:115)

This superb text gives the keys to a classification in which unrelated languages are placed on the same level as related ones, or close to it. One might compare, for instance, different systems of noun classes, or the various expressions of grammatical number that are functionally analogous. Such an in-depth effort on a general theory of linguistic structures, concerned more with meaning than forms—the integration of linguistic descriptions into models rather than a single universal scheme—seems to open to the researcher a bountiful source of directions and learning. It expresses better than many texts more formalized and up-to-date the concern of new anthropological linguistics.

I would like to conclude with an example showing the intricate interplay of linguistic and cultural categories: a seven-page article by Benveniste, on the item *rex* 'king' in the second volume of his work, *Le vocabulaire des institutions indo-européennes*. It appears to be a purely comparative study, but is really a model of anthropological linguistics. If we chose this example from within the Indo-European domain, it is precisely because it best illustrates the spirit of the author's method and the respective roles played by linguistic and cultural meanings. It should be obvious that the description of a language, if one conceives of it not as a given object, self-contained and similar to a monologue, but as one of the possible answers to a series of conceptual problems, will benefit a great deal from this model.

Benveniste studies the concept of *roi* 'king' at the opposite ends of the Indo-European world: Italoceltic and Indo-Iranian, conservative areas "where institutions and words elsewhere abolished persisted for a long time" (Benveniste 1968:10). His analysis bears upon the Latin *rēx* and the Sanskrit *rāj-*. The nominal theme shared by the two roots is **rēg-*. What is the semantic base of the concept? A vestige of another Indo-European language, namely the Greek verb ὀρέγω 'spread,' is the beginning of the thread that leads him to the meaning of **reg*. Most of the article is meant to demonstrate phonetically the similarity between this term and the **reg* domain. We are not directly concerned with this part. The second part establishes the exact meaning of the verb, which is to "draw out a straight line starting from one's position" or "to move forward in a straight line." This leading thread brings Benveniste back easily to Latin to explain *regio* (first "the point reached," then "the area delineated by straight lines"), *rectus* ("what is physically and morally right"), and *rēgula* ("ruler," instrument used to draw a line, and moral rule).[9] In the Roman expression "*regere fines*," the verb *regere* means "draw the frontiers in straight lines," which is "what the High Priest does for the construction of a temple or of a town when he draws out on the site the consecrated space."

The agentive referring to this action is *rex*, "the one who draws the line, or the guideline." The notion of Indo-European royalty is thus brought to light: the Indo-European *rex* is more a religious than a political figure. He holds no power, but he sets the rules and determines what is right. This notion bears relation to the priest colleges, whose duty was the perpetuation of rites.

The accurate contents of the word *rex*, the king, in terms of what he does and may do in later times and in the various societies is left by Benveniste to the investigation of historians, anthropologists, or sociologists. The demonstration does not rest on any extralinguistic assumption; and what is successively *referred to* by the word, its *denotata*, should not be taken into account.

And yet, using a comparison between two languages, Latin and Greek,[10] and a commentary on Homer, he describes augury practices, explains a moral constellation, characterizes the founder of towns or temples, talks about magics and customs, and undertakes the study of a social organization. By defining the notions of king and kingdom, and leaving to history the numbering and explicitation of successive *denotata*, he reaches the deepest level of meaning and understanding.

Such an endeavor on grammar and culture and their major common concerns (space, time, number, deixis, aspect, persons, and so forth), even on a different ground and with a different method from the one exemplified above, could only be most enlightening and therefore justify Benveniste's hopes that "any people who follow to the very end the exposition of our work may find in it materials for general reflections, particularly regarding the application of some of the models described herein to the study of those languages or cultures which, having no written documents, lack the historical perspective" (Benveniste 1968:12).

Once again associated, the language and culture of a society are seen as realities, not homologous but not heterogenous either. The tenuous intuition that "there is something common" between the two can be developed and tested. Though the past uses of phrases such as "spirit of a people" or "national character" are to be rejected, it is still legitimate to explore the dark and unconscious origin of a human group's language and culture. The apparent paradox of discrepancies is accounted for: "Considered as empirical and historical data, language and culture in their relationships show no sign of having analogical structures" (Benveniste 1974:91); or again: "We have seen that, between an historical language and an historical society, no necessary correlation may be established. However, at the fundamental level,[11] homologies can be perceived immediately" (1968:94).

Language here is conceived as a system of significant forms interpreting society, capable of reflecting social changes while keeping its structure unscathed. The most difficult task will always be to sort out the manifestation of meaning from the essence of meaning. In any case, avoiding the confusion between the empirical and the conceptual meanings is the true path in the maze of signification, leading to the glorious dawn of a properly semantic typology of languages. "The correlation between the two domains will neither be structural . . . nor typological . . . historical . . . or genetic," the common features of social practice and speech will have to be searched for "in this relationship of inter-human communication" (1966:114).

NOTES

1. This paper was translated by C. Siegel and revised by P. Menget.

2. My first linguistic fieldwork was on Trumai, a language isolate of central Brazil, spoken by a tribe of fewer than thirty people. The Trumai belong to what the anthropologists call the "Xingu pluriethnic society." This society involves about ten village communities defined by their languages. Four different families are represented: Tupi, Carib, Arawak, Gê, plus the unrelated Trumai.

My second fieldwork dealt with a few languages of the Mayan family, Tzeltal in particular. I studied the rhetorical figures found in the oral tradition of rituals (and possibly in the Maya scriptural tradition). Not only is this study comparative, but it rests on an idea of a pan-Maya system which is fairly credible and on which many studies by American scholars have been based.

3. "Anthropological linguistics" does not translate exactly the French word *ethnolinguistique*, but it comes close.

4. For further details on several early comparatists, see Droixhe (1984), which is devoted to studies carried out in Europe between the sixteenth and the eighteenth centuries.

5. Meillet is aware of the paradox of a diversity of languages expressing one material and intellectual civilization. He calls this an "anomaly" which is bound to disappear.

6. It was mostly the missionaries and the colonizers of North America who, when faced with unexpected linguistic realities difficult to handle in their Latin models, wrote about the discovery of a society together with its language, and on the necessity of living in "huts" rather than in the missions.

7. Pragmatics is understood in various ways in Europe and in the United States. Two major trends might be to consider the action "of" speech: tradition of the English analytical school; and to consider the action "with" speech: tradition related to sociolinguistics or the ethnography of speech, and the American pragmatic school. In all cases, "the meaning of the language is only an indication of the meaning of speech" (Ducrot 1980:32) and this concept is closely related to enunciation theories.

8. The minimal interpretation of the Sapir-Whorf hypothesis consists in comparing specialized vocabularies on the language side and a techno-economical situation on the culture side to deduce that language and culture categories corre-

spond with each other. It is actually a very special case of coincidence—explained by the necessity for mankind to deal with the environment—and not a general case: most of the facts contradict the direct and mechanical inferences from one field to the other, as do the situations where different languages exist in a homogenous cultural zone (or vice versa) (see Benveniste 1974:91–92). If the Sapir-Whorf intuition is right, it may be that the state of the linguistic theory at the time did not enable them to demonstrate it properly.

9. The passage to the moral sense is attested to by a Persian precept.

10. This is supported by Gothic, Old Persian, Finno-Ugrian, Basque, Armenian, Hittite, Chinese, Gallic, Gaelic, French, Germanic, Japanese, and Polynesian.

11. "As systematic comparisons of language and society were made, discrepancies appeared. It was discovered that the correspondence between the two was constantly disturbed by the major fact of diffusion, both in the language and in the social structure, so that societies with the same culture would have heterogenous languages, or conversely, closely-related languages would express entirely different cultures. Further study showed specific problems inherent in the analysis of either language or culture, as well as in the *signification problems* which they share. . . . The problem will be to find out the common basis to language and society, the principles that govern both structures, and first of all to determine in each of them the units to be compared in order to establish their interdependence" (Benveniste 1966:15).

REFERENCES

Austin, John L.
   1965   *How To Do Things with Words*. Oxford: Clarendon Press.
Benveniste, Emile
   1966   *Problèmes de linguistique générale*, Vol. 1. Paris: Gallimard, coll. Bibliothèque des Sciences Humaines.
   1968   *Le vocabulaire des institutions indo-européennes*. 2 vols. Paris: Editions de Minuit.
   1974   *Problèmes de linguistique générale*, Vol. 2. Paris: Gallimard, coll. Bibliothèque des Sciences Humaines.
Chomsky, Noam
   1970   *Le langage et la pensée*. Paris: Payot.
Cohen, Marcel and Antoine Meillet, compilers.
   1952   *Les langues du monde*. Paris: Champion.
Descartes, René
   1637   "Le discours de la méthode." In *Descartes, œuvres et lettres*. Paris: Gal-
   [1949]   limard, coll. La Pléiade.
Droixhe, Daniel, Pierre Swiggers et al.
   1984   "Genèse du comparatisme indo-européen." *Histoire, Epistémologie, Langage*. Vol. 6, fasc. 2. Lille: Presses Universitaires de Lille.
Ducrot, Oswald
   1980   *Les mots du discours*. Paris: Editions de Minuit.
Ducrot, Oswald and Tzvetan Todorov
   1972   *Dictionnaire encyclopédique des sciences du langage*. Paris: Le Seuil.

Greenberg, Joseph H.
    1968   *Anthropological Linguistics: An Introduction*. New York: Random House.
Hagège, Claude
    1985   *L'homme de parole*. Paris: Fayard.
Hymes, Dell, ed.
    1964   *Language in Culture and Society: A Reader in Linguistics and Anthropology*. New York: Harper and Row.
Kristeva, Julia
    1981   *Le langage, cet inconnu: une initiation à la linguistique*. Paris: Le Seuil.
Lounsbury, Floyd G.
    1965   "Another view of the Trobriand kinship categories." *American Anthropologist* 67.5 : 142–85. Special publication: *Formal Semantic Analysis*. Menasha: American Anthropological Association.
Meillet, Antoine
    1924   *La méthode comparative en linguistique historique*. Oslo: Aschehoug.
    [1984] Translated by G. B. Ford as *The Comparative Method in Historical Linguistics*. Paris: Champion.
Monod-Becquelin, Aurore
    1984   "La parole et la tradition amérindiennes dans les récits des chroniqueurs aux XVIe et XVIIe siècles." *Amerindia 6: Pour une histoire de la linguistique amérindienne en France*. Paris: Association d'Etudes Amérindiennes.
Paulhan, Jean
    1926   *La mentalité primitive et l'illusion des explorateurs*. Paris: Nouvelle Re-
    [1966] vue Française.
Ruwet, Nicolas
    1975   "Synecdoques et métonymies." *Poétique* 23. Paris: Le Seuil.
Sapir, J. David and J. Christopher Crocker, eds.
    1977   *The Social Use of Metaphor: Essays on the Anthropology of Rhetoric*. Philadelphia: University of Pennsylvania Press.
Tedlock, Dennis
    1983   *The Spoken Word and the Work of Interpretation*. Philadelphia: University of Pennsylvania Press.
Tyler, Stephen
    1979   *Cognitive Anthropology*. New York: Holt, Rinehart and Winston.
Verdier, Yvonne
    1979   *Façons de dire, façons de faire*. Paris: Gallimard.

Marilia Facó Soares and Yonne Leite

Vowel Shift in the Tupi-Guarani Language Family: A Typological Approach

ABSTRACT

This chapter deals with the vowel shifts that occur in the Tapirapé, Asurini, Guajajara, and Araweté languages of the Tupi-Guarani family (Brazil). It reviews previous approaches to internal classification such as the tree diagram and degree of participation in an extrinsically ordered set of rules. The push-chain mechanism is examined and criticized, and a simultaneous changes approach is proposed, with reassignment of allophony to resolve categorial conflicts.

Introduction

It is common among Brazilian scholars to complain that classifications of Brazilian Indian languages are based on insufficient material, and that they do not satisfy the requirements of the classical comparative method. In fact, the classifications available for some families sometimes show great divergences among themselves. In general, the classificatory work is the result of a superficial inspection of the lexicon; because of the quality of the descriptive data, the establishment of constant sound-meaning correspondence is not attempted. In addition, there is no continuity of effort, each work being the result of individual interest—sometimes even a sporadic incursion by the investigator into the field of historical linguistics. So there is no natural progression of knowledge built on the revision of previous work in order to enlarge it, confirm it, or invalidate it.

Within this general pattern, the study of the Tupi-Guarani family is an exception. It benefits from good descriptive analysis and from the continuous comparative and lexicostatistic studies of Rodrigues (1955, 1964, 1985); the reconstructions of protoforms by Lemle (1971) and Jensen

(1984); and the revisions of rules by Leite (1982), Soares (1978, 1979), and Viveiros de Castro (1984). Each author has answered a question raised in a previous work.

In this paper we will reexamine the vowel shift that occurred in some of the Tupi-Guarani languages, the change subsumed in Lemle's tree diagram as "change of *a"; it is reviewed by Leite (1982), Soares (1978, 1979), and Viveiros de Castro (1984).

Lemle's Tree Diagram and Shared Innovations

Based on phonemic data from Asurini (As), Guajajara (Gj), Kokama (Ko), Parintintin (Pt), Kamayurá (Km), Urubu (Ub), Guarani (Gn), Guarayo (Gy), Sirionó (Si), and Tupinambá (Tb), after reconstructing 221 lexical items through the systematic establishment of cognates, Lemle (1971:128) draws the tree diagram in Figure 1. However, as Lemle (1971:129) writes:

> Tapirapé (data from Yonne Leite) has much in common with Asurini, including the loss of contrast between *u and *o, the merging of certain other vowels with *a, and the phonetic manifestation of /y/ as [y] in syllable-final position and as [č] in other environments. However, its inclusion in the same section of the diagram as Asurini is difficult, since vowel nasalization remains as a phonemic feature of Tapirapé but not of Asurini and Guajajara.

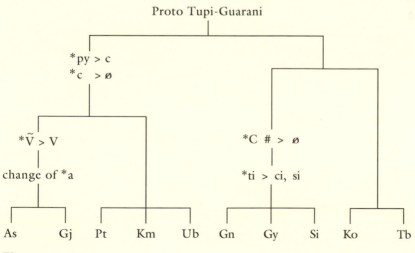

Figure 1

It is this difficulty in the tree diagram classification that Leite (1982) tries to solve with an approach using extrinsically ordered rules.

The following rules are formulated by Leite:

Rule 1

$$
V
$$

$$
\begin{bmatrix} + \text{bk} \\ + \text{lo} \\ - \text{rd} \\ - \text{nas} \end{bmatrix} \rightarrow [- \text{lo}] \quad / - \begin{bmatrix} \text{C} \\ + \text{nas} \end{bmatrix} \text{ in As, Tap, Gj}
$$

*a goes to ə in Asurini, Tapirapé, and Guajajara

Rule 2

$$
V
$$

$$
\begin{bmatrix} + \text{bk} \\ + \text{lo} \\ - \text{rd} \\ + \text{nas} \end{bmatrix} \rightarrow [- \text{lo}] \quad / \text{ in As, Tap, Gj}
$$

*ã goes to ə̃ in Asurini, Tapirapé, and Guajajara

Rule 3

$$
V
$$

$$
\begin{bmatrix} + \text{bk} \\ - \text{hi} \\ - \text{lo} \\ - \text{nas} \end{bmatrix} \rightarrow [+ \text{hi}] \quad / \text{ in Gj except in env. } \_\_(\text{Co}) \#
$$

*o goes to u in Guajajara except in syllable final or in penultimate syllable preceding o.

Rule 4

$$
V
$$

$$
\begin{bmatrix} + \text{bk} \\ - \text{hi} \\ - \text{lo} \\ - \text{rd} \\ - \text{nas} \end{bmatrix} \rightarrow [+ \text{hi}] \text{ in As, Tap}
$$

ə goes to i in Asurini and Tapirapé

Rule 5

$$
V
$$

$$
\begin{bmatrix} + \text{ bk} \\ - \text{ hi} \\ - \text{ lo} \\ - \text{ rd} \\ + \text{ nas} \end{bmatrix} \rightarrow \begin{bmatrix} [+ \text{ rd}] \text{ in As} \\ [+ \text{ hi}] \text{ in Tap} \end{bmatrix}
$$

ɔ̃ goes to õ in Asurini and to ɨ̃ in Tapirapé

Rule 6

$$
V
$$

$$
\begin{bmatrix} + \text{ bk} \\ + \text{ lo} \\ - \text{ rd} \end{bmatrix} \rightarrow \begin{bmatrix} - \text{ hi} \\ + \text{ nas} \end{bmatrix} \text{ in Tap}
$$

*a goes to ɔ̃ in Tapirapé

Rule 7

$$
V
$$

$$
\begin{bmatrix} + \text{ bk} \\ - \text{ hi} \\ - \text{ lo} \\ + \text{ rd} \\ - \text{ nas} \end{bmatrix} \rightarrow \begin{bmatrix} + \text{ lo} \\ - \text{ rd} \end{bmatrix} \begin{bmatrix} \underline{} \text{ in Tap} \\ \underline{}(Co) \text{ in As} \end{bmatrix}
$$

*o goes to *a* in all environments in Tapirapé and only in syllable final or in penultimate syllable preceding *o* in Asurini

Rule 8

$$
V
$$

$$
\begin{bmatrix} + \text{ bk} \\ + \text{ hi} \\ + \text{ rd} \end{bmatrix} \rightarrow [- \text{ hi}] \quad \text{in As and Tap}
$$

*u merges to *o* and *ũ to õ in Asurini and Tapirapé

Rule 9

$$
V
$$

$$
[+ \text{ nas}] \rightarrow [- \text{ nas}] \quad \text{in As and Gj}
$$

Nasality of vowels is lost in Asurini and Guajajara

Tapirapé and Asurini can be shown to be closely related by their participation in a great number of rules. Leite also observes that the loss of vowel nasality may have occurred independently in Asurini and Guajajara. In Guajajara, the loss is unordered with respect to rules 1 and 2; in Asurini, it has to be ordered after rule 5 but is unordered with respect to rule 8.

Soares (1979) studies the process of loss of vowel nasality in Guajajara, Asurini, and Kokama and the vocalic changes associated with it. She concludes that the loss of vowel nasality is a natural process, explained in acoustic and perceptive terms, so it should not be taken as a criterion for determining affiliation among languages. She also claims that it is necessary—and an urgent task—to isolate the factors that can cause sound change in order to avoid the indiscriminate use of shifts of different nature either to construct tree diagrams or to prove relationship among languages by establishing a relative chronology of rules.

Vowel Shift and Push-Chain

The proto system as reconstructed by Lemle has six oral vowels (i e ɨ a u o) and six nasal vowels (ĩ ẽ ɨ̃ ã ũ õ).

Guajajara (Gj), Asurini of the Xingu (AsX), Asurini of the Tocantins (AsT), Tapirapé (Tap), Parakanã (Par), and Araweté (Ar) are languages of the Tupi-Guarani language family that have undergone vowel shift and changed that system.

The shared innovations of these languages are:
- raising of *a to ɨ in Asurini of the Tocantins, Asurini of the Xingu, Parakanã, and Tapirapé
- nasalization of *a to ã in Tapirapé and Araweté
- lowering of *o to a in Asurini of the Xingu, Asurini of the Tocantins, Parakanã, Tapirapé, and Araweté
- neutralization of the contrast between *u and *o in Asurini of the Tocantins, Parakanã, and Tapirapé
- nasality loss in Asurini of the Tocantins, Asurini of the Xingu, Parakanã, and Guajajara.

Specific changes of each language are:
- raising of *a and *ã to ə and of some *o to u in Guajajara
- rounding of *ã to o in Asurini of the Tocantins
- raising of *ã to ɨ in Tapirapé

- raising of *a and *ã to *i* and *ĩ,* fronting of *ɨ and *ɨ̃ to *i* and *ĩ,* centralization and unrounding of *u and *o.

According to Leite, these shifts are not language-specific; as we have seen in the first section, they are shared innovations that can be formulated as gradual changes that take place one at a time.

So the raising from *a to *i* in Asurini and Tapirapé passed an intermediate step *a > ə > *i* (rules 1 and 4 above). The same graduality occurs in the shift *ã to *o* in Asurini: *ã > ə̃ > *õ* > *o.*

The interpretation of the process as a gradual change makes it possible to postulate rules shared by the various languages, even though the final result is quite different in each of them. Rules 1, 2, 4, and 5 say that Tapirapé, Asurini, and Guajajara are closely related: the change of *a began at the same time in the three languages and it ended up by differentiating Guajajara from Tapirapé and Asurini because Guajajara stopped the process in the intermediate step *ə while Asurini and Tapirapé continue their way toward *õ* and *ĩ* (rules 4 and 5).

Viveiros de Castro has applied this notion of gradual sound change and participation in rules to relate Araweté intimately to Guajajara, Asurini of the Tocantins, and Tapirapé. So the raising of certain *a and *ã to *i* in Araweté has taken place following rules 1, 2, 4, and 5 slightly modified in the context of application. Only after that, Araweté had a change of its own merging *ɨ and *ɨ̃ into derived *i* and *ĩ* and change both to *i.*

Leite's proposal has the merit of focusing on the process of change itself. However, it is connected to chronologically ordered rules and a push-chain result, so that the merger of a phoneme into another opens a hole in the pattern that has to be filled by a sound resulting from another change. This push-chain is exemplified in Tapirapé as shown in Figure 2. (The dotted line indicates partial and context-sensitive change.)

As can be seen in the diagram after rule 5 there is a hole in the pattern (*a); it causes rule 6 (nasalization of *a), which in turn causes rule 7 (*o → a), which in turn causes rule 8 (*u → o, *ũ → õ).

This sequence accounts for the changes in Tapirapé only. The change is unmotivated for Guajajara and Asurini (see Figure 3). In Guajajara, rules 1, 2, and 3 do not open holes in the pattern. Rules 1 and 3 are context-sensitive developments that affect only the distribution of allophones, while rule 2 only changes the pronunciation of the phone.

The Asurini shift allows a closer examination of the difficulties inherent in this approach. First, with the exception of rules 5 and 8, no hole in the pattern is opened. The changes accounted for by rules 1, 2, 4, and 7 are

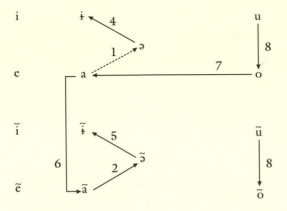

Figure 2

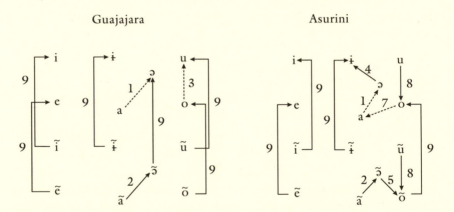

Figure 3

primary splits: the system itself does not change. Second, rules 1 and 2 may be an artifact; it is possible to suppose that the pronunciation of *a in the environment of a nasal consonant as well as of *ã was [ə] in the proto system. Third, there is no motivation, other than the one mentioned above, for an intermediate step *ə in the change of *ã to *o*. Fourth, the segments are merged with no subsequent change.

Araweté data confirm this state of affairs. It shares rules 2, 5, 6, and 7 with Guajajara, Asurini, and Tapirapé and it has as its own, rules 10, 11, 12, and 13 as Figure 4 displays.

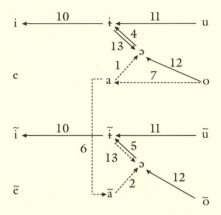

Figure 4

The rules that open a hole in the pattern and that are triggered by a push-chain mechanism are 10, 11, 12, and 13; however, rules 11, 12, and 13 are synchronic rules that account for the present fluctuations [u ~ ɨ], [o ~ ə] (rules 11 and 12), and [ɨ ~ ə] (rule 13).

It rather seems that the mechanism proposed by Leite for measuring degrees of genetic affinity is circular: the proof of close relationship lies in the greater participation in a set of extrinsically ordered rules, and the rules are ordered the way they are to prove the relationship. This circularity weakens the push-chain explanation.

The Phonetics of the Phonological Systems

Lemle (1971) and Leite (1982) have developed their proposals without taking into consideration the phonetics of the systems under comparison. They worked on a strictly phonemic level.

A closer examination of the phonetics of these systems leads to a reformulation of both the proto system and the explanation given to vowel shift using a mechanism of extrinsically ordered rules.

The vast majority of Tupi-Guarani Languages (Juma, Kamayurá, Kayabi, Kokama, Kayoá, Urubu, Parintintin, Oyampi, and Tupinambá, for instance) reproduce the vocalic proto system: six oral vowels (i e ɨ a u o) and six nasal vowels (ĩ ẽ ɨ̃ ã ũ õ). Oyampi is an exception, since it has five nasal vowels and six oral vowels.

Asurini of the Tocantins and Tapirapé[1] have five oral vowels: i e ɨ a o (Harrison 1961; Leite 1977). Tapirapé has the same vowels as nasalized phonemes and Asurini has no phonemic nasal vowels.

As for Awareté, which has a five or six vowel system, it is uncertain whether the language has the contrast between [u] and [o], or the contrast between [ɨ] and [ə] that fluctuates with [u] and [o].[2] It has five phonemic nasal vowels.

Guajajara is the only language that has a seven vowel system (with no phonemic nasal vowels): i e ə ɨ u o.

The differences among the phonemic systems described above can be summed up as (1) presence or lack of the contrast between [u] and [o]; (2) one or two central vowels; (3) presence or lack of nasality as a distinctive feature of vowels.

The available data now allow us to go further and to characterize phonetically those systems. Six vowel systems with the opposition [u] and [o] have the phonetic outputs[3] shown in Figure 5.

Subsystem Ia is an archetype based on Kayabi (Weiss and Dobson 1975); Oyampi is quite similar (Harrison and Olson n.d.). Subsystem Ib is derived from Parintintin (Pease 1962); Urubu (Kakumasu 1977) and Kamayurá (Silva 1981) are linked to it. What is typical of the six vowel system is the possibility of a phonetic output [ɔ] attributed to /o/, and [o] attributed either to /u/ or to /o/.

Five vowel systems have the phonetic outputs in Figure 6. In these languages there is no [ɔ] as a phone.

Another point that should be emphasized is the possibility of having [ë] and [ʌ] as outputs of /o/ (Harrison 1961). Weiss and Dobson (1975) in

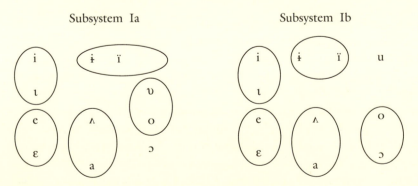

Subsystem Ia   Subsystem Ib

Figure 5. Circles indicate allophonic variation.

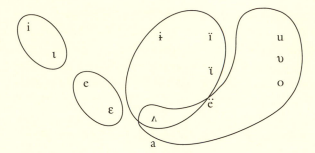

Figure 6

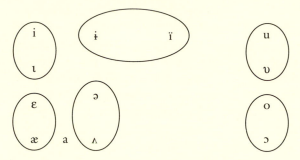

Figure 7

their description of Kayabi vowels have labeled back vowels as slightly rounded, and the same description is given by Harrison for Asurini /o/ (Harrison n.d.). This reducing of roundness is increased and systematized in Araweté, ending up as the fluctuation [u ~ ɨ] and [o ~ ə].

In Guajajara, the seven vowel system is found in the phonetic outputs in Figure 7 (Gudschinsky 1959; Bendor-Samuel 1961). Once more [ɔ] is present; the contrast between /u/ and /o/ is also found, as in subsystem Ia and Ib.

The correlation between the presence of the /u/:/o/ contrast and the output [ɔ], and the lack of the contrast and non-occurrence of [ɔ], is confirmed if we look at the tree classification of the Tupi branch and bring onto the scene the Macro-Tupian languages.

In Aweti (Monserrat 1975) and Sateré-Mawé (Graham and Graham 1961) there is the /u/ and /o/ contrast, and the allophone [ɔ] is a submember of /o/. According to the distribution of back vowels, Sateré-Mawé belongs to subtype Ia (Figure 5).

Cinta Larga (Sandberg 1977), Gavião (Moore 1976), and Suruí (Bontkes and Bontkes 1973), languages of the Mondé family, have a five vowel system: there is no contrast between [u] and [o] and the phone [ɔ] does not occur.

Munduruku (Braun and Crofts n.d.) has a five-vowel system (i e i a u), without the contrast between [u] and [o] and also without the phone [ɔ]. Preceding a /y/ coda, /u/ has an unrounded vowel as an allophone. So the Munduruku and Mondé languages are closely connected to the five vowel systems exemplified in Figure 6.

It is important to note that the data that made this mapping of phonemic systems into phonetic feasible were found in tentative phonemic analyses that were in general unpublished. These are the impressions of first surveys, when the analyst had not yet phonemized the material. This freshly heard material was written with a kind of transcription that, according to Abercrombie's distinction (1967), can be labeled impressionist and not systematic.

Reformulation of the Proto System

The facts presented thus far call for a reinterpretation of the proto system and of the rules transcribed above.

In the languages of five vowel systems, it would be more appropriate to have /u/ instead of /o/ as a norm of the back vowel. This is not a mere transcription decision, but derives from the fact that Tupi-Guarani languages that have an /o/ phoneme also have a phone [ɔ] as a phonetic output; this does not happen in languages where the contrast between /u/ and /o/ is neutralized. The allophony of the back vowel in these languages is very similar to that of the phoneme /u/ in languages with a six vowel system. By the same token, it would be more appropriate to have as norms of the proto system, as well as of the modern systems with six vowels, the symbols ɛ and ɔ instead of e and o.

Taking into account the allophony of the modern systems, it is possible to postulate allophonic variations in the proto system. Combining Figures 5, 6, and 7, we can propose the diagram in Figure 8 as phonetic output of the proto system.

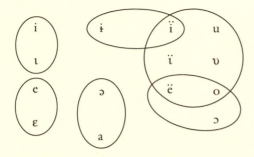

Figure 8

To conceive of the proto system as already having degrees of round-ness for back vowels and a low quality for the non-high back vowel ex-plains why there is in the various languages the change to a lesser or greater extent, more or less systematic, of *ɔ to *a.[4] Furthermore, it is possible to discard rules 11 and 12 of Araweté and to interpret the variation of back and central vowels as an extension and systematization of an allo-phony already existent in the proto system that is maintained in Araweté. This variation is not implemented in the other languages. Thus there is no motivation for a push-chain in Araweté that changes *u to *i since the domain of /ɨ/ has never been empty.

If the norm of the back phoneme in Tapirapé and Asurini is /u/ in-stead of /o/, rule 8, which merged *u and *o into *o, can also be discarded, and a push-chain mechanism is again unnecessary, since the domain of *ɔ continues open.

The concept of a nonhomogeneous proto system leads to a revision of Leite's (1982) explanation of vowel shift. Now we can leave out some of the rules, and these are exactly the ones that were pushing the chain to fill the holes. Furthermore, the push-chain explanation is based on the as-sumption that the changes occurred to restore the balance of the original system, but it does not explain why this balance was broken leaving an asymmetry.

Within a typological framework, there would be no need for such a strong mechanism as extrinsically ordered rules. If asymmetry and allo-phony are already present in the proto system, we can suppose that each language is just reassigning allophones simultaneously in order to solve the original conflict of uneven categorization.

Vowel Shift: A Typological Proposal

If roundness and backness are not considered independent acoustic and perceptual dimensions—that is, if less roundness is taken as directly connected to less backness and vice versa—Figure 8 can be simplified and the vocalic proto system will have the phonetic configuration of Figure 9.

This array is justified also by data from Kamayurá, a language for which there is a more detailed phonetic study. The display of Kamayurá vowels (Silva 1981), in comparison to Jones's cardinal vowels (1932:31–38), confirms that the central high unrounded vowel has as its domain of articulation the back area, close to *u*, as shown in Figure 10.

The main difference between the matrix here proposed and the system presented by Lemle is that here it is unbalanced and asymmetric: there is the categorial distinction between the high back rounded vowel and the unrounded one (*u [u]:*ɨ [ɯ]). This distinction does not hold for the other back vowels, that is, there is no categorial distinction between [ɣ] and [o] and [ɣ] and [ʌ]—all of them being linked to a single unit *ɔ.

This unbalanced system is maintained in the languages with a six vowel system, while the five vowel systems have tried to restore balance by

i   ɯ   u

e   ɣ   o

ɛ   a   ʌ

Figure 9

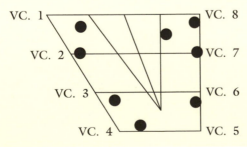

Figure 10

the reassignment of allophones in the dimension of height and area of articulation.

Guajajara focused on the dimension of height. It was shown above that in Guajajara some *a have been raised to [γ] and with that, the distinction between [γ] and [o] begins, since at times [γ] becomes a part of the domain of /a/. Furthermore, at times *o was raised to [u] and at other times it went to the domain of /ɔ/.[5] It is the process of nasal vowel loss that gave rise to a seven vowel system: all *ã were raised and lost nasality.

Asurini and Tapirapé tried to solve the asymmetry by conjoining the dimensions of height and area of articulation. In Asurini some *ɔ patterned to /a/, some *a raised to /i/ and at other times *a lined up to [o] and the output [ɔ] was lost. Besides that, every *a leveled to [o] in a joint process of raising and changing the area of articulation. Today, [γ] belongs to the same domain of [u] and [o]. In Tapirapé there has been a preference of height over place of articulation. All *ɔ became /a/ and only some *a raised to /ɯ/ while others became nasalized. All *ã were raised to /ũ/ and [γ] became a part of the domain of /ɯ/. Nowadays there is a fluctuation between [u ~ o], [ɯ ~ γ], [ũ ~ γ̃].

Araweté's choice has been in the dimension of area of articulation, although there have been some changes due to raising. In this way, some *ɔ lined up to /a/ and *ɨ became /i/ in a clear process of displacement of area of articulation. The same process happened in the fluctuation [u ~ ɯ] and [o ~ γ].

Figure 11 shows this redistribution of allophony in Guajajara, Asurini, and Tapirapé.

Depending on its four or five vowel system, Araweté would have the redistribution of allophones shown in Figure 12.

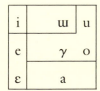

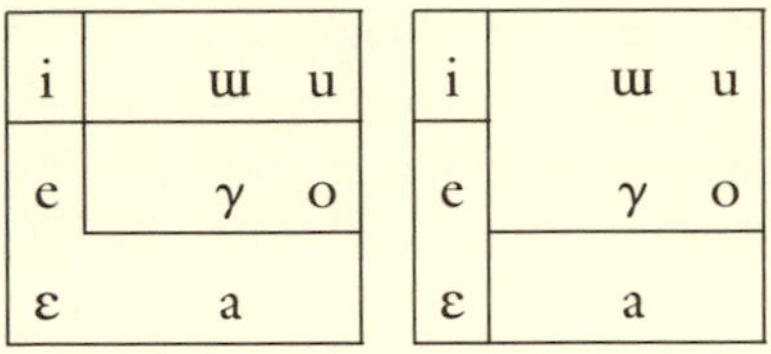

i	ɯ u
e	ɣ o
ɛ	a

i	ɯ u
e	ɣ o
ɛ	a

Figure 12

Conclusions

The actualization of the mechanisms of change explained above can be independent of the order in which each one took place. The changes can occur simultaneously. The main concern is the redimension of the phonological domains through the handling of allophones already present in the proto system: thus the original matrix has an inherent asymmetry. This asymmetry favors certain changes, but some languages may choose to remain with the unbalanced system.

The idea of simultaneous change is implicit in Rodrigues (1980:3). For him, the shift that occurred in Tapirapé and resulted in *u to *o*, *o to *a* and *a to *ã* can be explained as the phonological increase of one degree of compactness[6] in back vowels. This shift is handled by the following rule:

$$\begin{matrix} \text{V} \\ \begin{bmatrix} + \text{ posterior} \\ \text{n compact} \end{bmatrix} \end{matrix} \rightarrow [\text{n} + 1 \text{ compact}]$$

The potential for change is then circumscribed in the proto system, and universal acoustic, perceptual, and articulatory principles that govern sound change limit the possibilities of shifts. The paths each language can follow, then, are not numerous; and the similarity of vowel shift processes found in different languages should not be taken as evidence for determining closer relationships.

In fact, the historical studies of Brazilian Indian languages are still in their infancy. Better descriptive analyses are still needed. And in phonemic studies, an attitude of nonreductionism, with careful phonetic investigation and description of allophones, surely could contribute greatly to the study of sound change and lead to a deeper understanding of the relationship between synchrony and diachrony.

NOTES

1. Parakanã (Aberdour 1975) and probably Asurini of the Xingu (Nicholson 1982) could be added to this list. However, the available material does not allow use of the data for the present purposes.

2. Viveiros de Castro, personal communication.

3. Only oral vowels will be dealt with henceforth. The phonetic symbols used by most of the authors are reproduced as is. In the last section, the International Phonetic Alphabet will be used.

4. As was shown above, Tapirapé changed *ɔ to *a*. In Asurini and Araweté, the rules have restrictions in their environments. In Kayabi (Soares 1978) the change is sporadic, unsystematic, and less frequent.

5. The change of *o* to *u* has probably had its implementation in vocalic harmony. The change of *ɔ to *a* in Asurini may also be interpreted as implemented by vowel harmony. This topic deserves more attention in Tupi-Guarani linguistics.

6. According to Rodrigues (1980:3), nasal vowels are one degree more compact than the corresponding oral vowels.

REFERENCES

Abercrombie, David
1967   *Elements of General Phonetics.* Edinburgh: Edinburgh University Press.
Aberdour, Catherine
1975   *Formulário dos vocabulários padrões para estudos comparativos preliminares nas línguas indígenas brasileiras.* Rio de Janeiro: Museu Nacional.
Bendor-Samuel, David
1961   "Guajajara phonemics." Manuscript.
Bontkes, Willem and Carol Bontkes
1973   "Tentative Phonemic analysis of Suruí." Manuscript.
Braun, Ilse and Marjorie Crofts
n.d.   "Phonemic statement" (Munduruku). Manuscript.
Graham, Albert and Susan Graham
1961   "Phonemic statement of Sataré" (Tentative). Manuscript.
Gudschinsky, Sarah
1959   "Notes on Guajajara (Tupi) language (Posto Indígena Gonçalves Dias)." Manuscript.
Harrison, Carl
1961   "Report of Asurini survey." Manuscript.
n.d.   "The phonemics of Asurini; a language of Brazil." Manuscript.
Harrison, Carl and Gary Olson
n.d.   "Notas sobre regularidades fonéticas na língua Wãyãpí." Manuscript.
Jensen, Cheryl
1984   O desenvolvimento histórico da língua Wayampi. M.A. dissertation. São Paulo: Universidade Estadual de Campinas. Mimeograph.

Jones, Daniel
    1932   *An Outline of English Phonetics.* Cambridge: W. Heffer & Sons Ltd.
Kakumasu, James
    1977   "Formulário-Padrão Tupi" (Urubu). Manuscript.
Leite, Yonne
    1977   *Aspectos da fonologia e morfofonologia Tapirapé. Série Lingüística* VII,
            Rio de Janeiro: Museu Nacional.
    1982   *A classificação do Tapirapé na família Tupi-Guarani. Ensaios de Lingüística* 7 : 25–32. Belo Horizonte: Universidade Federal de Minas Gerais.
Lemle, Miriam
    1971   "Internal classification of the Tupi-Guarani linguistic family." *Tupi Studies* I, ed. David Bendor-Samuel, pp. 107–29. Norman, Okla: Summer Institute of Linguistics.
Monserrat, Ruth
    1975   "Formulário dos vocabulários padrões para estudos comparativos nas línguas indígenas Brasileiras." Rio de Janeiro: Museu Nacional. Manuscript.
Moore, Dennis
    1976   "Dados preliminares de língua dos Índios Gavião do Território de Rondônia (Brazil)." Manuscript.
Nicholson, Velda
    1982   "Breve estudo da Língua Asurini do Xingu." *Ensaios Lingüísticos* 5, Brasília: Summer Institute of Linguistics.
Pease, Helen
    1962   "Tentative phonemic statement for Parintintins." Manuscript.
Rodrigues, Aryon Dall'Igna
    1955   "As línguas 'impuras' da família Tupi-Guarani." *Anais do XXXI Congresso Internacional de Americanistas:* 1055–71. São Paulo.
    1964   "A classificação do tronco lingüístico Tupi." *Revista de Antropologia* 12. 1–2 : 99–104. São Paulo.
    1980   Contribuições das Línguas Brasileiras para a fonética e fonologia. Paper read at the XII Reunião Brasileira de Antropologia, Rio de Janeiro. Mimeograph.
    1984–85   "Relações internas na família lingüística Tupi-Guarani." *Revista Brasileira de Antropologia* 27–28 : 33–53. São Paulo.
Sandberg, Peter
    1977   "Formulário dos vocabulários padrões para estudos comparativos preliminares nas línguas indígenas Brasileiras." Rio de Janeiro: Museu Nacional. Manuscript.
Silva, Marcio
    1981   A fonologia segmental Kamayurá. M.A. Dissertation. São Paulo: Universidade Estadual de Campinas. Mimeograph.
Soares, Marilia Facó
    1978   "A classificação interna do Kayabi na família Tupi-Guarani." Manuscript.

1979   A perda da nasalidade e outras mutações vocálicas em Kokama, Asur-
         ini e Guajajara. M.A. dissertation, Rio de Janeiro: Universidade Fed-
         eral do Rio de Janeiro. Mimeograph.
Viveiros de Castro, Eduardo
1984   Araweté: uma visão da cosmologia e da pessoa Tupi-Guarani. Appen-
         dix 1. Ph.D. thesis. Rio de Janeiro: Museu Nacional. Mimeograph.
Weiss, Helga and Rose Dobson
1975   "Phonemic statement of Kayabi." Manuscript.

María Eugenia Villalón

A Spatial Model
of Lexical Relationships Among
Fourteen Cariban Varieties

Abstract

A brief summary of the history and distribution of the Cariban speakers and a short review of earlier classificatory work introduce a lexicostatistical study of fourteen Cariban varieties, based on a slightly modified 100-item word list. It was found that the percentages of homosemantic cognates do not conform well to a hierarchical structure, leading to the hypothesis that the pattern of Cariban lexical differentiation may reflect, instead, a cline structure.

A spatial tridimensional model generated through the application of the multidimensional scaling technique revealed the existence of both types of structure, with a clear predominance of cline relationships. This model correlates well with the geographical distribution of the sample languages and suggests tentative internal groupings that differ substantially from those postulated in recent works on Cariban classification.

The results of the multidimensional scaling show a basic core (east)/periphery (west) differentiation within the family that corresponds to the degree of divergence found among the types tested. It is construed that the greater homogeneity manifested by the core languages probably reflects a combination of later splits and sustained contacts accomplished through participation in regional networks. Finally, the scaling outcome, aided by selected glottochronological measures, becomes the basis for an inferred model of Cariban diffusion.

Introduction [1]

In 1955, Norman McQuown suggested that probably the most urgent task facing the student of the Cariban linguistic family was "to work out the lines of internal differentiation" (1955:562). There are several ways of dealing with this task. Reviewing the different methodological approaches to language grouping, Key (1979:15) distinguished between the inspection of vocabulary similarities (mass comparison) and the classical comparative method. In this paper I employ preferentially the first without entirely disregarding the second, undertaking a lexicostatistical study of 14 Cariban languages in order to address the priority cited by McQuown. As a first step, the glottochronological technique developed by Swadesh was used to estimate the degree of similarity existing among the varieties. Subsequently, multidimensional scaling, as applied by Black (1974) to linguistics, was used to generate a more sophisticated model of their internal relationships. The object of these lexicostatistical applications was two-fold: (1) to outline a provisional classification and (2) to shed light on selected aspects of Cariban prehistory, such as the probable center of origin and dispersal paths of its speakers. The varieties included in this study are the following: Yabarana (YA); Kamarakoto (KA); Panare (PA); Pemon or Arekuna (PE); Bakairi (BA); Makushi (MI); Taurepan (TA); Makiritare or Ye'kwana (MA); Carib, Kari'ña, or Galibi (CA); Cumanagoto (CU); Hianacoto-Umaua (HO); Chaima (CH); Oayana or Rucuyen (OA); and Macoita or Yukpa (MT). With the exception of Chaima and Cumanagoto, all the languages are currently spoken. The status of Hianacoto-Umaua is uncertain (cf. Durbin and Seijas 1973a; Durbin 1977).

History and Distribution of the Cariban People

Cariban is one of the great linguistic families of South America, encompassing dozens of languages spoken by the Caribs, carriers of a vigorous culture that left a profound and permanent imprint on northern South America. They are manioc cultivators, master canoe builders, and expert navigators; these skills allowed them to engage in successful raiding and to build up extensive trading networks. A historical quirk immortalized these people (*caribales*) in our English term "cannibal," although the existence of this practice among them has never been definitely proven. Sued-Badillo (1978) has recently argued that the term "Carib" was abused by the chroniclers and came to identify any native group that opposed or resisted the process of colonization.

Columbus first encountered "Carib" people (i.e., people to whom he attributed man-eating habits) in the Lesser Antilles during his second voyage; however, the real ethnic or linguistic identity of those people was never conclusively ascertained. Recent investigations tend to show that Cariban-speaking groups did not establish permanent settlements in the

Antilles during pre-conquest times, in spite of the fact that their raids may have taken them as far north as Florida. Allaire (1980), after carefully reviewing the ethnohistorical and archaeological data, found no acceptable evidence of prehistoric Carib settlements and migrations from the mainland into the Windward Islands. As a result, he concluded that the expression "Island Carib" could not be correlated or associated with any particular site, culture, or prehistoric group of people (Allaire 1980:243). Elaborating on his findings, he stated that the term applied most properly and exclusively to a linguistic entity (an Arawakan-based language with heavy Kari'ña borrowings):

> The island population belonged properly to one ethnic group whose distribution included both the islands as far north as Guadeloupe and a section of the Guiana coast between the Corentyne and Oyapoc rivers. This ethnic group, despite its cultural uniformity, was essentially bilingual in speech, although perhaps in the process of assimilation to the Cariban language of the mainland. (Allaire 1980:243)

Durbin seemed to hold a similar opinion when he contended "that there was no Carib language in the islands outside of that spoken by invading Carib males for a generation or so after the invasions" (1977:29), a view advanced by Taylor (1954) many years before. Expressing ideas that stand in sharp contrast to those above, Landar (1968) postulated the existence of Carib settlements on the southern Texas coast, claiming that the extinct Karankawa was in fact a member of the Cariban linguistic family, which he believed could be included in the Hokan stock. The evidence he presents for such far-reaching allegations, however, is inconclusive and uneven in quality. Although the likelihood of such a tentative reconstruction is not to be denied out of hand, and stands as a working hypothesis, the facts presently available do not seem to warrant the full acceptance of such greatly enlarged frontiers for Cariban.

As the human geography of the newly discovered lands became better known during the centuries following the conquest, Cariban speakers were found on the Atlantic coast of the mainland, from the northern mouth of the Amazon[2] to Cumaná (Hoff 1968:9) and the environs of present-day Caracas. In this area, they did not make up a continuous population block, but were interspersed mostly among Arawaks and Waraos. The largest inland concentration of Cariban speakers was centered in the Guiana Highlands, forming enclaves that extended as far as the western shore of Lake Maracaibo and the eastern slopes of the northern tip of

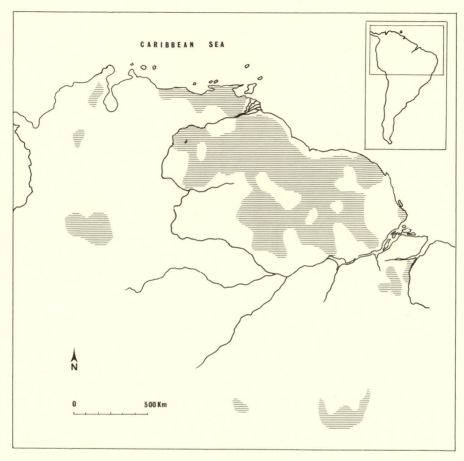

Map 1. Maximum distribution of Cariban languages.
Adapted from Rowe (1974b), Loukotka (1968), and Durbin (1977).

Colombia. South of the Lower Amazon were scattered the Arará, Parirí, and the Apiaká. The Palmella were located on the Guaporé River (between Bolivia and Brazil) and the Carijona between the Vaupés and Caquetá rivers (Lathrap 1970; Durbin 1977). On the Upper Xingú and the headwaters of the Tapajós River were settled the Bakairi and Nahukwa, the southernmost Cariban-speaking people.

Map 1 gives an approximate picture of the early distribution of Cariban speakers and clearly illustrates their wide scattering. According to many authorities, this widespread arrangement came about as a result of successive and fairly recent migrations:

> In the Amazon-Orinoco area, most of the societies with a tropical-forest-village type of culture belong to a comparatively few, widely distributed, and fairly undifferentiated language groups—Cariban, Arawakan, Tupí-Guaraní, and Panoan. The homogeneity of these language groups and the comparative uniformity of their cultures suggest that the wide distribution of these people was brought about by fairly recent and rather rapid migrations. (Steward and Faron 1959:26)

Following a generalized assumption, Lanning has lately suggested that "the last major expansion in the tropical forest was that of the Cariban peoples, which was vigorously carried out when the Europeans arrived in the area" (1974:100, cited in Allaire 1980:238). This belief is shared by most culture historians who frequently claim that the Cariban speakers, supposedly a warlike and expansionist population, fanned out from the heart of lowland South America in a predominantly northerly direction, conquering and displacing the original populations (mostly Arawakan). The evidence supporting this assumption is not decisive however, and allows for more than one interpretation. Durbin apparently concurs with established views when he writes that

> it would seem almost certain that the Caribs replaced Arawaks, since we see the Guiana Carib languages boxed in among Arawaks on all sides—north and south, east and west. Just as recent Tupi and Yanomamö expansions began to dislodge Caribs from various areas, we would hypothesize that the Caribs pushed Arawaks north into the Antilles, to the west, and deep into southern Brazil. (Durbin 1977:34)

In order to explain how the Caribs might have reached the southern coast of the United States, Landar speculated on the possibility of successive migration waves which, after securing bases in Honduras, Nicaragua, and Panama, finally landed on the Texas coast:

> The migration resulted from a very early, possibly a late 15th century Kaliña naval raid. This raid antedated the loss of the Kaliña grammatical core in the Antilles and possibly the Kaliña conquests in the Antilles. . . . The migration route was from the homeland north of the Amazon to the coast and Lesser Antilles to parts of Central America to Tamaulipas and Texas (Landar 1968: 257, 258).

On the other land, we have already seen that Allaire (1980) has questioned the historicity of at least some of the Carib migrations. To him the weight of the evidence calls for a radically different interpretation, suggesting that

if one posits Arawak incursions into Carib territories—especially along
the continental coastline—rather than Carib invasions, then the interpretation of Carib warfare would change from that of an expansion strategy
to one of territorial protection (Allaire 1980:246).

In spite of the contrasting views, one fact stands out in the early history of the Cariban people: they constituted one of the dominant elements
in the huge and ongoing process of acculturation which, by the time it
ended abruptly with the conquest, had given the tropical lowlands its basic
cultural homogeneity in the presence of an astounding linguistic and ethnic diversity. Peaceful and progressive acculturation, raids, migrations, the
search, structuring and securing of trade networks, occupation of new territories, protection of one's own homeland, and strategic political alli-
ances, must all have played a part in shaping the pattern of Cariban
distribution observed in Map 1.

This picture was to be radically altered as the colonization of the
mainland proceeded. Today, all the Cariban speakers have disappeared
from the Venezuelan coast. According to Humboldt, the Kari'ña (Carib)
took refuge around 1720 in the lands bordering the Middle Orinoco,[3]
where they were evangelized and where they remained after the demise of
the missions (Hoff 1968:11). Their congeners continue to inhabit the
coasts of Surinam, the western half of Guyana, and the westernmost coast
of French Guiana (Hoff 1968:11–12). Other Cariban speakers are presently
found in the Sierra de Perijá, which divides Venezuela and Colombia, on
the Vaupés River, throughout most of the Guiana land mass, and on the
Xingú.

The assumption of prehistoric Carib migrations as the more likely
explanation for their widespread distribution leads us to the question concerning their original homeland and center of dispersal. In this respect
there has been no lack of alternatives set forth. Rochefort (1681), for example, was unique in identifying the Caribs with the Cofachites and plac-
ing their original home on the southeastern shores of the United States,
from whence they had supposedly spread wedgelike over South America.
Von Steinen (1892) suggested the Upper Xingú as the probable homeland,
a belief shared by Rivet and Loukotka (Tovar 1961:134). Landar is ambiguous on the point for, immediately after proposing the area north of the
Amazon, he quoted Rivet, who thought that the center of dispersal lay
between 10° and 12° latitude (between the Upper Xingú and the Upper
Tapajós) (1968:258). Steward and Faron suggested the general area of
Guiana as the probable center of diffusion (1959:289), while Durbin

pointed to the Guiana area of Venezuela, Guyana, Surinam, or French Guiana, excluding as improbable Brazilian Guiana (1977:35). To Lathrap, on the other hand, "the weight of historical and linguistic evidence suggests that the ancient home of Proto-Cariban was on or adjacent to the Guiana Highlands possibly along the north shore of the Lower Amazon" (1970:82–83). Furthermore, he associated the Carib expansion with a ceramic tradition that spread gradually out of the northeast quadrant of the Amazon Basin into adjacent parts of South America about A.D. 500 (Lathrap 1970:165). These conflicting opinions make it evident that many lengthy and comprehensive investigations must be carried out before this question can be elucidated. Indeed, it is in this field that linguistic studies can make a significant contribution to the culture history of some of the most important Southern American ethnic groups. McQuown was quite correct in pointing out that rather urgent and "necessary studies for tracing migration history via language distribution need to be carried out in Cariban" (1955:564).

Cariban External Affiliations

The essential and original unity of the Cariban stock was recognized in fairly early times. The Capuchin missionary Francisco de Tauste, for example, noted in 1680 mere dialectical differences among Chaima, Cumanagoto, Core, Quaca, Paria, and "Varrigones," reporting that although Carib was understood throughout the Province of Cumaná (i.e., from the Gulf of Paria to Caracas) it was more "proper and natural" to the last mentioned groups (1680 [1888]:1). Father Gilij, who named the linguistic family, reported in the mid-eighteenth century on the affinities he had observed among the Orinoco tongues, admitting that his knowledge of Tamanaco enhanced his comprehension of other Cariban languages (1782 [1965]:171). Proving to be a surprisingly good comparativist, he grouped all the languages spoken along the Orinoco River into nine separate "mother tongues" and distinguished the following Cariban "dialects": "Tamanaco, Pareca, Uokeári, Uaracá-Pachilí, Uara-Múcuru, the language of the women without men [Amazons], Payuro, Kikirípa, Mapoye, Oye, Palenco, Maquiritare, Akerecoto, Avaricoto, Pariacoto, Cumanacoto, Guanero, Guakíri, Areveriana," the languages spoken on the Paria coast, and the environs of Caracas (Gilij 1782 [1965]:174). Additionally, Gilij recalled having perceived very early in his career lexical affinities between the land Caribs and the "cannibals of the Antilles" (Gilij 1782 [1965]:174).

Thereafter, the autonomous position of the Cariban family has remained unaltered, although suggestions for more inclusive groupings have not been lacking. For example, Schuller (1919–20) proposed including Cariban and Arawakan in a broad linguistic phylum along with Chibchan and Mayan. Mason also believed that Arawakan might prove to be ultimately related to Cariban (Steward and Faron 1959:25), while De Goeje hinted at a possible relationship between Cariban, Tupian, and Arawakan (1909:2). Rodrigues, a contemporary student, has argued for the existence of "a quite close relationship between Tupian and Cariban" (1974:56) although Hoff, rejecting such a notion, has called attention to the numerous borrowings found between Tupi and Carib (1968:13). Greenberg (1962) tentatively suggested an encompassing Ge-Pano-Carib phylum, and we have already commented on Landar's claims affiliating Cariban to the Hokan stock. Up to the present, however, none of the attempts to establish wider genetic relationships for Cariban has proved entirely successful. Thus it seems most convenient for the purpose at hand to treat Cariban as an independent linguistic entity. This way, the scope of the present discussion is held within manageable bounds and our attention focused on the problems concerning the composition of the Cariban family.

Cariban Internal Subdivisions

Until very recently, most of the Cariban internal classifications were based on geographical rather than linguistic considerations. This applies to Mason's (1963), Tovar's (1961), and Simpson's (1940) classifications, which followed essentially the same lines. These attempts have been largely superseded by Greenberg's (1962), Loukotka's (1968), Girard's (1971), Durbin's (1977), and Migliazza's (1980) work. Greenberg divided the Macro-Carib group into northern, southern, and northwestern branches. All the languages included in this paper fall within his Northern Branch except Bakairi and Macoita, which are listed as members of the southern and northwestern branches respectively. Key, who based her work on Greenberg's typological classification, skips these subdivisions and instead draws on the work of Durbin and Seijas, who posited, among others, a Western Carib group (Colombia and Venezuela) and a Southern Division embrac-

ing Hianacoto of southeastern Colombia, Maquiritare of southern Venezuela, and Bakairi of the Upper Xingú in Brazil (1979:103). Loukotka
(1968) presented an overly complex and unrealistic picture of the Cariban
family, listing 256 languages and dialects arranged in 24 "groups." Yet 153
of these lacked any documentary evidence whatsoever and for many others
only a few extant words or phrases were on record (cf. Rowe 1974a). More
than half of the subgroups proposed were not supported by adequate
data, and represented, in reality, merely the educated guess of this emi-
nent scholar. Girard's (1971) provisional classification, based on language-
specific phonological features, included 14 groups whose members bore
a relatively close kinship, plus a miscellaneous category: (1) Cumana,
(2) Makiritare, (3) Pemon, (4) Oayana, (5) Waiwai, (6) Carib, (7) Tiriyó,
(8) Yabarana, (9) Aparai, (10) Paushiana, (11) Bonari, (12) Arará, (13) Bakairi, (14) Motilon, and (15) Opon-Carare, Panare, Palmella, and Pimenteira.

Durbin's (1977), and Migliazza's (1980) partial groupings represent
the most satisfactory work on Cariban classification presently available.
Since Durbin's groupings constitute a fundamental reference point for the
discussion that follows, they are reproduced in Table 1 as originally published. This classification establishes a basic division between Northern
and Southern Cariban, reflecting the changes that Proto-Cariban *p has
undergone in the latter languages. Migliazza (1980), who recently assessed
the status of the languages of the Orinoco-Amazon watershed, agreed
with most of Durbin's subdivisions but added some important modifications of his own. He placed Wayumara among the East-West Guiana Carib
languages and transferred Waiwai to the Southern Guiana Carib division,
arguing that it closely resembles Hishkaryana and exhibits a change from
Proto-Cariban *p to h (Migliazza 1980:123). Henley and Mattei-Muller
have challenged this assertion, claiming that the available evidence on this
point is ambiguous, and thus Waiwai must be considered a borderline case
in whichever group it is included (1982:82–83). Additionally, Migliazza
pointed out that Sapara, Yawapery, Pauxiana, Wayumara, and Purucoto
are all extinct[4] and correctly identified Brazil as the former location of the
latter two. Lastly, he detected some redundancies in Durbin's classification, observing that "Wabui" is a general name for the people of the Nha-
munda River who otherwise speak Hishkaryana, as is likewise Parukoto a
common reference term for the aforementioned groups as well as for Waiwai and other tribes of the northern Pará region (Migliazza 1980:122;
Gama Malcher 1964:27–28). Similarly, Yawapery, Crichana, and Waimirí
seem to be synonymous terms (Migliazza 1980:123; Gama Malcher 1964:

TABLE 1. DURBIN'S CLASSIFICATION OF CARIB LANGUAGES

I. NORTHERN CARIB
  A. Coastal Carib
    1. Venezuelan Coastal Carib
      a. Chaima*
      b. Cumanagoto*
      c. Yao*
      d. Tamanaco*
    2. Sierra de Perijá
      a. Japreria
      b. Yukpa
      c. Yuko
    3. Opone-Carare*
  B. Western Guiana Carib
    1. Mapoyo
    2. Yabarana
    3. Panare
    4. Quaca*
    5. Pareca*
  C. Galibi
  D. East-West Guiana Carib
    1. Oayana-Aparai
    2. Roucouyene
    3. Aracaju*
    4. Trio-Rangu
    5. Wama (Akuriyo)
    6. Urukuyana
    7. Triometesen
    8. Kumayena
    9. Pianakoto
    10. Saluma
    11. Pauxi*
    12. Cachuena
    13. Chikena
    14. Waiwai
    15. Paravilhana*
    16. Wabui
      17. Sapara
      18. Yauapery
      19. Waimiri
      20. Crichana*
      21. Pauxiana
      22. Bonari*
      23. Makusi
      24. Purucoto
      25. Pemon
      26. Patamona
      27. Akawaio
      28. Arinagoto*
  E. Northern Brazilian Outliers
    1. Palmella*
    2. Pimenteira?*
    3. Yaruma*
    4. Txicão
    5. Paríri*
    6. Apiaka*
    7. Arara*
    8. Yuma*
II. SOUTHERN CARIB
  A. Southeastern Colombian Carib
    1. Hianacoto-Umaua*
    2. Guaque*
    3. Carijona
  B. Xingu Basin Carib
    1. Bakairi
    2. Nahukwa
  C. Southern Guiana Carib
    1. Ye'kwana
    2. Wayumara-Azumara
    3. Parukoto
    4. Hishkaryana
    5. Warikyana (Kashuyana-Kahuyana-Ingarune)

Source: Durbin 1977.
* extinct

45), although the scant evidence presented by Loukotka (1968:207–8) could easily lead one to think otherwise.

Cariban Lexicostatistics

In order to estimate the degree of lexical similarity obtaining among the members of our language sample, percentages of glottochronologic cognates or "sames" (cf. Hymes 1960:18) were calculated employing Swadesh's 100-item word list, to which the following modifications were made: the term *claw* in the standard list was replaced by *nail,* and the terms *knot* and *bark* were replaced by *hammock* and *manioc,* two terms that must be considered part of the basic vocabulary for the geographical area concerned. The criterion employed in selecting the sample was the availability of satisfactory lexical material up to 1976, when the computations were carried out. Given the number of spoken Cariban languages and the geographical distribution of its speakers, this sample cannot be considered an optimal one. Nonetheless, all of the major divisions and subdivisions proposed by Durbin are represented except Opon-Carare and the Northern Brazilian Outliers (see Table 1), all of which are presently extinct. Map 2 shows the location of the sample languages as reported in the published sources employed to compile the test lists.[5] The Panare data were gathered from my own field notes.

Because of the high number of synonyms encountered, particularly in the older sources, two cognate counts were performed: one which tended to maximize the number of shared cognates among the sample languages and one which tended to minimize it. Tables 2 and 3 show the respective cognate percentages obtained from the two counts, which on the whole do not show great disparities. When differences do occur they usually do not exceed 3 or 4 percentage points. The maximum variation between the two counts was found for the Makushi-Cumanagoto and Taurepan-Cumanagoto pairs, which show a change of 6 and 7 points, respectively, attributable, in a considerable measure, to the multiplicity of forms recorded by Tauste (1680 [1888]). Unless otherwise specified, the discussion that follows and the ciphers cited therein are all based on the high count.

In compiling the measures of shared cognates presented in Tables 2 and 3, due account was taken of sound correspondences and morpheme boundaries. Strict semantic equivalences were adhered to and most forms compared exhibited a VCV or a CVCV structure. Thus the possibility of

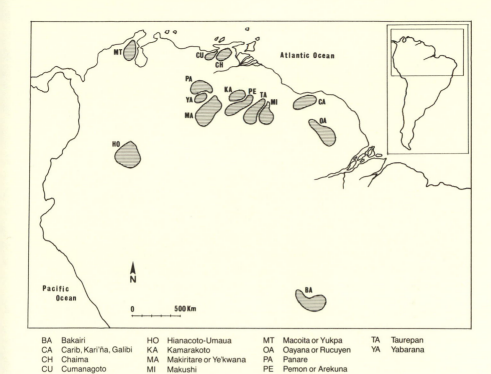

BA	Bakairi	HO	Hianacoto-Umaua	MT	Macoita or Yukpa	TA	Taurepan
CA	Carib, Kari'ña, Galibi	KA	Kamarakoto	OA	Oayana or Rucuyen	YA	Yabarana
CH	Chaima	MA	Makiritare or Ye'kwana	PA	Panare		
CU	Cumanagoto	MI	Makushi	PE	Pemon or Arekuna		

Map 2. Distribution of the sample languages.
Adapted from Rowe (1974b).

TABLE 2. PERCENTAGES OF SHARED COGNATES AMONG 14 CARIBAN LANGUAGES (HIGH COUNT)

	YA	KA	PA	PE	BA	MI	TA	MA	CA	CU	HO	CH	OA
KA	49												
PA	51	43											
PE	52	76	47										
BA	51	51	51	52									
MI	55	77	49	84	54								
TA	54	76	47	89	53	83							
MA	59	55	52	58	57	62	60						
CA	58	57	44	58	52	60	60	61					
CU	59	56	56	60	58	69	63	65	62				
HO	52	48	48	49	48	51	51	50	59	53			
CH	60	59	55	60	60	69	62	65	64	77	53		
OA	58	55	48	51	56	56	54	60	60	62	53	62	
MT	48	47	37	46	43	46	47	48	51	42	43	43	48

TABLE 3.   PERCENTAGES OF SHARED COGNATES AMONG 14 CARIBAN
LANGUAGES (LOW COUNT)

	YA	KA	PA	PE	BA	MI	TA	MA	CA	CU	HO	CH	OA
KA	46												
PA	49	43											
PE	49	79	46										
BA	51	49	50	48									
MI	53	77	47	80	51								
TA	51	76	46	84	52	81							
MA	55	53	51	53	57	59	59						
CA	53	57	43	56	51	58	60	60					
CU	57	53	53	55	56	63	56	62	58				
HO	51	48	45	48	48	52	51	51	59	49			
CH	57	57	55	58	56	64	59	62	63	77	52		
OA	56	55	47	50	57	56	54	60	60	59	54	61	
MT	45	44	34	42	40	43	44	46	48	42	42	43	45

including spurious matches (due to onomatopoeia, chance, or sound symbolism) was kept to a minimum (cf. Campbell 1973).

One of the main applications of glottochronology is the estimation
of linguistic time depth. In this regard some claims have been made for
Cariban that seem to be in need of revision. Layrisse and Wilbert (1966),
after computing strictly preliminary lexicostatistics for Akawaio, Kari'ña,
Makushí, Panare, Kamarakoto, Taurepan, Ye'kwana, Yabarana, and Macoita, all Cariban languages spoken in Venezuela, concluded that they

> appear to have been united 4500 years ago, when they formed a single lin-
> guistic community. The languages with maximum divergences are Panare
> and Bacaïri of the upper Xingú. . . . They seem to have been separated some
> 4800 years ago, and 7 m.c. earlier than Yukpa (Macoita) separated from Ba-
> caïri. (106)

Durbin expressed a similar opinion, stating that his data also suggested
such a line of development (1977:36). Our results, however, disagree with
these estimates. The deepest time span within our language sample was
obtained between Macoita and Panare, which apparently began to diverge
from a common parent language approximately 3,290 years ago—considerably less than the span propounded by Layrisse and Wilbert. Similarly,
the divergence times among Bakairi, Panare, and Macoita appear to be

overestimated, for our calculations suggest that Macoita and Bakairi began to separate from a common ancestor approximately 2,800 years ago, and Panare and Bakairi 2,200 years ago. These latter two languages, moreover, do not appear to be as closely related as Layrisse and Wilbert thought (1966 : 67). In fact, our data indicate that, lexically at least, both are significantly more distant from one another than each is from Proto-Cariban,[6] showing that they developed independently, as would be expected from their large geographical separation and relative and longstanding isolation from mainstream Cariban (Guiana heartlands and coasts).

Other glottochronological statistics have been computed by Mattei-Muller and Migliazza (Migliazza 1980; Henley and Mattei-Muller 1982) in an attempt to estimate the degree of linguistic differentiation existing among Panare, Yabarana, and Mapoyo (Wanai). Given the presence of some discrepancies between these two sources, I undertook the reckoning of cognate percentages for the three languages in question. Table 4 summarizes the results obtained and compares them with those furnished by the cited authors. While Henley and Mattei-Muller have suggested that Mapoyo and Yabarana "could be considered dialectical variants of a single language" (1982 : 81–82), my own calculations imply that both were a single homogeneous speech community approximately 1,090 (±180) years ago (68% confidence level). As far as the differentiation Mapoyo/Panare is concerned, both Mattei-Muller and Migliazza estimated a time depth of approximately 2,000 years on the basis of a cognate count per-

TABLE 4.   PERCENTAGES OF SHARED COGNATES
FOR THREE CARIBAN VARIETIES

	Panare	Mapoyo
Yabarana	51	72 (80)[a]
Mapoyo	49 (42)[b]	
	(45)[c]	
	(60)[d]	

[a] Mattei-Muller's calculation. No list specified (in Henley and Mattei-Muller 1982 : 81).

[b] Mattei-Muller's calculation from the 200-item word list (Migliazza 1980 : 126).

[c] Migliazza's calculation from the 200-item word list (Migliazza 1980 : 126).

[d] Migliazza's calculation from the 100-item word list (Migliazza 1980 : 126).

formed with the 200-item word list, while Migliazza obtained half that
amount employing the 100-item word list (Migliazza 1980:126). My own
calculations performed with the latter list suggest that Panare and Mapoyo
began to diverge from a common ancestor 2,360 (±320) years ago (68%
confidence level).

In sum, the data presented so far reflect splits within our Cariban
sample ranging from 390 years (Pemon and Taurepan) to 3,290 years
(Panare and Macoita).

Besides their application to dating language splits and estimating
chronological depth, percentages of shared cognates have proved useful as
a tool of linguistic classification, with the assumption that this measure of
lexical similarity is presumably an indicator of overall affinity. Two models
of mapping or synthesizing linguistic variation have usually been distinguished: the hierarchical or "tree" model and the continuous (spatial) or
"wave" model (Anttila 1972). In the pages that follow both will be considered in an effort to determine the most satisfactory model of Cariban
interrelationships.

Figure 1 depicts, in the classical branching mode commonly employed
in comparative linguistics, a gross outline of the internal relationships im-

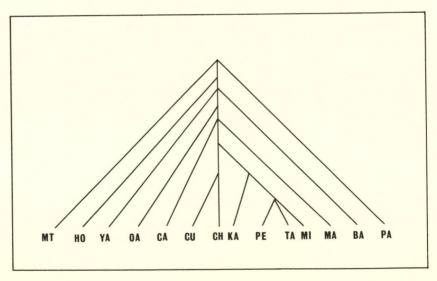

Figure 1. Approximate tree model of lexical relationships among 14 Cariban
varieties.

plied in Table 2. This tree, it must be emphasized, is not intended to be a formal map, but merely a summary of the similarity matrix produced by simple inspection. The lexicostatistics presented therein readily reveal, on the one hand, a close resemblance among Pemon, Taurepan, Kamarakoto, and Makushi, and between Chaima and Cumanagoto on the other, two clusters whose members share "critical percentages" (Dyen 1962:153). Thus, on the basis of cognate percentages alone, it seems reasonable to consider them separate subgroups. Additionally, the comparative extreme positions of Panare and Macoita, and to a lesser extent, of Hianacoto-Umaua, is clearly observable. However, other linguistic boundaries are not so well delineated, for once the two or three outliers and the two subgroups have been isolated, the picture blurs considerably. For this reason the tree presented in Figure 1 is not regarded as well motivated or particularly informative. In fact, as will be explained next, it conceals serious shortcomings.

How well a given set of cognate percentages conform to a tree structure and are thus most appropriately described by a hierarchical classification depends, according to Black, on the extent to which they satisfy the constraint of "ultrametric inequality" (1974:6). This condition is minimally satisfied when the two lowest of three percentages in a triad are equal (for a discussion, see Black 1974). A glance at the Cariban percentages reveals triplets that fulfill this condition as well as others that do not. Table 5 reproduces the percentages of cognates shared by Taurepan, Kamarakoto, and Pemon. This information can be adequately and fully depicted by means of a branching structure (Figure 2) because it satisfies the aforementioned condition. Assuming that the percentage differences are significant, the tree shows the closer relationship that Pemon and Taurepan share, as well as the more distant one that both have with Kamarakoto.

Just the opposite situation is exemplified in Table 6, where the lexicostatistical percentages for Macoita, Carib, and Cumanagoto are presented.

TABLE 5. PERCENTAGES OF SHARED COGNATES
AMONG TAUREPAN, KAMARAKOTO, AND PEMON

	Kamarakoto	Pemon
Pemon	76	
Taurepan	76	89

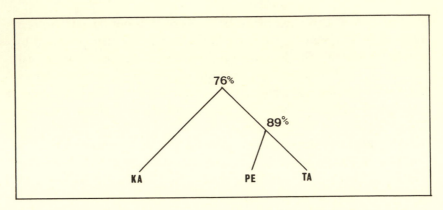

Figure 2. Cognate percentages among Kamarakoto, Pemon, and Taurepan.

TABLE 6.   PERCENTAGES OF SHARED COGNATES
AMONG MACOITA, CARIB, AND CUMANAGOTO

	Macoita	*Carib*
Carib	51	
Cumanagoto	42	62

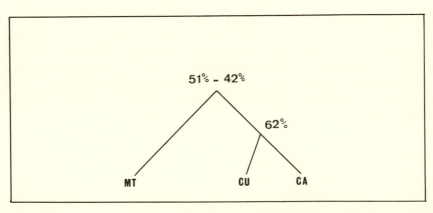

Figure 3. Cognate percentages among Macoita, Cumanagoto, and Carib.

Rendered graphically, the resulting tree (Figure 3) is capable of displaying the greater similarity existing between Carib and Cumanagoto, but it fails to show that the former is more closely related to Macoita than the latter, assuming the percentage differences to be significant. Cases such as the one detailed above indicate that the Cariban percentages do not conform well to a hierarchical representation or subgrouping. A tree or another type of branching structure, therefore, would not provide a very useful base for interpretation or inference.

Multidimensional Scaling

Black (1974) has demonstrated the usefulness of multidimensional scaling in the investigation of nonhierarchical linguistic relationships. This technique allows for the representation of underlying language affinities (as reflected in cognate percentages) in some sort of spatial configuration of varying dimensions. Or, in slightly different terms, it enables the researcher to test for the existence of linguistic clines, "considered to be characterized by potentially continuous variation in some sort of meaningful space" (Black 1974:6). We shall test the hypothesis that Cariban linguistic variation shows a predominantly cline arrangement. If multidimensional scaling can represent the Cariban varieties in a spatial model of n dimensions that correlate highly with their geographical distribution, then it will be considered that the cognate percentages do in fact conform to a cline structure.

The aim of multidimensional scaling is to represent linguistic (lexical) differences (proportions of noncognate homosemantic words) as distances among points (languages) in the smallest acceptable number of dimensions (Kirk and Epling 1973:60). In our particular application of this statistical procedure, Kruskal's MDSCAL multidimensional scaling computer program was employed, the cognate percentages shown in Table 2 having provided the input data. In a most general way, this and other similar computer programs start out with an initial configuration and modify it iteratively until no small change can improve further its fit with the original percentages, within certain preset limitations (Black 1974:21). The resulting configuration is then printed with an index of "stress" or a measure of the "goodness of fit" between the scaling and the original percentages on which it is based. In more precise terms, the stress index is the sum of the squares of the deviations between distances among the points in the final scaling and the "ideal distances" for the input percentages. Ideal distances are values that satisfy the constraint of nonmetric scaling (decreasing monotonicity: i.e., higher percentages have to be represented by smaller ideal distances) and at the same time are closest (as measured by stress) to the actual distances used to represent the percentages in physical space (Black 1974:22–23). As a rule of thumb, a stress measure above .10 is considered an indication of relatively poor fit.

Figure 4 shows the "best" bidimensional spatial representation of Cariban lexical relationships obtained after the application of multidimensional scaling. The peripheral positions of Panare, Macoita, and

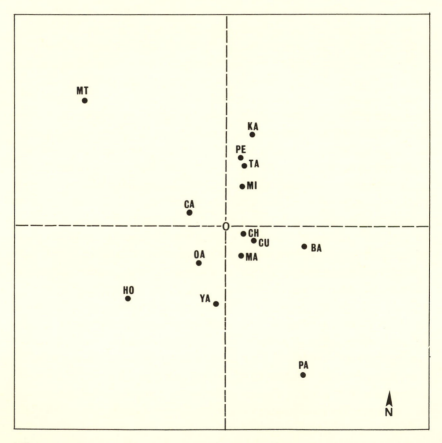

Figure 4. Bidimensional representation of lexical relationships among 14 Cariban varieties (stress = .098).

Hianacoto-Umaua stand out clearly, as do two distinct clusters: Taurepan, Pemon, Kamarakoto, and Makushi (Gran Sabana group), on the one hand, and Chaima and Cumanagoto (the coastal group) on the other, close to which now appears Makiritare.

Since Figure 4 can be interpreted as a kind of surface map of the northern half of South America, it has been superimposed (with a slight rotation) on Map 2, in order to gauge how well the scaling positions correlate with the actual geographical distribution of the sample languages (see Figure 5). At first glance, it is obvious that the correspondence is very poor, worse indeed than a stress index of .098 would have led us to believe. While Hianacoto-Umaua and Macoita fall very near their true placements and the members of the Gran Sabana group appear not too distant, having preserved their relative positions albeit with a reversed compass orientation (NE to SW instead of NW to SE), all of the remaining points, save Panare, have been "pulled" excessively toward the center of the axes: Chaima and Cumanagoto are aligned inversely and show up quite to the south of their attested locations; Carib and Oayana are veered inordinately to the west; Bakairi appears far to the northwest of its Xingú base, while Panare and Yabarana, in contrast, have undergone a great shift southward, and Makiritare a lesser one.

It would have been desirable to test whether the essentially hierarchical positions of Hianacoto-Umaua, Macoita, and Panare were affecting the scaling of the finer relationships, for the possibility exists that the primary split between the latter two (which in most trial configurations surfaced opposite each other) could be interfering with a more sensitive evaluation of the interrelationships obtaining among the remaining variants (Black 1974). This could have been accomplished by means of a new application of multidimensional scaling, utilizing a trimmed sample, but the depletion of the allotted computer time prevented such an undertaking. Nevertheless, several earlier runs performed with an initial sample of 11 languages, in which Panare and Bakairi represented the more extreme varieties, demonstrated that pruning them from the sample enhanced somewhat the overall fit of the new 9-point configuration and lowered the stress index, but it also evidenced that most of the improvement occurred in the areas of least interest, namely, the coastal group and the Gran Sabana cluster. Hence, it is reasonable to suppose that perhaps not much would have been gained by this added manipulation.

So far our results indicate that a two-dimensional scaling of linguistic distances within Cariban, measured by the degrees of lexical differentia-

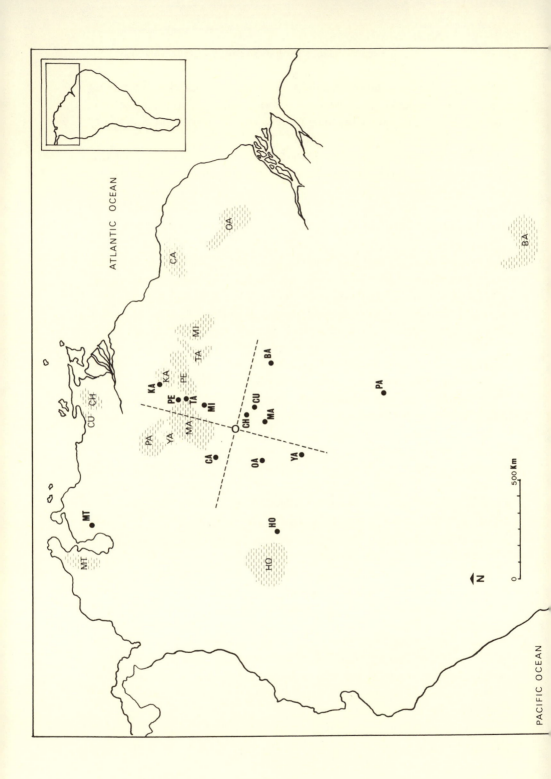

tion that reflect the percentages of homosemantic cognates among 14 varieties, bear little relationship to geographical reality. Therefore, our initial hypothesis stands unproved. The rather poor fit and a stress index (.098) approaching the limits of the acceptable suggest, however, that two dimensions may be insufficient to portray adequately the Cariban interrelationships. If this assumption is correct, then a third dimension must be introduced in order to test for the existence of clines and generate a satisfactory model of internal affiliations and development.

Figure 6 depicts a three-dimensional scaling of the percentages presented in Table 2, in the form of a triaxial diagram. Each point (or language) in it should be visualized as "suspended" in the space described by the cube, whose "floor" and "ceiling" can be interpreted as a "flattened" and smaller version of the surface plane shown in Figure 4. This tridimensional model of Cariban lexical relationships has a stress index of .048, a measure equivalent to a 50 percent drop from the previous scaling, which augurs a markedly improved fit.

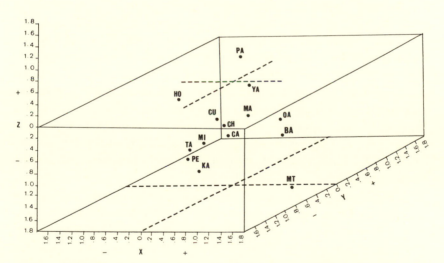

Figure 6. Tridimensional model of lexical relationships among 14 Cariban varieties (stress = .048).

Figure 5. Two-dimensional scaling of 14 Cariban varieties compared to their geographical distribution.
Adapted from Rowe (1974b).

In effect, a comparison with Map 2 reveals an enhanced arrangement of the points in space relative to one another. This time Panare, Yabarana, and Makiritare appear aligned in a manner that reflects their true geographical distribution. Chaima and Cumanagoto are grouped toward the "northernmost" corner, the latter showing up correctly to the "northwest" of the former, and Carib to the "southeast" of both. Oayana also manifests a better placement, figuring to the "southeast" of Makiritare and Carib. Bakairi appears located more accurately toward the "south" of Oayana, as well as Hianacoto-Umaua, which now is situated to the "southwest" of Panare and Yabarana. In contrast, the relative collocation of the Gran Sabana cluster and Macoita seems to have deteriorated. Careful inspection of the configuration, however, reveals that this assessment is not entirely correct, for while Macoita is indeed misplaced, the grouping of the cluster is actually better, figuring to the "south" of the coastal group (Chaima and Cumanagoto) and "west" to "northwest" of Carib and Oayana. Finally, it may be noticed, concerning the internal sorting of the group's members, that our model has generated exactly their mirror image; that is, if Makushi, Taurepan, Pemon, and Kamarakoto were to be reflected on their own axes,[7] their arrangement would appear precisely as shown on Map 2.

These results indicate that a three-dimensional model of Cariban interrelationships is definitely superior to its two-dimensional counterpart, for in spite of its increased interpretative difficulty, it does correlate highly with the comparative geographical distribution of the sample languages, even if it does not reflect adequately the extent of the physical distances involved. Hence, it suggests strongly the predominance of a cline arrangement in Cariban coexisting, nevertheless, with a few hierarchical relationships. These aside, the outstanding feature of the array is a gradual variation through space without sharp splits.

As intimated above, the shift to a higher dimensionality imposes the added task of formulating an acceptable description of the third dimension. Figure 7 shows the graph of its values, corresponding to those registered along the Z axis of Figure 6. It is important to first notice that the interlanguage variation is small toward the center and that all scores, taken together, describe a soft elongated S-curve that jumps sharply at the opposite ends of the distribution, where Panare, Yabarana, Macoita, and Hianacoto-Umaua fall. It is these extreme values (in conjunction with those that determine their position along the X and Y axes) that tend to "push" toward the "ceiling" or the "floor" of the configuration of the

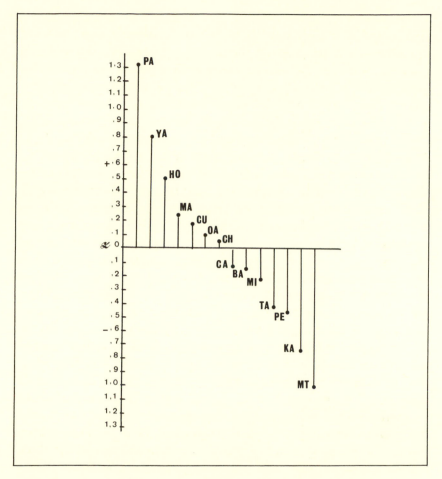

Figure 7. Values of the third (Z) dimension of the scaling configuration in Figure 6.

aforementioned varieties. Three of them, it will be recalled, assumed clearly peripheral positions in the bidimensional scaling, on account of which they were preliminarily identified as outliers. The significance of their spatial location "above" or "below" the others will soon be clarified. We are now in a better position to attempt a more refined interpretation of our three-dimensional model and to draw some tentative historical inferences.

Conclusions

Our results do not corroborate the presence of a basic north-south division in Cariban (cf. Table 1). It will be recalled that this dichotomy was formulated after grouping in a southern division all languages whose *p had undergone certain changes, mostly fricativization (Durbin and Seijas 1972, 1973a; Durbin 1977). The sharing of a single phonological innovation, however, does not seem sufficient evidence on which to establish such a major split, for commonly a cluster of shared related changes is required in order to discard independent innovation (duplication) or borrowing as alternative explanations (Anttila 1972; Hoenigswald 1960). Moreover, it could be argued that a shift from *p to h, φ, f, or w is a rather trivial marker of language splits, due to the fact that it is a fairly recurrent phenomenon attested under a wide variety of conditions and environments. Indeed, several "northern" languages exhibit a similar tendency. Waiwai, it has been remarked above, furnishes a borderline case as to its affiliation in any one of the two main divisions proposed by Durbin. Similarly, several dialects of Panare, a language in which *p > p is solidly established, exhibit p ~ h in noninitial positions. Until further evidence is forthcoming, these considerations lead me to grant priority to our results based on lexical evidence, which, if correctly interpreted, do not uphold the classification of Hianacoto-Umaua, Makiritare, and Bakairi in a single southern branch.

Secondly, our scaling configuration does not accord with the composition of the various subgroups proposed in Table 1. As far as it indicates, the classification of the Sierra de Perijá varieties (Macoita) and the Venezuelan Coastal Carib (Chaima and Cumanagoto) in a Coastal Carib unit (Durbin and Seijas 1972; Durbin 1977) doesn't appear to be particularly well motivated, nor does the classification of Oayana and the Gran Sabana cluster in an East-West Guiana Carib group (Table 1). In order to summarize visually the extent of the differences discussed, the classification presented in Table 1 and the tridimensional configuration of 14 Cariban languages are compared in Figure 8.

In contrast, our results suggest the existence of a central core of languages surrounded by four outliers, two of which constitute remote varieties, linguistically as well as geographically speaking (Hianacoto-Umaua and Macoita). The situation is portrayed in Figure 9, where the inner core languages[8] have been inscribed within the smaller cube, around which are positioned the four "topmost" and "bottommost" variants: Hianacoto-

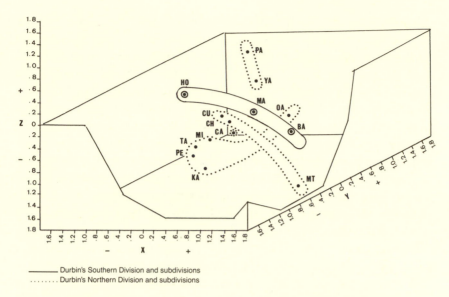

Durbin's Southern Division and subdivisions
.... Durbin's Northern Division and subdivisions

Figure 8. Tridimensional model of Cariban interrelationships and Durbin's 1977 classification.

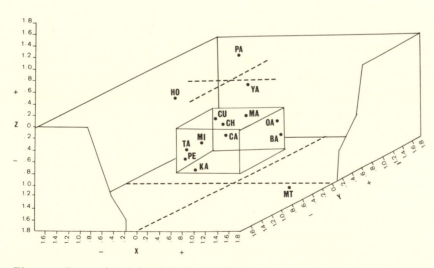

Figure 9. Core and peripheral Cariban varieties.

Umaua, Panare, Macoita, and Yabarana. The first three, in particular, should be regarded as unique sorts for, scaling results apart, they are not significantly closer to any of their nearest configuration neighbors (see note 6). Each one stands in an essentially ranked relationship vis-à-vis the nuclear languages and the rest of the outliers. Yabarana may constitute a borderline case, while Makiritare seems to represent a transitional type between the core and the periphery. Within the nucleus, contrastingly, greater overall affinity prevails among the constituents. In this manner, our three-dimensional configuration of lexical variation within Cariban reveals a mixture of cline and hierarchical relationships, corresponding to the "core"/"periphery" distinction just proposed. The components of the latter show the greatest divergence, unlike those of the core, among which predominate the more gradual and continuous variation characteristic of linguistic clines.

When translated into geographical terms, the core/periphery dichotomy acquires its fullest significance, owing to the fact that all peripherals without exception lie toward the western edge of the Cariban distribution, with Macoita and Hianacoto-Umaua conforming its boundaries (Map 3). It is not without relevance either, that Makiritare, identified tentatively as a transitional variety, holds a similar position in geographical terms (see Map 3). In sum, the core/periphery distinction coincides with a west/east division within Cariban, this being about the only clearly defined break suggested by the scaling results: toward the periphery ("west"), linguistic divergence is considerable; toward the core ("east"), it is slight.

Finally, it remains to be determined whether any subrelationships can be detected among the nuclear specimens, leading to the identification of subgroups. In this regard, our tridimensional scaling has preserved the well-known clusters comprised by Makushi, Taurepan, Pemon, and Kamarakoto, on the one hand, and by Cumanagoto and Chaima on the other. Together they constitute the only two demarcated sets within our sample. For further exploration, several triadic tests (see note 6) were run with the following results:

(1) Chaima and Cumanagoto are significantly closer to each other than to Makiritare or Carib.

(2) Oayana and Makiritare are significantly closer to each other than to Bakairi (i.e., the latter is not significantly closer to either of the two).

(3) No pair in the triad Makiritare-Cumanagoto-Carib is signifi-

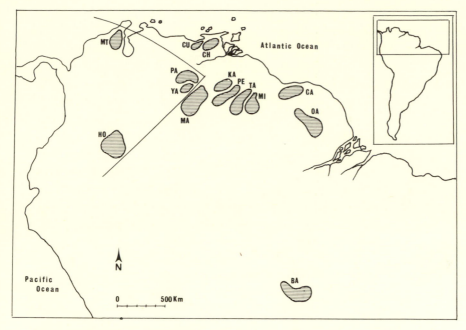

Map 3. Peripheral and core varieties.
Adapted from Rowe (1974b).

cantly closer to each other than to the third (i.e., MA is not significantly closer to CU than to CA; CU is not significantly closer
to MA than to CA; and CA is not significantly closer to CU than
to MA).

(4) No pair in the triad Carib-Makiritare-Oayana is significantly
closer to each other than either is to the third.

(5) As expected, Pemon and Taurepan were found to be significantly
closer to each other than to Makushi or Kamarakoto, but both
were found to be significantly closer to Makushi than to
Kamarakoto.

These outcomes, in conjunction with those derived from the multidimensional scaling of lexical distances measured by percentages of homosemantic cognates, imply a classification of the fourteen varieties tested
similar to that shown in Table 7.

TABLE 7.   CLASSIFICATION OF 14 CARIBAN
LANGUAGES DERIVED FROM
MULTIDIMENSIONAL SCALING

PERIPHERAL *(Outliers or Western Division)*
  I.   Macoita
 II. Hianacoto-Umaua
III. Panare
IV. Yabarana

CORE *(Eastern Division)*
  V. Makiritare
      Carib
      Oayana
      Bakairi

      Makushi
      Taurepan
      Pemon
      Kamarakoto

      Cumanagoto
      Chaima

Interpretation and Inferences

The greater homogeneity discerned among the core or nuclear languages probably reflects a combination of later splits, postseparation contacts, and participation in a dialect chain. It is conceivable that our configuration might have "recovered" the "fossil" evidence of a former state of affairs that stood in sharp contrast to the modern situation characterized by wide linguistic gaps due to the extinction of intermediate forms and diminished intertribal interaction. Having discussed selected aspects of time depth within Cariban in an earlier section of this chapter, we turn next to a review of some of the evidence pointing to the existence of dialect chains, pervasive cultural contacts, and extensive trade networks among the aborigines of northern Venezuela and the Orinoco (Morey 1975; Morales and Arvelo-Jiménez 1981; Lathrap 1973).

    For example Gilij (1782 [1965]), who was well acquainted with the aboriginal Cariban population occupying the Middle Orinoco in the eighteenth century, observed that, allowing for the "expected small differences," it all shared practically the same language as that spoken on the Paria coast and the environs of Caracas (174). He reported, additionally, that "the Makiritare, Areverianos, Cumanacotos and the inhabitants of Paria could be called Tamanacos [extinct speakers of a Middle Orinoco Cariban variety]" (Gilij 1782 [1965]: 172). On account of their presumed close resemblance, relatively speaking, several current authors have grouped Tamanaco with Chaima and Cumanagoto (Loukotka 1968; Girard 1971; Durbin 1977). Girard, for example, noticed that Tamanaco's consonant cluster reduction rules seemed to occupy a position in between the Cumana group, which retained the clusters intact, and the Makiritare group, which reduced them to ʔS (Girard 1971:206–7). In analogous manner, Civrieux (1980) has remarked on the manifest affinity between *sotto*, the Makiritare word for "person," "twenty," "human being," and *choto* (or *shoto*), generalized with identical meaning among the northern Cariban tribes:

> The central tribes of the Northern Cariban Area [Map 4] (Cumanagoto), and the eastern ones (Chaima) called themselves *Choto* (people, human being) and spoke dialects of a common tongue (*Chotomaimu*) which allowed for mutual communication. It is probable, but not proven, that the westernmost Cariban (Caracas, Meregoto) were also *Choto* and spoke dialects of the *Chotomaimu*. (Civrieux 1980:40, my translation)

In Civrieux's opinion, this unique isolexicality bespeaks a degree of kinship between Makiritare and the northern Cariban tribes (Civrieux 1980:38).[9] Thus, the evidence gathered by a number of researchers employing different methods and data provides some support for the postulated existence of a historical dialect area bounded at the north by Coastal Cariban and to the south by Guiana Cariban. Midway between the two stood as linkages Tamanaco and the other defunct languages of the Middle Orinoco. Noteworthy in this respect is the fact that Makushi, another Guiana core language, shares with Cumanagoto and Chaima its largest percentage of homosemantic cognates outside its own subgroup (69%). Upon application of the triadic method (see note 6), it was found that Makushi is significantly closer to Cumanagoto than it is to Makiritare, though it is significantly closer to the latter than to Oayana. Indeed, here may lie the explanation for the inversion that presents the Gran Sabana quartet in both configurations, where Makushi appears repeatedly "pulled" toward the coastal cluster and Carib, reversing the actual geographic orientation of the chain.

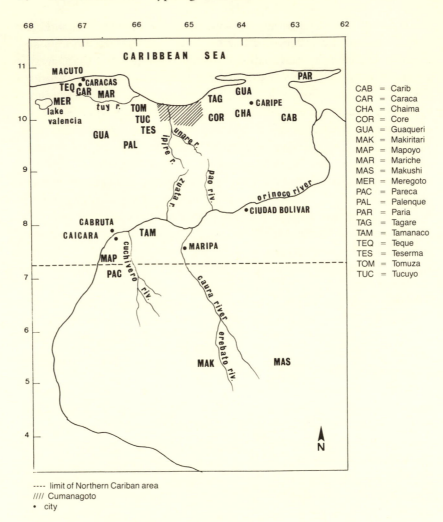

Map 4. Focal area of a major Cariban network.
Adapted from Civrieux (1980).

One of the most pertinent regions to consider in the examination of sustained interethnic contacts as a significant factor in the evolution of the core or "eastern" languages is the "Northern Cariban Area," which stretched, according to Civrieux (1980), in an easterly direction from Borburata and Lake Valencia to the Paria Peninsula (Map 4). This region was the home of numerous tribes that were fairly homogeneous in language and culture and clearly distinguishable from the Caribs (Kari'ña or Galibi). Halfway through the Northern Cariban belt were located the Palenque and the Cumanagoto, between the Chaima to the east and the Tomuza and its neighbors to the west. The Palenque, who were deft navigators, figured as trade intermediaries between the coastal people, including the Cumanagoto, and the Orinoco tribes. The region comprising the headwaters of the Unare, Ipire, Pao, and Zuata rivers (Map 4) constituted a strategic node in the fluvial and trade network linking them. From the Unare Lagoon, where the Palenque and surrounding peoples sought salt and dried and salted fish, flowed these and other items (Civrieux 1980:50–51) in the Palenque canoes, effectively structuring a socioeconomic web that linked vast territories and set the stage for sustained interethnic contacts.

A similar role was played by the Caribs, who, before the advent of the Europeans, exchanged gold and "Amazon stones" throughout Guiana, traveling up and down the Orinoco water system and the Rio Branco as well (Hoff 1968:17, 18–19). When the demand for European items rose among the Indian groups, the Caribs became the key middlemen, bartering foreign goods from the coastal towns deep into the interior country. According to Morey (1975:257), by the seventeenth century they were bringing in large amounts of European goods to the regional markets of the Llanos and exchanging them for slaves. The Caribs also used to participate in the crowded trade fairs that were held annually at the several "trade centers" that developed along key spots on the Orinoco, where highly prized natural resources were gathered at certain times of the year (Morey 1975:269). The turtle beaches of the Middle Orinoco and the fish markets of the Atures Rapids were two examples. In the latter,

> tribes from the east and south met those from the Llanos, especially during the dry season. As early as 1584 Antonio de Berrío was told by the natives that this area was the center of trade between Guayana and the Llanos (Ojer 1960:54). The Carib made this place one of their regular trading stops on their expeditions up the Orinoco. Here they not only bought provisions for their journey, but met other groups with whom they traded their European articles for slaves. (Morey 1975:271)

It is quite possible (although we lack direct evidence) that the Makiritare and other Guiana Cariban tribes participated in some of these networks, representative of the several regional systems of interaction that were active centuries ago. The idea is not entirely far-fetched, for the Makiritare, who are excellent canoeists and merchants, traveled to Angostura (Ciudad Bolívar) before the end of the eighteenth century in search of iron tools, textiles, and guns. In 1840 the explorer Robert Schomburk met a party of Makiritare from the Cunucunuma River (on the Upper Orinoco) on its way to Georgetown to trade (Coppens 1971:35). The Makiritare oral tradition describes the Indians who inhabited Caicara, a port on the Middle Orinoco (Map 4) and preserves the memory of those who intermarried with these strangers. Similarly, their lore makes reference to those Makiritare who married among the coastal Macuto people (Map 4) and tells how their descendants later dispersed. Lastly, a Makiritare esoteric chant makes numerous allusions to prominent topographical features of the valley of Caracas and surrounding areas. Naturally, the content of an oral tradition cannot be taken in its literal sense or accepted uncritically. Nevertheless, it is not totally devoid of significance for, at the very least, it expresses a point of view about a particular aspect of a distant past epoch (Vansina 1973:20).

Altogether, the evidence reviewed confirms the existence of far-flung pre-Columbian regional networks that sprang up in the presence of a vast web of navigable waters capable of sustaining a brisk traffic of peoples and goods. The character of this natural system of communication favored those who, like the Caribs, Cumanagoto, Makiritare, and Pemon, possessed the required navigational skills, and bypassed or neglected others who, like the Panare, did not. This reconstructed probable course of affairs may provide a partial explanation for the peripheral positions of Panare and Yabarana, neighboring varieties of Makiritare, which bespeak long periods of relative isolation and independent evolution.

To conclude the interpretation of the tridimensional scaling results, we will address the problem of determining a likely center of origin and the most plausible dispersal routes for Cariban. In order to do so, it seems convenient to recall briefly some generally accepted principles. The two main postulates of migration theory state that (1) the area of origin of related languages is continuous and (2) the probabilities of different reconstructed migrations are inversely related to the number of reconstructed language movements that each requires (Diebold 1960; Dyen 1956). Additionally, it is generally believed that the home of a protolanguage can be safely identified with the area where linguistic differentiation is greatest (Anttila 1972).

In accordance with these axioms, our results suggest the following model of Cariban development: (1) The center of dispersal of the sample languages lay somewhere in the Venezuelan Guiana. Within this general area, the slopes which give birth to the Caura, Cuchivero, and Ventuari watersheds, north of the junction of the sierras Parima and Pacaraima, seem the most likely site of the ancestral home of the Cariban speakers. (2) From this area or thereabout, a very early migration possibly ensued, giving rise to the Yukpa-Macoita enclave. Opon-Carare, farther south, is usually regarded as an extension of this northwesternmost Cariban variety (Durbin and Seijas 1973b). (3) A later cleavage and migration probably gave rise to the Hianacoto-Umaua-Carijona enclave. (4) After these two outward waves were accomplished, or possibly coincident with the second, Yabarana and Panare began to pursue a comparatively independent course of evolution. (5) Concurrently, Cariban initiated a gradual expansion toward the north, south, and east. (6) Among those that followed the southern route (possibly along the Rio Branco) figured, most likely, the ancestors of the Caribs and the Bakairi. The latter, representing the last major split, probably headed straight south, while the Carib branch may have veered northward after its southern sojourn, eventually to wedge between the eastwardly expanding Cariban groups and the coastal population of the Guianas. Or, alternatively, they may have settled on the Atlantic shores and later displaced inland (cf. Allaire 1980). This last reconstruction seeks to incorporate the implications of Hoff's analysis of Carib and Tupi borrowings:

> . . . formerly the area of habitation of the Caribs may well have extended further southwards. An indication of the correctness of this view is perhaps the considerable borrowing that has taken place between Carib and the unrelated Tupi language. . . . Among the loan-words there is a strikingly large proportion of names of plants and animals, far outnumbering words for items of material culture. This supports the assumption that the borrowing was not only the result of long trade travels, but also of a formerly shorter geographical distance between Caribs and Tupi. (Hoff 1968 : 13)

Map 5 summarizes this reconstructed prehistory of Cariban.

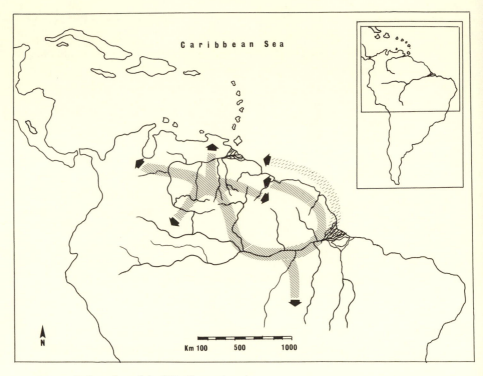

Map 5. Inferred model of Cariban migration.

Acknowledgments

A first version of this chapter was prepared for a course in quantitative methods in linguistic classification taught by Robert L. Oswalt at the University of California, Berkeley, in the fall of 1975. At that time, he suggested that I revise my paper for publication and to that end made detailed comments and suggestions, most of which I incorporated into the second draft many years later. In spite of the time elapsed, he was kind enough to referee this chapter and send his very useful comments. For all this, for his continued interest, and for arranging my use of computer time in 1975, I owe him a debt of gratitude. The Computer Center of the University of California, Berkeley, subsidized the computer time. Finally, Henry E. Corradini deserves special credit and thanks for the beautifully done maps and drawings that accompany the text.

Appendix

COORDINATES OF THE THREE-DIMENSIONAL SCALING OF 14 CARIBAN VARIETIES.

	X	Y	Z
Yabarana	.051	.353	.800
Kamarakoto	−.176	−.501	−.774
Panare	.879	−.668	1.325
Pemon	−.347	−.514	−.467
Bakairi	1.066	−.059	−.156
Makushi	−.159	−.455	−.239
Taurepan	−.333	−.457	−.424
Makiritare	.308	−.101	.233
Carib	−.390	.324	−.128
Cumanagoto	.102	−.324	.198
Hianacoto-Umaua	−1.124	.314	.514
Chaima	.150	−.214	.048
Oayana	.324	.610	.103
Macoita	−.351	1.691	−1.023

NOTES

1. A shorter and slightly modified Spanish version of this material appeared in *Antropológica* 68 (1987): 23–47.

2. The evidence for the presence of Caribs in Brazil at the beginning of the seventeenth century is contradictory. For a discussion see Hoff (1968:8–11).

3. For a fuller account of the Kari'ña retreat see Civrieux (1976).

4. It was mentioned earlier that the status of Hianacoto-Umaua, classed as extinct by Durbin (1977), is uncertain. In addition, see Loukotka (1968); Key (1979), Schindler (1977); and Castellvi and Espinosa Perez (1958).

5. Armellada (1943); Goeje (1946); Hildebrandt (1958); Hoff (1968); Koch-Grünberg (1908, 1928); Méndez-Arocha (1959); Ruiz Blanco (1888); Steinen (1892); Simpson (1940); Tauste (1680 [1888]); Williams (1932); Yangues (1683 [1888]); Ahlbrinck (1931).

6. In order to determine whether a particular variety was significantly closer to a second than to a third, the triadic method developed by Oswalt (1973) was applied. This technique of judging relationships involves an analysis of the cognate distribution among a chosen triplet of related languages, followed by a one-tailed test of significance. For example, in considering if A is significantly closer to B than to C, one must determine first the number of cognates which A shares with B but not with C, as well as the number which A shares with C but not with B. Then the probability of getting such a split is determined at a chosen level of significance (0.100 in our case). With the aid of this procedure "probability measures" of the degree of lexical interrelationships are obtained at levels of significance which help in decision-making (Oswalt 1973:330).

7. Multidimensional scaling plots can be rotated and/or reflected according to need or preference since they merely represent a scaling of points spaced and oriented relative to one another and without reference to any external condition or relationship (see definition, above).

8. These languages were consistently "pulled" toward the center of the distribution in all trial scalings performed to generate two- and three-dimensional configurations.

9. The Chikena speakers, located in the southeast corner of Guyana, also share this morph (cf. Loukotka 1968:205).

REFERENCES

Ahlbrinck, W.
   1931   *Encyclopaedie der Karaiben,* Verhandelingen der Koninklijke Akademie van Wetenschappen te Amsterdam, afdeeling letterkunde, n.r. Deel 27.1.

Allaire, Louis
   1980   "On the historicity of Carib migrations in the Lesser Antilles." *American Antiquity* 45.2:238–45.

Anttila, Raimo
   1972   *An Introduction to Historical and Comparative Linguistics.* New York: Macmillan.

Armellada, Cesáreo de
   1943   *Gramática y diccionario de la lengua Pemón. Vol. 2: Diccionario.* Caracas: Artes Gráficas.

Black, Paul
   1974   *Multidimensional Scaling Applied to Linguistic Relationships.* Murray Hill, N.J.: Bell Laboratories. Mimeographed.

Campbell, Lyle
   1973   "Distant genetic relationship and the Maya-Chipaya hypothesis." *Anthropological Linguistics* 15.3:113–35.

Castellvi, Marcelino de and Lucas Espinosa Perez
   1958   *Propedeútica etnioglotológica y diccionario clasificador de las lenguas indoamericanas.* Madrid: Consejo Superior de Investigaciones Científicas, Instituto "Bernardino de Sahagún."

Civrieux, Marc de
   1976   *Los Caribes y la conquista de la Guayana Española (Etnohistoria Kari'ña).* Caracas: Universidad Católica "Andrés Bello."
   1980   "Los Cumanagotos y sus vecinos." In *Los aborígenes de Venezuela Vol. I, Etnología antigua,* ed. Walter Coppens, pp. 27–239. Caracas: Fundación La Salle.

Coppens, Walter
   1971   "Las relaciones comerciales de los Yekuanas del Caura-Paragua." *Antropológica* 30:28–59.

Diebold, Richard A., Jr.
   1960   "Determining the centers of dispersal of language groups." *International Journal of American Linguistics* 26.1:1–10.

Durbin, Marshall
  1977   "A survey of the Carib language family." In *Carib-speaking Indians: Culture, Society and Language,* ed. Ellen B. Basso, pp. 23–38. Tucson: University of Arizona Press.
Durbin, Marshall and Haydée Seijas
  1972   "The phonological structure of the Western Carib languages of the Sierra de Perijá." *Atti del XL Congresso Internazionale degli Americanisti* (Estratto): 69–77.
  1973a   "Proto-Hianacoto: Guaque-Carijona-Hianacoto-Umaua." *International Journal of American Linguistics* 39.1:22–31.
  1973b   "A note on Opon-Carare." *Zeischrift für ethnologie* 98.2:242–45.
Dyen, Isidore
  1956   "Language distribution and migration theory." *Language* 32.4: 611–26.
  1962   "The lexicostatistically determined relationship of a language group." *International Journal of American Linguistics* 28.3:153–61.
Gama Malcher, José M.
  1964   *Indios. Grau de integração na comunidade nacional, grupo linguístico logalização.* Rio de Janeiro: Ministerío da Agricultura, Conselho Nacional de Proteção aos Indios.
Gilij, Felipe Salvador
  1782   *Ensayo de historia americana.* Vol. 3. Transl. Antonio Tovar. Caracas:
  [1965] Biblioteca de la Academia Nacional de la Historia, vol. 73.
Girard, Victor
  1971   Proto-Carib Phonology. Ph.D. dissertation. University of California.
Goeje, Claudius Henricus de
  1909   *Etudes linguistiques Caraïbes.* Verhandelingen der Koninklijke Akademie van Wetenschappen te Amsterdam, afdeeling letterkunde, n.r. 10.3.
  1946   *Etudes linguistiques Caribes,* Vol. 2. Verhandelingen der Koninklijke Akademie van Wetenschappen te Amsterdam, afdeeling letterkunde, n.r. 2.
Greenberg, Joseph H.
  1962   "Provisional classification of aboriginal languages of Latin America." [chart]. *Encyclopaedia Britannica, Vol. 12.* Chicago: Encyclopaedia Britannica Inc.
Henley, Paul and Marie-Claude Mattei-Muller
  1982   "Comentarios (Languages of the Orinoco-Amazon watershed: Some comments on Migliazza's classification)." *Antropológica* 57:79–90.
Hildebrandt, Martha
  1958   *Lenguas indígenas de Venezuela I. Sistema fonémico del Macoita.* Caracas: Ministerio de Justicia, Comisión Indigenista.
Hoenigswald, Henry M.
  1960   *Language Change and Linguistic Reconstruction.* Chicago: University of Chicago Press.

Hoff, B. J.
    1968   *The Carib Language*. Verhandelingen van het Koninklijk Instituut voor Taal-, Land- en Volkenkunde 55. The Hague: Martinus Nijhoff.

Hymes, D. H.
    1960   "Lexicostatistics so far." *Current Anthropology* 1.1 : 3—44.

Key, Mary Ritchie
    1979   *The Grouping of South American Indian Languages*. Ars Linguistica, 2. Tübingen: Gunter Narr.

Kirk, Jerome and P. J. Epling
    1973   "Taxonomy of the Polynesian languages." *Anthropological Linguistics* 15.1 : 42—70.

Koch-Grünberg, Theodor
    1908   "Die Hianákoto-Umáua." *Anthropos* 3 : 1—112.
    1928   *Vom Roroima zum Orinoko, Vol. IV*. Stuttgart.

Landar, Herbert
    1968   "The Karankawa invasion of Texas." *International Journal of American Linguistics* 34.4 : 242—58.

Lanning, Edward
    1974   "Eastern South America." In *Prehispanic America*, ed. S. Gorenstein, pp. 87—109. New York: St. Martin's Press.

Lathrap, Donald W.
    1970   *The Upper Amazon*. New York: Praeger.
    1973   "The antiquity and importance of long-distance trade relationships in the moist tropics of pre-Columbian South America." *World Archaeology* 5 : 170—86.

Layrisse, Miguel, and Johannes Wilbert
    1966   *Indian Societies of Venezuela: Their Blood Group Types*. Caracas: Fundación La Salle.

Loukotka, Čestmír
    1968   *Classification of South American Indian Languages*, ed. Johannes Wilbert. Latin American Center Reference Series, vol. 7. Los Angeles: University of California.

McQuown, Norman A.
    1955   "The indigenous languages of Latin America." *American Anthropologist* 57.3 (June): 501—70.

Mason, John Alden
    1963   "The languages of South American Indians." In *Handbook of South American Indians*, ed. Julian H. Steward, vol. 6, pp. 157—317. New York: Cooper Square.

Méndez-Arocha, Alberto
    1959   "Yabarana con apuntes fonémicos." *Antropológica* 7 : 63—84.

Migliazza, Ernest C.
    1980   "Languages of the Orinoco-Amazon Basin: Current status." *Antropológica* 53 : 95—162.

Morales, Filadelfo and Nelly Arvelo-Jiménez
    1981   "Hacia un modelo de estructura social Caribe." *América Indígena* 41.4 : 603—26.

Morey, Nancy K. C.
1975 Ethnohistory of the Colombian and Venezuelan Llanos. Ph.D. dissertation. University of Utah.

Oswalt, Robert L.
1973 "A triadic method of judging linguistic relationships." *Anthropological Linguistics* 15.7:328–36.

Rochefort, Charles de
1681 *Histoire morale des îles Antilles de l'Amérique.* Rotterdam.

Rodrigues, Aryon Dall'Igna
1974 "Linguistic groups of Amazonia." In *Native South America,* ed. Patricia J. Lyon, pp. 51–58. Boston: Little, Brown.

Rowe, John Howland
1974a "Linguistic classification problems in South America." In *Native South America,* ed. Patricia J. Lyon, pp. 43–50. Boston: Little, Brown.
1974b "Indian Tribes of South America" [Map]. In *Native South America,* ed. Patricia J. Lyon. Boston: Little, Brown.

Ruiz Blanco, Matias
1888 *Arte y tesoro de la lengua cumanagota* [Algunas obras raras sobre la lengua Cumanagota publicadas de nuevo por Julio Platzmann, Vol. III]. Leipzig: B.G. Teubner.

Schindler, Helmut
1977 "Carijona and Manakïnï: An opposition in the mythology of a Carib tribe." In *Carib-speaking Indians: Culture, Society and Language,* ed. Ellen B. Basso, pp. 66–75. Tucson: University of Arizona Press.

Schuller, Rodolfo R.
1919–1920 "Zur sprachlichen Verwandtschaft der Maya-Qu'itsé mit der Carib-Aruác." *Anthropos* 14–15:465–91.

Simpson, George Gaylord
1940 "Los Indios Kamarakotos." *Revista de Fomento* 3.22–25:201–660.

Steinen, Karl von den
1892 *Die Bakaïri-Sprache.* Leipzig: K.F. Koehler's Antiquarium.

Steward, Julian H. and Louis C. Faron
1959 *Native Peoples of South America.* New York: McGraw Hill.

Sued-Badillo, Jalil
1978 *Los Caribes: Realidad o fábula.* Río Piedras (Puerto Rico): Editorial Antillana.

Tauste, Francisco de
1680 *Arte bocabulario doctrina christiana y catecismo de la lengua de Cumana*
[1888] [Algunas obras raras sobre la lengua Cumanagota publicadas de nuevo por Julio Platzmann, Vol. I]. Leipzig: B.G. Teubner.

Taylor, Douglas
1954 "Diachronic note on the Carib contribution to Island Carib." *International Journal of American Linguistics* 20.1:28–33.

Tovar, Antonio
1961 *Catálogo de las lenguas de América del Sur.* Buenos Aires: Editorial Sudamericana.

Vansina, Jan
    1973   *Oral Tradition: A Study in Historical Methodology.* London: Penguin
            Books.
Williams, James
    1932   "Grammatical notes and vocabulary of the language of the Makuchi
            Indians of Guiana." *Anthropos* 8.
Yangues, Manuel de
    1683   *Principios y reglas de la lengua Cumanagota* [Algunas obras raras sobre
    [1888] la lengua Cumanagota publicadas de nuevo por Julio Platzmann, Vol.
            II]. Leipzig: B.G. Teubner.

III

Comparative Linguistics

Ana Fernández Garay

The Phonology of Ranquel and Phonological Comparisons with Other Mapuche Dialects

ABSTRACT

This chapter describes the phonemes of Ranquel, a Mapuche dialect, and compares the system with other Mapuche dialects spoken in Argentina and Chile. Ranquel was spoken some years ago in the province of La Pampa, Argentina. Nowadays there remain some speakers, but they seldom use their mother tongue. The fricative series of Ranquel is compared with other Mapuche varieties spoken in Argentina.[1] The labial and dental fricatives /v, ð/ are generally voiced consonants, in contrast to the other dialects wherein voiceless fricatives prevail. Finally, the chapter shows the relationship between Ranquel and Picunche, the northern Mapuche dialect of Chile.

Introduction [2]

This chapter was prepared using data collected during fieldwork conducted on October 17–27, 1983, in the province of La Pampa, Argentina.[3] During this period, the following places were visited: Santa Rosa (the capital of La Pampa); Victorica (in the department of Loventué, 150 km from Santa Rosa); Telén (a rural settlement 12 km from Victorica); Santa Isabel (a rural town in the department of Chalileo, in the northwest of the province, 312 km from Santa Rosa); Colonia Emilio Mitre (in the department of Chalileo, 18 km from Santa Isabel and 294 km from Santa Rosa). We concentrated our work in Colonia Emilio Mitre, for it is an exclusively indigenous settlement and the only place where we could find a Ranquel group. In 1983 the colonia had approximately 120 inhabitants, but the population varies frequently because of the periodic or continual migrations of the people who abandon the reservation to look for work. Colonia Emilio Mitre is about 400 km from Chile, at about the latitude of Chillán,

Chile, which coincides with the northernmost area of Mapuche speakers in Chile. Ethnographical information on the Ranquel is given in Fernández Garay (1988).

Background of the Studies

The names of the Ranqueles (they call themselves Ranquelinos) come from the words *raŋkïl* 'reed-grass' and *če* 'people'. They were known from the earliest times from the book written by Lucio V. Mansilla in 1870: *Una excursión a los indios ranqueles*. He called them an Araucanian group:

> tribus de indios araucanos que, habiendo emigrado en distintas épocas de la falda occidental de la cordillera de los Andes a la oriental, y pasado los ríos Negro y Colorado, han venido a establecerse entre el río Quinto y el río Colorado, al naciente del río Chalileo. (Mansilla 1870[1966]:66)

According to Rodolfo Casamiquela, the Ranqueles were the transition group of the west area of the Querandíes, "Araucanized" by the Mapuche tribes from the north of Neuquén, that is, the Pehuenche group. The old Querandí language, in Casamiquela's view, should be related with the Gününa-küne, that is, the northern austral Tehuelche (Casamiquela 1982:21−22). Cooper classified the Ranqueles as belonging to the Mapuche, who were called Araucanians by the Spanish conquerors; the name comes from Arauco (*raï* 'clay' and *ko* 'water'), a region in central Chile. The same position was taken by the missionary Sánchez Labrador, who worked in Pampa and Patagonia about the middle of the eighteenth century. The few Ranqueles who survive nowadays are found in the Colonia Emilio Mitre, in the Pampean desert. According to the data collected in situ, this group could have come from La Blanca, near Luan Toro, in the northeastern area of the province, where they would have arrived from Villa Sarmiento or Sarmiento Nuevo, in Río Cuarto, Córdoba, Argentina. Although it is not the goal of this chapter to search for the mysterious origin of the group, the linguistic analysis could bring forth some evidence about this interesting subject through the phonological comparison of Ranquel with other Mapuche dialects.

Ranquel has not been well documented up to the present. We only have the "Vocabulario Rankelče" by A. V. Frich, compiled by Loukotka in "Contribuciones a la lingüística sudamericana" (1929). Frich's vocabulary was collected in General Acha, La Pampa, far from the Ranquel area, and it is quite different phonetically from what I have observed. Today, Ranquel is in an advanced state of extinction, as it is being replaced by Spanish.

The present study is based on the corpus obtained in Colonia Emilio Mitre from bilingual speakers: Juana Cabral de Carripilón (75 years old); Veneranda Cabral de Cabral (77 years old); Marcelina Baigorrita (nearly 100 years old) and Juana Carripí de Lima (75 years old). They are considered to be the last Ranquel-speakers of the community. A basic vocabulary of 200 to 600 words and 200 phrases was elicited from the informants, and this forms the corpus for this work.

Phonological System of Ranquel

The inventory of Ranquel phonemes is as follows:

Consonants	Labial	Dental	Alveolar	Retroflex	Palatal	Velar
Stop and affricate	p	t		tʳ	č	k
Fricative	v	ð	s	r		
Lateral			l		λ	
Nasal	m		n		ñ	ŋ
Semivowel	w				y	

Vowels	Front	Central	Back	
High	i	ï	u	
Low	e	a	o	

Description of the phonemes:

/p/   is articulated as a bilabial, oral, voiceless stop.

/t/   is articulated as a postdental, oral, voiceless stop.

/tʳ/   is articulated as a retroflex, oral, voiceless affricate. In the idiolect of Veneranda Cabral, it alternates with an apico-alveolar, voiceless stop: [tʳ] ~ [ţ].

/č/   is articulated as a palatal, voiceless affricate. In Juana Cabral and Marcelina Baigorrita's speech, it alternates with an apico-alveolar, voiceless stop: [č] ~ [ţ]. This [ţ] is a stylistic variation, of affective nature.

/k/   is articulated as a velar, oral, voiceless stop when it precedes central and back vowels. Contiguous to front vowels, it advances its point of articulation closer to the palatal region.

/v/   is articulated as a labiodental, oral fricative, with voiced and voiceless realizations: [v] ~ [f]. The voiced one prevails.

/ð/   is articulated as an interdental, oral fricative, with voiced and voiceless realizations: [ð] ~ [θ]. The voiced one prevails.

/s/   is articulated as a predorso-alveolar, oral, grooved, voiceless fricative. Due to its low frequency and to its appearance in loanwords from Spanish, we can assume that this sibilant is a foreign sound lately incorporated into Ranquel because of continuous contact with the Spanish language. The oldest studies of Mapuche do not include /s/ in their descriptions of the pronunciation of its sounds. Valdivia (1606) says "Finalmente en esta lengua raras vezes se hallan estas sylabas: ga, gue, gui, go, gu, al modo que nosotros las pronunciamos. Ni ça, çe, çi, ço, çu. Ni fa, fe, fi, fo, fu. Ni ja, je, ji, jo, ju. Ni ra, re, ri, ro, ru con la fuerza que nosotros las pronunciamos, ni sa, se, si, so, su. Ni xa, xe, xi, xo, xu" (Valdivia 1606 [1887]: Cap. 1, De la pronvnciacion y orthographia).

Febrés, in the eighteenth century, confirmed this statement: "No usan en la lengua el ja, jo, ju, ni el ge, gi castellano, ni la s, x, z, ni tampoco la b, ni la f" (Febrés 1765 [1884]: 34). In this century, Moesbach insists on the nonexistence of this sound: "Faltan, pues, en comparación con el alfabeto español; la b, c, d pura, g, h, j, s pura, x, z" (Moesbach, 1962: 25).

/r/   is articulated as a retroflex, oral, voiced fricative. Sometimes it becomes voiceless in front of voiceless stops. In Juana Carripí's idiolect, the fricative alternates with the flapped, apico-alveolar voiced vibrant due to contact with Spanish.

/l/   is articulated as an apico-alveolar, voiced lateral. Next to back vowels, and near retroflex and velar consonants, it is articulated as a retroflex.

/λ/   is articulated as a palatal, voiced lateral.

/m/   is articulated as a bilabial, voiced nasal.

/n/   is articulated as an apico-alveolar, voiced nasal. When it occurs in the same syllable with a retroflex consonant, it is articulated in the prepalatal region.

/ñ/   is articulated as a palatal, voiced nasal.

/ŋ/   is articulated as a velar, voiced nasal. It becomes palatalized next to front vowels.

/w/   is articulated as a labio-velar, voiced semivowel.

/y/   is articulated as a palatal, voiced semivowel. In some cases, it may sound like a grooved fricative: [pun'puya] ~ [pun'puža] 'armpit', much like the sound heard in Argentinian Spanish.

/i/ is articulated as a high, front, unrounded vowel. Sometimes it becomes short when it occurs next to another vowel, according to the position of the accent. Occasionally, the articulation may become slightly relaxed, and it partially lowers: [pi'či] ~ [pI'či] 'little'. Sometimes it develops a consonant as an element of transition: [ṭa iñ ḵe'wĭn] ~ [ṭa yiñ ḵe'wĭn] 'my mouth'.

/e/ is articulated as a low, front, unrounded vowel. It raises slightly before /i/ and after the palatal semiconsonant /y/.

/ï/ is articulated as two variations conditioned by the accent. In an accented syllable, /ï/ becomes [ï], a high, back, unrounded vowel. In an unaccented syllable /ï/ becomes [ə], a mid, central, unrounded vowel. It generally is shortened when preceded by a vowel. It can develop a consonant as an element of transition: [ku'ï] ~ [ku'ɤï] 'hand'.

/a/ is articulated as a low, central, unrounded vowel. Sometimes it raises slightly before /i/: [nie'lai] ~ [nie'lɛi] 'there is not'.

/u/ is articulated as a high, back, rounded vowel. It may become short when it occurs next to another vowel, according to the position of the accent. Before retroflex consonants, it may lower slightly: [pʊ'ra] 'eight'; [kʊ'tʳan] 'illness'. Sometimes it develops a consonant in transition: [u'le] ~ [wu'le] 'tomorrow'.

/o/ is articulated as a low, back, rounded vowel. It becomes short when it occurs next to another vowel.

Distribution:

In final position, only the following consonants may occur:

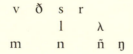

     v ð s r

            l   λ

   m   n   ñ ŋ

Comparison of Ranquel with Other Mapuche Dialects

Only the fricative series will be taken into consideration here. First of all, I will summarize briefly other modern studies done in the Mapuche areas of Argentina, that is, in the provinces of Río Negro, Neuquén, and Colonia Emilio Mitre, of La Pampa. Suárez, Golbert, and Acuña worked in Neuquén, the province with the highest concentration of Mapuche residents.

Suárez (1958 [1988]) described the phonological system of the Manzaneros, who live in Quila Quina, by Lacar Lake. In this dialect, the fricative phonemes are /f θ š/ and a vibrant series that includes /r/. From the phonetic point of view, Suárez says, "La mayor parte de los fonemas (del sistema) tienen un solo alófono, cuyo valor fonético es en general, el común para los signos empleados" (Suárez 1958 [1988]:1). Thus he does not find the voiced counterpart of /f/ and /θ/. Though he creates a new series, Suarez describes the /r/ as fricative, sometimes retroflex.

Golbert (1975) collected data in Rucachoroy, 18 km from Aluminé and 20 km from the Chilean border toward the west, in the central area of the province. For this group, the fricative series has the following phonemes: /f θ s r š x/

/f/   has four varieties: [f] labiodental voiceless fricative; [v] labiodental voiced fricative; [ɸ] bilabial voiceless fricative; [β] bilabial voiced fricative. They vary freely, though the voiceless are more frequent.

/θ/   has two varieties: [θ] interdental voiceless fricative, and [ð] interdental voiced fricative, which vary freely; in this case, Golbert does not point out which prevails.

/s/   is a phoneme of very low frequency; it appears in loans from Spanish and in very few Mapuche words.

/r/   includes two articulations: one more fricative than the other, and both apico-prepalatal, voiced, and retroflex, in free variation.

/š/   is a dorso-palatal voiceless fricative.

/x/   is a Spanish loan.

Acuña (1984) worked on the reservation Ancatruz, toward the south of Neuquén, by the Limay River. She presents the following fricative series: /f θ r š/. It may be noted that: /s/ and /x/ do not appear in the system; /f/ does not have a voiced realization; /θ/, on the other hand, has both a voiced and voiceless realization, though the voiced one is very scarce; /r/ has a retroflex variety and another that is not retroflex; and /š/ alternates in affective situations with almost all the stop and fricative sounds. According to Acuña, /š/ was not a phoneme earlier, but has been incorporated lately.

From Río Negro, I presented the phonological system of the Mapuche group settled in Anecón Grande, 200 km from San Carlos de Bariloche, an important tourist city in the province (Fernández Garay 1982). The following phonemes constitute the fricative series /f θ s r š/.

/f/   and /θ/ have voiced and voiceless variations, with voiceless ones prevailing.

/s/   is a phoneme of very low frequency; it appears in Spanish loans and in very few Mapuche words.

/r/   is a retroflexed, voiced fricative.

/š/ is also a phoneme of low frequency, but it appears in words of every-day use: *kuše* 'old woman'; *kišu* 'he, alone'; *šumel* 'shoes'.

In comparing these dialects, one notes that, in Río Negro and Neu-quén, the phonemes /f/ and /θ/ either have a unique voiceless realization or can be articulated with voiced or voiceless variations, in which case the voiceless one absolutely prevails. The same obtains in La Pampa, outside of Colonia Emilio Mitre, according to my field notes. The Mapuche of La Pampa, who do not belong to the Ranquel group, differ from them in the articulation of their fricatives /f/ and /θ/, which are voiceless. On the other hand, in Ranquel the phoneme /v/, except in Marcelina Baigorrita's idio-lect, is usually articulated as a voiced sound, with a dominant frequency of fifteen [v] to one [f]. It must be said that Señora Baigorrita's mother was Azulera, (from Azul, in the province of Buenos Aires) and thus did not belong to the Ranquel community; her dialect would have been the Ma-puche spoken by the groups settled in the center of Buenos Aires before the Desert Conquest. This then is the reason that, in her idiolect, /f/ appears with a frequency of three voiceless for each voiced fricative. As for the other Ranquel phoneme /ð/, the voiced variation prevails in the four idio-lects with a frequency of six to one against the voiceless one.

The sound /s/ has been considered a phoneme of the Ranquel group, though it appears mostly in Spanish loans and in a few Araucanian words. This situation is repeated in Rucachoroy and Anecón Grande. As has already been noted, /s/ is a sound that has not been attested by either Valdivia or Febrés in the past, nor, more recently, by Moesbach. The as-sumption that it is a sound incorporated into Ranquel from Spanish con-trasts with Key's interpretation (1978a). She thinks that it might have been a phoneme in pre-Mapuche and that it later disappeared, remaining only as a paralinguistic feature for special circumstances, to express emotional connotations.

The phoneme /r/ appears in all the dialects without exception. The phoneme /š/ occurs in all the dialects described in Río Negro and Neu-quén. The descriptions agree about the low frequency of the phoneme and on the doubts originated by the fluctuations[4] of /š/ with /s/, /č/, and /θ/. In La Pampa, it is heard in Colonia Emilio Mitre, as a stylistic affective varia-tion. It seems quite clear that it is an Araucanian sound, since it has been recorded by Febrés as an affective realization: "Suelen los indios mudar algunas letras por otras, v.g. . . . la r en d, y más en el ja, jo, ju catalán, ó gia italiano, ó ge, gi francés, para hablar melindroso" (Febrés 1765 [1884]:35).

Thus we see, in comparing the material, that Ranquel is a dialect that differs in some respects from the other Mapuche varieties of Argentina. As far as we know now, it is the only dialect in which the voiced fricatives predominate.

The distinctiveness of this dialect in Argentina has been demonstrated. Now let us look at Ranquel in relation to the dialects of Mapuche in Chile. There, Lenz determined the existence of four Mapuche dialects: Picunche (from the north), Huilliche (from the south), Pehuenche (from the eastern side of the Cordillera, the Araucaria area), and Moluche (next to the Pehuenche). Moluche and Pehuenche do not have many linguistic differences, according to Lenz (1895–97:134), so that three dialects may be considered. From the dialect of the north or Picunche, Lenz writes: "El dialecto de los picunches es el que ha conservado con mayor fidelidad el estado fonético primitivo del idioma. La pérdida del sonido de la voz que es tan característico para los huilliches, sólo se muestra en los principios del desarrollo" (Lenz 1895–97:68). Thus, Picunche was beginning to lose the voicing in the fricative series, even though the voiced sounds predominated. In the dialects of the central area there is a great variation between voiced and voiceless fricatives, according to Lenz, while in the dialect of the south, the Huilliche, the fricatives have completely lost the voicing. Thus we can affirm that in this respect, Ranquel appears to be closer to Picunche, which has maintained voicing in the fricatives. According to Lenz, "La lei fonética que distingue los dialectos del araucano se debe a la tendencia de cambiar v, d, zh, z', l, λ, en f, z, sh, s', l', λ', es decir suprimir el sonido de la voz en todos los sonidos fricativos" (Lenz 1895–97:xxiii). And, he adds later, "En el dialecto huilliche, d, j, r, así como v i más o menos completamente, l i ll han perdido el sonido de la voz, escribo el resultado: z, sh, s', f, l', i, λ'" (Lenz 1895–97:6).

Thus we have:

Older Araucanian	Picunche	Huilliche
d (ð)	d (ð)	z (θ)
j (ž)	zh (ž)	sh (š)
r	z' (ž)	s' (š)
v	β	f
l	l	l' (voiceless)
λ	λ	λ' (voiceless)

Of all the sounds described by Lenz for Picunche, only [ž] is not a phoneme of Ranquel; it is a variation of /y/. Concerning this sound Suárez writes, "no está claro cuáles pueden haber sido las razones que llevaran a Lenz a postular este sonido pues en Valdivia tan minucioso y exacto en la descripción fonética, no se encuentra ningún indicio de él" (Suárez 1958 [1988]:14). The other sounds occur in Ranquel, though the labial [β] is changed into a labiodental [v].

Croese (1980) establishes the boundaries of the Mapuche dialects of Chile, determining the limits among them and their mutual intelligibility. He distinguishes eight dialectological regions: the I and II regions form the northern branch; the III, IV, V, VI, and VII form the central branch; and the VIII region is considered the southern branch. He based his analysis on rigorous graphics and precise relations between the attested items collected in situ. Most significantly, his work confirms Lenz's statements, finding great differences between north and south and a central area with much variation. From Croese's graphic number 3 (Croese 1980:17–18) we may conclude that the Ranquel belongs, without doubt—from the phonic point of view—to Croese's northern branch that is, to the Picunche, according to Lenz. In contrast, the varieties described in Río Negro, Neuquén, and those of La Pampa that are not Ranquelinos, with great predominance of voiceless fricatives, are related with Croese's central branch, called Pehuenche and Moluche by Lenz. It remains to be seen whether, in the grammatical and lexical aspects, Ranquel is also close to Picunche, the northern Mapuche dialect of Chile. This similarity between Ranquel and Picunche (northern Chilean Mapuche) goes against Casamiquela's theory, which posits that the Ranqueles have been "Araucanized" by the Pehuenches (Casamiquela 1982:9). Now it remains to be seen how this "Araucanization" from the northern region of the Araucanía took place.

Appendix

LIST OF RANQUEL VOCABULARY OBTAINED IN COLONIA EMILIO MITRE IN 1983.

mouth	wïn	blood	moλvïn
tooth	voro	nerve	vïn
shoulder	vïri	face	aɲe
finger	saŋil	skull	loŋko
heel, ankle	λoŋkosewï	brain	mïlo ~ moλo
rib	kaði	neck	pel
navel	poðo	nape	topel

nail	wili	thorn	r̈ikav̈in
elbow	čoñokin	root	volil
fist	lipan	seed	ïtʳar
shoulder blade	krakra	pasture	kaču
kidney	kuðakuðaλ	hill	mawiða
heart	piuke	land, soil	mapu
leg	čan	ostrich	čoike
knee	luku	(*Rhea*	
foot	matʳa	*americana*)	
hip	tʳutʳe	small lizard	vilkuñ
skin	tʳïlke	cat	ñaiki
bladder	wiλeñ	flea	n̈ir̈im
vein	witʳur	fly (insect)	pïlï
perspiration	ïlwi	wildcat	ŋulus
voice	ðuŋun	hen	ačawaλ
river	leuv̈i	goat	kap̈ira
dew	m̈ilven	frog	poive
cloud	tʳavtʳomï	piche	kuntʳï
plain	lelv̈in	(animal;	
smoke	pitʳun	*Zaedyus*	
sky	wenu	*pichiy*)	
wind	kïr̈iv	toad	lavatʳa
moon	kïyen	hare	mara
night	pun	dog	tʳewa
afternoon	tʳavia	fox	ŋïr̈i
coal	kuyïl	zorrino	sañi
ashes	livtʳuvken	(skunk; *Co-*	
leaf	tapïl	*nepatus*	
caldén	witʳu	*chinga*)	
(tree; *Proso-*		peludo	kov̈ir
pis caldenia)		(animal;	
jarilla	koiwe	*Chaeto-*	
(bush; *Lar-*		*phractus*	
rea divari-		*villosus*)	
cata)		mouse	ðeẅi
piquillín	tʳïvtʳau	pigeon	maikono
(bush; *Con-*		falcon	kičikïčï
dalia micro-			
phylla)			

carancho	tʳaru	brother	peñi
(bird of		father	čao
prey; *Polybo-*		mother	ñuke
rus plancus)		uncle	čačañ
chimango	tʳiukï	aunt	ñaña
(vulture-		son	pīñeñ
like; *Mil-*		son	votïm
vago		daughter	ñawe
chimango)		grandfather	λako
viscacha	tʳïwi	grandmother	papa
(*Lagostomus*		son-in-law	λaλa
maximus)		daughter-in-	pïñmo
viper	čoča	law	
martineta	wari	white	pïlan
(partridge;		black	kurï
Eudromia		red	kelï ~ kolï
elegans)		green	nïkï
partridge	siλo	yellow	čoð
(*Nothura*		high	pïta
maculosa)		short	pïtï
bird	ïñim	sweet	koči
spider	tʳïtʳin	bitter	vïre
puma	tʳapial	salty	kotʳi
(*Felis*		good	kïme
concolor)		new	we
guanaco	luan	horn	mïta
(*Lama*		tail	kïlen
guanicoe)		meat	ilo
maize	wa	soup	korï
salt	čaði	grease	yuwin
carob bean	soi	knife	kučiλo
woman	ðomo	drum	kultʳun
man	wentʳu	town	waria
husband	vïta	yesterday	wiya
wife	kure	tomorrow	ule
old woman	kuðe ~ kuse	today	vačantï
old man	vïta	pot	čaλa
friend	weni	water	ko
sister	lamŋen	winter	pukem

summer	walïn	to be hungry	ŋiñin
medicine	lawen	to be thirsty	wïwïn
fire	kitʳal	to go	amuton
road	ripï	to come	kïpatïn
well (water)	riŋaŋko	to arrive	akutïn
stone	kura	to abandon	elkïnïn
feather	ŋïpï	to enter	konpan
egg	kuram	to walk	tʳekalen
fish	čaλwa	to climb	piran
potato	poñi	to come down	naupatïn
wine	pulku	to run	levïn
bread	kovke	to see	pen
sun, day	antï	to hear	aλkin
work	kiðau	to kill	laŋimïn
lie	koila	to bring	kïpalen
ugly	weða	to sing	ïlkantun
deaf	pilu	to say	veipin
dumb	ketʳo	to ask	niλatun
blind	tʳauna	to give	elun
to eat	ilotïn	to buy	niλan
to drink water	pïtokon	to knit	ŋiren

Notes

1. Since completing this study I have reassessed the status of [š]. My present analysis assigns it affective status in the Ranquel dialect.

2. I wish to acknowledge María Beatriz Fontanella de Weinberg for her constant support and her useful observations. I also want to express my appreciation to Martine Delahaye for her helpful remarks, and to thank Dr. Jorge Navas, from the Museo Argentino de Ciencias Naturales Bernardino Rivadavia, Buenos Aires, for his amiability in giving me the scientific names of certain plants and animals.

3. This was the first stage of the Linguistic Research Relief Project of the Mapuche Communities of La Pampa, supported by the Dirección de Cultura of the province and the Secretaría de Cultura de Presidencia de la Nación. Anthropologist María Inés Poduje took part in the fieldwork because she knows the area well and is acquainted with its inhabitants; she therefore greatly facilitated the development of the work. The results of this fieldwork were presented in the report "Informe definitivo del relevamiento lingüístico realizado en Comunidades Mapuches del oeste de la provincia de La Pampa" (1984), which outlined and explained the process of extinction of Ranquel.

4. For the concept of fluctuation, see Clairis (1981).

References

Acuña, Leonor
1984   Las consonantes del Mapuche. Paper presented at the III Congreso Nacional de Linguística, Morón, Argentina.
Augusta, Fray Félix José de
1903   *Gramática Araucana*. Valdivia.
Casamiquela, Rodolfo
1982   "Tehuelches, Araucanos y otros en los últimos 500 años de poblamiento del ámbito pampeano patagónico." Buenos Aires, *Síntomas* 4–5.
Clairis, Christos
1981   "La fluctuation des phonèmes." Istanbul, *Dilbilim* 6:99–110.
Cooper, John M.
1946   "The Araucanians." In *Handbook of South American Indians*, ed. Julian H. Steward, vol. 2. pp. 687–760. Washington, D.C.: United States Government Printing Office.
Croese, Robert
1980   "Estudio dialectológico del Mapuche." *Estudios filológicos* 15:7–38. Valdivia: Universidad Austral de Chile.
Echeverría Weasson, Max Sergio
1964   "Descripción fonológica del Mapuche actual." *Boletín del Instituto de Filología de la Universidad de Chile* 16:13–59.
Febrés, Andrés
1765   *Gramática Araucana, o sea Arte de la lengua general de los Indios de*
[1884] *Chile*, Reproducción de la edición de Lima de 1765, con los textos completos por Juan Lársen. Buenos Aires: Impreso por Juan Alsina.
Fernández Garay, Ana
1982   "Rogativas Mapuches." *Amerindia* 7:109–44.
1988   Relevamiento lingüístico de hablantes Mapuches en la Provincia de la Pampa. Santa Rosa, La Pampa: Depto. Investigaciones Culturales, Dirección General de Cultura, Subsecretaría de Cultura y Communicación Social.
Golbert, Perla
1975   *Epu Peñiwen*. Buenos Aires: Centro de Investigaciones en Ciencias de la Educación, (CICE).
Key, Mary Ritchie
1976   "La fluctuación de fonemas en la teoría fonológica." *Signos: Estudios de lengua y literatura* 9.1:137–43.
1978a   "Linguística comparativa Araucana." *VICUS: Cuadernos-linguística* 2:45–56.
1978b   "Araucanian Genetic Relationships." *International Journal of American Linguistics* 44.4 (October):280–93.
Lagos Altamirano, Daniel
1981   "El estrato fónico del Mapudungu(n)." *Nueva revista del Pacífico* 19–20:42–66.

Lenz, Rodolfo
    1895–97   *Estudios araucanos*. Santiago de Chile.
Loukotka, Čestmir
    1929   "Contribuciones a la lingüística sudamericana." *Revista del Instituto de Etnología de la Universidad de Tucumán* 1:409–15.
Mansilla, Lucio Victorio
    1870   *Una excursión a los indios ranqueles*. Buenos Aires: Kapeluzs.
    [1966]
Moesbach, Ernesto Wilhelm de
    1962   *Idioma Mapuche*. Padre Las Casas. Imprenta San Francisco, Chile.
Salas, Adalberto
    1978   "Mapuche-Español. Análisis fonológico contrastivo." *VICUS: Cuadernos-linguística* 2:57–86.
Sánchez Labrador, José
    1936   *Los indios pampas, puelches, patagones*. Buenos Aires.
Suárez, Jorge A.
    1958   "Observaciones sobre el dialecto Manzanero." Monograph, Instituto
    [1988] de Linguística, Universidad de Buenos Aires. Reprinted in *Estudios de lenguas indígenas Sudamericanas*. Bahía Blanca: Depto. de Humanidades, Universidad Nacional del Sur.
    1959   "The phonemes of an Araucanian dialect." *International Journal of*
    [1988] *American Linguistics* 25.3:177–81. Reprinted in *Estudios de lenguas indígenas Sudamericanas*. Bahía Blanca: Depto. de Humanidades, Universidad Nacional del Sur.
Valdivia, P. Luis de
    1606   *Arte y Gramatica General de la Lengva que corre en todo el Reyno de*
    [1887] *Chile, con un Vocabulario y Confessonario, compuestos por el Padre Luys de Valdivia de la Compañia de Iesus en la Prouincia del Piru* . . . En Lima por Francisco del Canto. Año 1606. Facsimile edition prepared by Julio Platzmann. *Arte, Vocabulario y Confesionario de la Lengua de Chile, compuestos por Luiz de Valdivia*. Edición Facsimilar. Leipzig: B. G. Teubner.

Bruce Mannheim

Southern Peruvian Quechua Consonant Lenition

ABSTRACT

The Cuzco-Collao dialect of Southern Peruvian Quechua is distinguished from the Ayacucho-Chanca dialect by a series of syllable-final lenitions. The sequence of the lenitions is reconstructed by means of (1) internal reconstruction; (2) variation in the modern subdialects of Cuzco-Collao Quechua; and (3) written records from the late sixteenth until the late nineteenth centuries. The changes are shown to follow an orderly course through the word, subject to phonological and grammatical constraints.[1]

Introduction

Comparative reconstruction, particularly of native American languages, tends to emphasize uniformity in several respects. For methodological reasons, linguists must strive to construct as general a model as possible of the diversity of the attested cognate forms with which they work. This requires a uniformitarian view of the reconstructed prototype speech community—a view which is particularly misleading when we consider that it is often incorporated into nonlinguistic interpretations of the culture history of the speakers.[2] Also, comparative reconstruction—again for cogent methodological reasons—requires as general as possible a model of the processes by which the daughter languages diverged from the reconstructed prototype (or *proto*) language. Thus, if several similar-seeming processes of change can be subsumed structurally in a single statement, we assume that they represent a single set of historical events. This is required by Occam's razor. To assume otherwise would needlessly complicate the reconstructed model, in other words, needlessly complicate both reconstructed prototype language and reconstructed history. These uniformitarian assumptions are irrefutable as methodological principles go. They have led several generations of scholars to handle complex and variable evidence in a cogent and orderly way. This is again particularly true of North American languages, which once—early in this century—seemed inordinately diverse, and of South American languages, which appear that way today.

In this chapter, I wish to show that the orderliness obtained in a comparative reconstruction must be supplemented by other kinds of evidence: by historical records of the language change, and by contemporary dialect variation. Once we do so, the changes that once seemed straightforward and neat acquire a much more multiform cast. Where a comparative reconstruction could posit a single set of regular correspondences as a model of the changes from parent to daughter language, a model of change that incorporates philological and dialectological evidence must treat the changes in a much more piecemeal fashion. On the other hand, once we have done so, regularities of change emerge that are of a different order from the regularities assumed by the comparative method. These regularities have to do with the ways in which sound change takes place (cf. Chen and Wang 1975) and with the nature of the relationship between the processes. I intend to demonstrate this point by examining the lenitions of syllable-final consonants in the Cuzco-Collao variety of Southern Peruvian Quechua from the reconstructed parent language, Common Southern Peruvian Quechua, to the present. To do so, I use historical documentation of the language which begins in the middle of the sixteenth century as well as evidence from contemporary dialectal variation.

Southern Peruvian Quechua

Southern Peruvian Quechua is spoken by about two million inhabitants of the six southeastern departments of Peru, Apurímac, Arequipa, Ayacucho, Cuzco, Huancavelica, and Puno (Mannheim 1985b). It is a member of the peripheral branch of the Quechua family ("Quechua A" in the classification of Parker, 1963, 1969–71; "Quechua II" in the classification of Torero, 1964), and most closely related to varieties spoken in Bolivia. In this article, I refer to three levels of grouping of Quechua languages, from least to most inclusive: Common Southern Peruvian, the reconstructed ancestor of modern Southern Peruvian Quechua; Southern Quechua, including Southern Peruvian Quechua and the varieties spoken in Bolivia, Northern Argentina, and Northern Chile; and Common Quechua (or "proto Quechua"), the reconstructed ancestor of all of the Quechua languages.

Modern Southern Peruvian Quechua is divided into two dialects that have similar morpho-syntactic systems but very different sound systems. One dialect, Cuzco-Collao Quechua, includes an ejective (glottalized) and an aspirate stop series—thought to he borrowed from its Jaqi neighbors—in its segmental inventory (Mannheim 1985b). The other, Ayacucho-Chanca Quechua, does not. Conversely, the range of consonants that may appear in syllable final position is restricted in Cuzco-Collao Quechua and quite free in Ayacucho-Chanca. Ayacucho-Chanca Quechua syllable final stops correspond to Cuzco-Collao spirants. Some time after distinctive ejectives and aspirates were incorporated into the phonological system of Cuzco-Collao Quechua, the final consonants of syllables began to weaken. Stops weakened to spirants, and most distinctions between places of articulation were lost. Should these changes continue along the same trajectory, it appears likely that Cuzco-Collao Quechua will eventually have only open, consonant-vowel syllables. In this chapter I use comparative reconstruction of the common ancestor of the Southern Peruvian Quechua dialects, written texts that document about four hundred years of the history of the language, and contemporary dialectal variation to reconstruct the sequence of linguistic events by which the Cuzco-Collao Quechua syllable finals changed. These events reveal general principles that constrain the ways in which sound changes expand their domain of application. Comparative evidence suggests that they apply at least to other Quechua languages as well. But they make sense in terms of some very general properties of Quechua morpho-syntax, and so should turn out to constrain the expansion of change in other unrelated languages of the same morpho-syntactic type.

The systematic correspondences between the Cuzco-Collao and Ayacucho-Chanca dialects was first observed by Rowe in his classic article "Sound patterns in three Inca dialects" (1950). He compared these dialects with early seventeenth-century Cuzco-Collao Quechua as described by Gonçález Holguín (1607, 1608) and observed that the Ayacucho-Chanca dialect lacked the ejectives and aspirates present in modern Cuzco-Collao Quechua and obliquely attested in Gonçález Holguín's *Vocabulario,* while the modern Cuzco-Collao dialect showed a narrower range of segments in syllable-final position than either Ayacucho-Chanca or colonial Cuzco: The Ayacucho-Chanca and colonial Cuzco-Collao syllable-final stops correspond to modern Cuzco-Collao spirants. From this evidence he reconstructed a prototype Southern Peruvian Quechua ("Classic Inca"; I shall refer to it here as Common Southern Peruvian Quechua) with both the full range of syllable-final consonants and ejectives and aspirates. Rowe (1950: 137) believed that, "the known modern dialects, including those of Cuzco and Ayacucho, derive from the form of the language spoken in Cuzco in the sixteenth century rather than preserving older local differences." This assertion has turned out to be inadequate in the light of more intensive work in the Central Quechua languages, which has demonstrated that the Quechua family is far more diverse than was believed in the 1940s and 1950s. The time depth of genetic reconstruction in Quechua is consequently larger than was then believed. Rowe's emphasis on colonial text rather than comparative reconstruction therefore seems misplaced, at least for a pan-Quechua horizon, for there are few colonial texts of secure provenience from outside of Cuzco, and the depth of differentiation of the Quechua family is far greater than the four and a half centuries that can potentially be documented with texts. He appears to have considered his reconstruction as deep and wide in scope as the evidence permitted. If it was not a family-wide reconstruction, it was an excellent study of Southern Peruvian Quechua phonological history, for which much of the detail has stood the test of time.

Rowe's key assumption for both the restoration of the finals and the ejectives and aspirates was procedural. When one segment in a witness consistently corresponded to two in another without apparent conditioning, he reconstructed it as a merger. His reconstruction of the finals has since been empirically supported by other evidence. His argument that the lenitions were innovations in Cuzco-Collao Quechua accounts for much of the dialect variation in the modern language, and by traces of the mergers in the synchronic phonology. Rowe's reconstruction of the finals also permits them to be reconstructed at a pan-Quechua level in an unproblematic way. The reconstructed syllable-finals correspond exactly in cognate forms to those of other, non-southern Quechua languages (Parker 1969–71; parts 1, 4, 5).

Rowe's assertion that Common Southern Peruvian Quechua had both ejectives and aspirates and that these were subsequently lost in Ayacucho-Chanca Quechua is less strong. From an external viewpoint, neither can be reconstructed outside Southern Quechua (Southern Peruvian, Bolivian, and Argentine varieties), although there are possible witnesses in Ecuador which may ultimately be of Southern Peruvian origin as well. Reconstruction of ejectives and aspirates is highly problematic even at the level of Southern Quechua, for there is considerable lexical variation in presence of glottalization and aspiration throughout the Southern Quechua languages (cf. Stark 1975). The distribution of ejectives and aspirates in modern Cuzco-Collao into patterned but variable phonesthematic sets suggests that the variability of these features is a result of a long-term process of lexical diffusion and split (Mannheim and Newfield 1982). There is a small amount of evidence that Ayacucho-Chanca Quechua once had these features also, in the form of an *h* that begins words that etymologically should begin with a vowel.

Words beginning with a vowel were preceded by a predictable glottal catch. But in the Southern Quechua languages that have ejectives and aspirates, there is a word-structure constraint that restricts glottalization to once per word. Words preceded by a glottal catch that also contain an ejective (glottalized) stop are incompatible with the constraint. The initial glottal catch was therefore replaced by an epenthetic *h* in such words. Some examples from contemporary Cuzco-Collao Quechua are listed in column A of Table 1.

Column B lists the Ayacucho-Chanca cognates (from Parker 1969b and Soto Ruíz 1976) to the Cuzco-Collao examples and column C lists cognates from a Central Quechua language, Ancash (from Parker and Chávez 1976).[3] (The Ancash cognates are from a dialect that has preserved etymological initial *h*.)[4] Each of the Ayacucho-Chanca words has an initial *h* whose presence is not accounted for by its usual etymological source, as the Ancash cognates attest. In one set, there is a dialect variant with the expected form (*hispay* ~ *ispay*); in another the initial *h* is in the process of being reinterpreted as a variant of the uvular spirant *q* (*hamka* ~ *qamka*).

TABLE 1

	A *Cuzco*	B *Ayacucho*	C *Ancash*
'to sneeze'	hačʔiy	hačiy	akčiwsaay
'roasted grain'	hankʔa	hamka ~ qamka	ankay
'toad'	hampʔatu	hampatu	ampatuy
'to catch'	hapʔiy	hapiy	
'how much'	haykʔa	hayka	ayka
'to urinate'	hispʔay	hispay ~ ispay	išpay

Each of them also corresponds to a stem in Cuzco-Collao Quechua which has an initial *h* that was conditioned by the ejective. These Ayacucho-Chanca stems (and others like them) were either borrowed from a variety that had ejectives or represent the residue of an epenthetic *h* that formerly was conditioned by the presence of glottalization in Ayacucho-Chanca Quechua. There is no independent evidence that these stems were borrowed. Thus it seems to me plausible, though far from certain, that Rowe was correct in assuming that Common Southern Peruvian Quechua had ejectives. It needs to be added, however, that the overwhelming majority of epenthetic *h* initials in Cuzco-Collao do not have corresponding *h* initials in Ayacucho-Chanca.

Rowe (1950:146ff.) also reconstructed two sibilants on the basis of the orthographies of Domingo de Santo Tomás (1560a, 1560b) and Gonçález Holguín (1607, 1608). Comparative and philological evidence (Landerman 1983; Mannheim 1988) now support the conclusion that colonial Cuzco-Collao Quechua had two sibilants even though all modern Southern Peruvian Quechua varieties show only one as a reflex of both. (Some varieties south of Cuzco do have two phonemic sibilants, /s/ and /š/, but the /š/ is from a more recent phonologization of the syllable-final reflex of *č > š* with the output of a dialectally restricted synchronic rule of sibilant palatalization before front vowels.

The paradigmatic segmental inventory in Figure 1 may be reconstructed for Common Southern Peruvian Quechua. (I have placed the ejectives and aspirates between brackets to indicate their problematic status.)

p	t	č	k	q	
[pʰ	tʰ	čʰ	kʰ	qʰ]	
[pʔ	tʔ	čʔ	kʔ	qʔ]	
m	n	ñ			
	s	ṣ			h
		r			
	l	λ			
u/w		i/y			
	a				

Figure 1. Segmental inventory of Common Southern Peruvian Quechua.

The distributions of Common Southern Peruvian Quechua segments were reconstructed on the basis of a "minimum common denominator" principle. When a process is attested for both modern varieties and not specifically contradicted by philological evidence, I assume that it was present in the common language. The canonical syllable structure was CV(C) with the initial consonant slot filled by a glottal catch for underlyingly vowel-initial words. Contextual variation of vowels was roughly the same as in modern Cuzco-Collao except (1) the modern processes that raise vowels adjacent to *y* were absent, and (2) the rule that lowers high vowels adjacent to a uvular was narrower in application. (In addition, certain morphologically governed vowel alternations and formative fusions have either expanded in scope or have been introduced since Common Southern Peruvian Quechua.) Glides were derived from underlying vowels, as in both of the modern varieties. The syllable-final consonants were reconstructed as they appear in modern Ayacucho-Chanca Quechua. All of the nonejective and nonaspirated stops occurred at the ends of syllables as stops, with the single possible exception of the uvular. It is impossible to tell from colonial texts whether it had become a spirant.[5] Nasals other than *n* occurred at the ends of syllables; *ñ* was restricted to pre-palatal position.[6] *n* was realized as [ŋ] before glides, nasals, and laterals. The retracted tap *r* was realized as [ɹ] word-finally. λ depalatalized before the alveolar series; *l* was infrequent.

Consonant Lenition: An Overview

The most striking change in the Cuzco-Collao dialect from Common Southern Peruvian Quechua to the present is that the final consonants of syllables have been systematically weakened. Not only have stops weakened to corresponding spirants, but a number of place distinctions have merged. Nasals and glides are in the process of disappearing at the ends of syllables as well. The language appears to be moving toward open consonant-vowel syllables in place of closed consonant-vowel-consonant syllables. Changes of this kind are common enough to pass without comment by the historical linguist. After all, consonant-vowel syllable structure is universally unmarked. Moreover, the processes that affected many of the syllable-final segments are similar enough that one may attempt to treat them as instances of a single, global correspondence; at least this would be true for the spirantizations of stops. Finally, the correspondences are regular enough to simply list as an unordered set of changes conditioned only by the syllable-final environment, particularly if one does the comparative reconstruction from a list of word stems. Thus, Rowe and Parker both accounted for these changes with lists of correspondences. A comparative reconstruction of the Common Southern Peruvian Quechua syllable finals, then, provides the appearance of an instantaneous, across-the-board shift from the conservative Ayacucho-Chanca-like arrangement of intact finals to the innovative Cuzco-Collao-like arrangement of weakened finals.

Nothing could be further from the truth. The finals weakened over centuries, one at a time. The spread of the changes across classes of linguistic formatives has also been uneven. As a result of both of these factors, the extent of the weakenings of finals is uneven from contemporary dialect to dialect, and from historical attestation to attestation. The variation between historical states of the language and between dialects is nonrandom. Variation in space and variation in time supply evidence that allows the chronology and mode of actuation of the changes to be reconstructed. Such a forward or "prospective" reconstruction in turn reveals a set of general principles that are accountable to further observations of contemporary dialect differences and historical attestations of the language. What we are after is a model of the innovations in Southern Peruvian Quechua grammars that lay behind the changes, a model of their structural properties, of the ways in which they were introduced into the grammar, and of the relationships they bear to one another. As a model, it is accountable to evidence of the same order as the evidence from which it was constructed; in this case it is accountable to further evidence from variation in time and social space. As a comparative reconstruction is accountable to principled differences between forms, so is a prospective reconstruction accountable to principled differences *between grammars*, between "system[s] where everything holds together" (*un ensemble où tout se tient*) (Meillet 1924 [1967]: 25–26).

Here is a brief summary of the syllable-final weakenings and mergers. Stops weakened along an acoustic gradient, from those that concentrated acoustic energy in relatively higher portions of the auditory spectrum (*acute*) to those that concentrated acoustic energy in the lower portion (*grave*), in order of increasing gravity. The stops have generally merged into the spirants *s* and χ. Tap *r* has weakened to [ɹ]. The frequency of *r* has also been reduced by restructuring individual lexical and grammatical formatives. Changes of individual formatives have also eliminated sibilants in the inflectional system, although all of these innovations continue to show dialectal variability. Nasals have assimilated to the place of articulation of the following obstruent and are velarized elsewhere. The nasality feature is in the process of shifting from the consonantal ends of syllables to vocalic nuclei. This change is also dialectally variable. The contrast between the laterals *l* and λ has largely been neutralized. Vowel-glide sequences are dialectally in the process of reanalysis as single vowels. Remember that each of these changes affected the ends of syllables.

These changes are clearly related one to the other, despite the fact that the standard descriptive and theoretical frameworks of historical linguists would treat the changes as unrelated to each other. Moreover, their spread is subject to several general conditions: If a particular change has taken place in stems, then it has taken place in the derivational morphology; if in the derivational morphology, then in the inflectional and discourse-level morphology, provided, of course, that the appropriate structural requirements for the change are met. If a change has taken place inside the word, then it has taken place at the ends of words, but not vice versa. Likewise, if a change has taken place inside of word stems, then it has taken place at the ends of word stems, but not vice versa. These general conditions are qualified below.

I used three kinds of evidence to reconstruct these changes, and to reconstruct the grammatical conditions that governed their spread: (1) Internal reconstruction from morphological alternations in the speech of modern-day speakers of Southern Peruvian Quechua. (2) Dialectal variability among speakers of Southern Peruvian Quechua living in the Department of Cuzco, Peru. This took the form of about two hundred hours of recorded speech samples, about a third of which came from a single parish in which I did ethnographic research. (3) Textual records of Southern Peruvian Quechua from as early as the late sixteenth century until the late nineteenth century. These included priest's manuals, books of sermons, and other religious literature; Quechua texts cited in colonial chronicles written by speakers of the language; grammars and dictionaries; and literary works, especially dramatic poems. In each case, I sampled several running passages from the text (in the case of dictionaries and grammars, running sequences of entries) and charted out the changes witnessed by the texts. The sample included a number of Republican-era texts, but my efforts were concentrated on the colonial-era materials where the evidence was more sketchy and more difficult to interpret. The colonial-era materials included the following: Santo Tomás (1560a, 1560b); Molina "el

Cuzqueño" (1575); Tercer Concilio Limense (1584, 1585); the anonymous *Vocabulario* of 1586; the anonymous manuscript that begins *Runa yn° niscap machoncuna* . . . (Anonymous, Huarochirí, early seventeenth century); an anonymous fragment of notarial records from 1605–8; Gonçález Holguín (1607, 1608); Santa Cruz Pachacuti Yamqui (1615); Pérez Bocanegra (1631); Aguilar (1691); Centeno (n.d.); and the anonymous dramatic poems *Usca Paucar* (Sahuaraura codex); and *Ollantay* (Sahuaraura and Justiniani codices).[7] I treated multiple texts by the same author as a single source. On the other hand, the different codices of the dramatic poems, including the two Sahuaraura codices, represented different states of the language, and so were treated as distinct sources. I will henceforth refer to this set of sources collectively as the "textual sample." I also sampled approximately twenty other colonial-era sources and an equal number of texts from the nineteenth and the first half of the twentieth centuries. This chapter relies primarily on dialectal and philological evidence. A synchronic grammar of syllable finals that covers much of the ground of a phonological internal reconstruction is in preparation.

Stops

Lenition of syllable-final palatals and, to a limited extent, of alveolars is attested as early as 1560 by Domingo de Santo Tomás. But there are difficulties with establishing dialect provenience for his work. Santo Tomás (1560a [1951]:15) explicitly stated that he drew the entries in his vocabulary indiscriminately from among the Quechua languages. Guaman Poma (c. 1615:1079) referred to Santo Tomás's work as "la lengua del cuzco chinchaysuyo quichiua todo rrebuelto." His citations of variation in sibilant usage, {x}~{s} ([š] ~ [ş]); the central/southern *hamuy ~ xamuy* ([šamuy]) lexical shibboleth; and both the central and southern words for four, *chusco* and *tagua*, respectively; all suggest that he worked with speakers of central languages as well as with a southern language which may have been Southern Peruvian Quechua. The problems of provenience make it unclear whether we are witnessing the same sound changes as those reported by others a century and a half later (perhaps because the others were reporting conservative speech) or a different basic variety of Quechua altogether. But Quechua language text was always written in Spanish orthography, almost always by nonnative speakers. The political oppression of Quechua speakers and legal maneuvers to prevent the growth of an indigenous literate class prevented language standardization of the growth of literary and orthographic traditions (Mannheim 1984). The lack of consistent scribal practice should rule out conservatism of reporting in later works in Quechua. Apart from Santo Tomás and besides archaic and very sporadic variation of syllable-finals (e.g., *cičpa* ~ *cispa* in Gonçález Holguín's *Vocabulario; huaynacauri* ~ *huaynacapri* in Pachacuti Yamqui's *Relación*), we do not find evidence of regular syllable-final lenitions until Juan de Aguilar's *Arte* of 1691. Aguilar has variable lenition of the final palatals in inflectional morphology and not at all in stems.

Syllable-final *č*, the least grave of the stops in a scalar sense, lenited to [š] at the ends of syllables (change i). This established a syllable-final [s] : [š] contrast which has reflexes in all modern Cuzco varieties.

(i)

č > [š] / __ $

The syllable-final [s] : [š] distinction has been eliminated entirely in suffixes and stem-finally; north of Cuzco and east of the Vilcanota River, it has also been eliminated in stems (sound change iii). The palatal fricative has a regular aspiration reflex by sound change (ii) in the following stop if the following stop is the first one in the word.[8]

(ii)

$$[\text{STOP}] > [\text{ASPIRATE}] / \left\{ \begin{array}{c} \text{š} \\ \text{č} \end{array} \right\} \text{—}$$

Palatal stops or fricatives induce aspiration on the following stop.

(iii)

š > s / __ $

For examples of (i), (ii), (iii), see Table 2. Notice that in the third example *pišqa* ~ *pisqa* does not have an aspirated *q* because it is not the first stop in the word.

TABLE 2

source	changes (i)–(iii)	
ačka	aškʰa ~ askʰa	'many'
učpa	ušpʰa ~ uspʰa	'ash'
pičqa	pišqa ~ pisqa	'five'

The fourth change in this group occurs in a rare environment. Jointly with (i) and (iii), it accounts for (as far as I know), two forms, the stem *inčik* > *inčis* 'peanut' and the inclusive plural *-čik* > *-čis*. Though the output of (iv) appears to have created new contexts for (i) and (iii) to apply, there are no attested intermediate forms.

(iv)

k > č /i __

Juan de Aguilar's *Arte de la lengua quichua* (1691 [1939]) showed (i) and (iii) to apply simultaneously in suffixes. Thus the enclitic *-čuč* 'perhaps' also appeared as *-čus*, but never as **-čuš*. They must nonetheless be formulated as separate changes in order to account for differential modern dialectal spread. Durative *-čka* also appears as *-ša*. But Aguilar lacked (iv) so there is no corresponding *-čis* inclusive attested. Centeno's *auto sacramental, El pobre más rico* (n.d.) shows the palatal lenition rule jointly with the *š* > *s* merger having gone to completion except for the postvocalic alternant of dubitative enclitic *-ča*, which regularly appears as *-č*, always in word-final position. The alternation between a postconsonantal CV form and a post-vocalic V form—which was paralleled by *-mi* → *-m* / V __ for the witness marker of scope of affirmation and *-si* → *-s* / V __ for the reportive—allowed the postvocalic *-č* alternant to be reconstituted by the speaker. In the *-ču* + *č* sequence, in which context it never alternated, *-č* (< *-ča*) followed the normal course of change to *s*. The resulting *-čus* was reanalyzed as a single morpheme. Ultimately, the alternation was dropped, thereby avoiding homophony with the reportive *-s* in the more frequent, postvocalic environment. The enclitic *-ča* was reassigned from the class of alternative enclitics (*-mi, -si*) to the nonalternating set (negative/yes-no question *-ču*, emphatic *-ya*, and so forth). Regularization of *-ča* is attested in the Sahuaraura codex of *Usca Paucar*. The *-čis* form of the inclusive plural (< *-čik* by [iv], [i], and [ii]) appears in *El pobre más rico* in word-final position only, that is, just the condition under which palatalization of *k* is regular. Word-medially it appears as *-čik*. In the Sahuaraura *Usca Paucar* manuscript the alternation was leveled to *-čis*. The aspiration reflex of the syllable-final palatals is first attested in an unequivocal form in *Usca Paucar*. By this time it was complete.

Syllable-final *t* did not occur in the suffix system. In stems it has regularly lenited to *s* ([v]; see examples in Table 3)[9] except idiosyncratically in a single place name, *Ccatca* [qʔaθqa] ~ [qʔasqa], for which the θ-form appears to be a spelling pronunciation introduced by Spanish speakers.

TABLE 3

source	t > s	
mutki-	musk^{h}i-	'to smell'
mitka-	misk$^?$a-	'to trip'
utqay	usq^{h}ay	'quickly'

Lenition of syllable-final t did not become regular in stems until the nineteenth century at the earliest.

(v)

$t > s / \_\_ \$$

Upon weakening, the syllable-final [grave] stops have gradually been converging upon [χ]. The modern-day synchronic reflex of these changes is a rule that realizes all non-strident occlusives as [χ]; it is widespread in the Department of Cuzco. Sound changes (vi), (vii), and (viii) represent three stages in the lenition and uvularization of syllable-final p. Stage (viii) has regularized in suffixes; all three are dialectally and lexically attested in stems in present-day Cuzco.

(vi)

$p > \phi / \_\_ \$$

(vii)

$ap > a^w\chi / \_\_ \$$

(viii)

$\phi > \chi / \_\_ \$$

Stages (vi) and (vii) are in competition in the more conservative dialects. Stage (viii) has been reached in suffixes and is currently diffusing across the lexicon, where its progress slows to avoid homonymy. For example, one of the most resistant words is *raϕra* 'wing', temporarily prevented from falling together with *raqra* 'split, to split'. But stage (viii) is further advanced in casual speech: A speaker who used the form *č$^?$aχra* 'plant' in an unguarded moment denied it when the word was elicited later in the day in a more formal setting as *č$^?$aϕra*.

Regular expansion of (viii) may be sidetracked by other sound changes that otherwise bear no relation to the sequence of syllable-final lenitions and mergers. In the center of Andahuaylillas (Quispicanchi), located some 35 km from Cuzco,[10] the aspirated labial [pʰ] has become spirant [ɸ], as in *ɸiñakuy* 'to get angry' as opposed to *pʰiñakuy* in the outlying communities in the district. (In the community of Lluthu, about 9 km from the center, I only heard the spirantized form used by a resident of the community speaking to a visitor from the center.) The new initial [ɸ] has been supported by other changes, such as the metathesis of *raɸra* to *ɸarɸa*. Uvularization of the syllable-final bilabials has stagnated at the same time as more recent changes (such as *uy > i*) have entered the grammar. In other words, syllable-final [ɸ] appears to have been held in place by the establishment of a /ɸ/ phoneme.

Neither stage (vi) nor stage (vii) are independently attested for suffixes in the older texts, although in the case of the (vi), this may be an accident of orthography. Uvularization (stage viii) first appears—variably, and in suffixes—in the Sahuaraura codex of *Usca Paucar*. Sahuaraura's *Ollantay* manuscript shows regular uvularization of the postvocalic genitive and frequent uvularization in switch-reference *-pti*. There is no change whatever in the stems. By the time of the Justiniani codex of *Ollantay*, uvularization was complete in suffixes. Uvularization presupposes spirantization of the labial and so also presupposes spirantization of the uvular. The gap—be it temporal or orthographic—between *El pobre más rico* and the two Sahuaraura manuscripts is too large to establish the sequence of these changes on other than internal implicational grounds. It is possible (though it is not attested) that the grave stops simultaneously became spirants, that is, that (vi) was actually a part of the more general sound change (ix).[11] Examples of (ix) appear in Table 4.

(ix)

[+ GRAVE] > [+ CONTINUANT] / __ $

Grave segments—labials, velars, and uvulars—became spirants at the ends of syllables

Nasals

Assimilation of syllable-final nasals to the following stop is attested variably in stems throughout the textual sample. Assimilation of $n \rightarrow m$ / __ *p*, is widespread in *El pobre más rico* and likely led to reanalysis of other occurrences of syllable-final *m* that were not involved in an alternation as underlying /n/. At the time of the *Usca Paucar* manuscript, the postvocalic

TABLE 4

source	(*ix*)	*x* >	(*vii*)	(*viii*)	
-q	-χ	—	—	—	'agentive nominalizer'
-pti	*-øti	—	—	-χti	'subordinating suffix'
maqčʔiy[a]	maχčʔiy	—	—	—	'to wash'
wakča[b]	waxča	—	—	—	'orphan'
*hapqʔiy	haøqʔiy	—	ha^{w}χqʔiy	haχqʔiy	'dig up'
qʔapñusqa[c]	qʔaøñusqa	—	qʔa^{w}χñusqa	qʔaχñusqa	'dented'
rapra[d]	raøra	—	—	raχra	'wing'
wak	wax	waχ	—	—	'several'

[a] Gonçález Holguín (1608 : 223), *macchhini ~ macchini.*

[b] Gonçález Holguín (1608 : 167), *huaccha.*

[c] Gonçález Holguín (1608 : 135), *kapñuscca.*

[d] Gonçález Holguín (1608 : 313), *rapra* as 'rama de arbol o ramo'.

alternant of the 'scope of affirmation, witness' suffix *-mi* is also attested as *-n*. Ultimately, the nasal neutralization rule was generalized to continuant environments. This final expansion occurred by the time the Sahuaraura codex of *Ollantay* was written.

r-Spirantization

Spirantization of tap /r/ began word-finally; this is a regular stage in the lenition process. The rule was generalized to "adjacent to a word-boundary," perhaps under the influence of a parallel rule affecting Spanish /r/, which in much of the Americas, including highland Peru, also under-goes spirantization. The /r/ is currently weakening in preconsonantal po-sition as well. The history of the /r/ lenition (which has a reflex in the synchronic grammar) demonstrates the dialectical nature of the evolution of grammatical rules: like the other spirantization processes, it appears to have begun at the ends of words and then of stems. The structural descrip-tion of the rule was generalized from "before" to "adjacent to" word and stem boundaries under the influence of a formally identical rule in lan-guage contact. This obscured the relationship between the form of the rule and its concomitant function. Further generalization of the rule to "before a syllable boundary"—which was the functionally consistent natural next step for the rule to take—became quite complicated from a formal point of view. With time, however, the functional motivation is coming to override it even at the cost of considerable formal complication.

Simplication of the Vowel-Glide Sequences

Three processes have contributed to simplication of vowel-glide sequences: (1) Back glides have fronted at the ends of syllables, following the regular pattern of change from derivational morphology to stems and from the ends of words and stems to stem-medially; (2) /ay/ diphthongs have coalesced to high vowels; (3) /uy/ diphthongs have simplified to [u]. The first of the changes is widespread, although still variable within stems, while the second and third are both changes in progress.

(x)

w > y / __ $

(xi)

ay > e: > i / __ $ except after a uvular

(xii)

uy > u / __ #

The shift of *w* to *y* is attested in the derivational suffix *-wsi-* 'to assist to', the only suffix in which it occurs, in the Sahuaraura manuscript *Ollantay*. The Justiniani manuscript, on the other hand, shows the change stem-finally as well. It is now complete in suffixes and stem-finally and lexically and dialectally variable stem-medially, as in Table 5.

Cuzco-Collao vowels are raised phonetically before a high, front glide, *y;* for /a/, this is *æ* → *ɛ*. Phonetic raising, like many coarticulatory effects, is normally attributed to the segment that induces the effect, in this

TABLE 5

source	w > y	
-wsi-	-ysi-	'to assist to'
pʔunčaw	pʔunčay	'daylight'
wawqi	wayqi	'brother of a male'

case the *y*. But many speakers are no longer attributing the effect to the adjacent *y*, and are treating the raised ɛ as basic and unmodified. In turn, the diphthong is coalescing (monophthongizing) around ɛ. Coalescence does not appear to be taking place in the suffix system. Moreover, in the sequence *-sqayki* 'I to you, future', the uvular prevents raising from taking place. The sequence is currently in the process of dropping the uvular, but even without the uvular, raising and coalescence do not take place. Rather, there is a competing change in which the *y* is lost regardless of whether the uvular is then dropped. This change, which is present only in suffixes, also affects the second person nominal form, *-yki*. But there is no evidence that the second person nominal form is being leveled to *-ki*.

Conditions on Sound Change

The lenitions and mergers of consonants at the ends of syllables are clearly related to one another, although that relationship is not a *formal* one. From the standpoint of the structural form of the processes, they reflect separate innovations, that is to say, separate historical events. The textual evidence bears this out. Although many of the correspondences are quite systematic, and can be collapsed into a very few, very general correspondence statements—for example, that all stops at the ends of syllables correspond to spirants in the modern Cuzco-Collao dialect—the textual record shows that the changes took place piecemeal. Apart from the possibility of (wrongly) collapsing these changes into more general correspondence statements, at a formal level they appear to be unrelated one to another. But the overall organization and sequence of these changes suggests that there is an underlying functional unity to them. They occur in an orderly, implicational sequence. Within the stops, the order of the weakenings is predictable from their acoustic characteristics. The stops which concentrate acoustic energy higher in the spectrum and have a smaller overall energy packet weaken first. Those stops which concentrate acoustic energy lower in the spectrum weaken later. The lenitions have also left a strong mark on the synchronic phonology of the language in the form of a clear, unifying orientation to a number of structurally discrete rules.

The syllable-final weakenings also show another kind of unity, which is ignored in a tabulation of sound correspondences but emerges in a historical reconstruction that is also accountable to dialectal and philological evidence. These changes do not take place equally in all classes of morphological formatives. Rather, they spread across the word, from morpheme class to morpheme class, and from narrower phonological environments to more inclusive ones. A reconstruction that simply tabulates regular correspondences cannot show this. The logical consequence of a reconstruction that is content with simple tabulation of correspondences is that instances of a phonological segment appear to change equally in all nonphonological linguistic contexts. Studies of sound change in progress and of lexical diffusion of phonological changes show that even if this is a good working assumption, it is an oversimplification (Wang 1969; Chen 1972; Chen and Wang 1975; Krishnamurti 1978; Labov 1981). In the case described here, we found that regular principles govern the spread of innovations from environment to environment. These principles constrain the set of possible transitions between any two grammars that are related by a single historical process. The principles bear up equally well in the textual sample (variation in time), dialectological evidence (variation in space), and internal reconstruction (variation in space/time). Here are informal statements of the principles: First, the syllable-final weakenings and mergers begin at the ends of words and word-stems and subsequently also take place word- and stem-medially. This has a straightforward phonological basis. Second, the syllable-final weakenings and mergers begin in the suffix system and spread into word stems. This seems to have a morphosyntactic motivation (cf. Mannheim and Newfield 1982). The principles may be stated as implicational hierarchies that constrain the class of possible language states relative to the output of a particular change. To put it more simply, they only permit sound changes to expand in certain ways. This restricts possible transitions between two historical or dialectal states.

(xiii)

1. If a sound change takes place word-medially, then it takes place word-finally.[12]
2. If a sound change takes place stem-medially, then it takes place stem-finally.

The first clause of condition (xiii) follows straightforwardly from the nature of the syllable. The changes in question occur at the ends of syllables. A phonological word must contain an integral number of syllables. The environment "word-final" is therefore a proper subset of the environment "syllable-final." Southern Peruvian Quechua does not resyllabify at word boundaries. For the syllable-final changes in Southern Peruvian Quechua, the environment "stem-final" is also a proper subset of "syllable-final." All verbs and some substantives end in vowels, and the addition of a suffix often adds a final consonant to the last syllable in a stem. Verbs are bound forms. But nouns that act as lexical stems are free, that is, may occur without suffixes. Many of these end in a consonant. Condition (xiii) may be accounted for formally by assigning the #-boundary to stems—it is independently required by other phonotactic contraints—and the ##-boundary to words. The ##-boundary also marks the domain of other phonological processes, including stress assignment. The ##-boundary is a proper subset of the $, syllable, boundary.

For the second clause of condition (xiii), the lenitions and mergers could be stipulated to spread from / __ # to / __ $. (I understand boundaries such as $ and # to be a linear notational shorthand for hierarchically organized constituents.) This clause may be attributed to individual analogical leveling of suffixed stems to their nonsuffixed counterparts. Southern Peruvian Quechua has a strong tendency for morphemes to be phonologically invariable. Very few grammatical formatives and *no* lexical or stem formatives are involved in regular, phonologically motivated alternations.[13] The second part of the condition contributes to the preservation of stem invariance.

The implicational hierarchies in (xiii) are consistent with the states summarized in rows a–d of Table 6, but not consistent with e–h. Here "+" means that the change has taken place in a particular environment and "−" that it has not ("+" includes cases in which the structural description of the change is not met in the environment). The inconsistent cases are marked with an asterisk (*).

Here is an example: The shift of syllable-final *w* to *y* took place in the

TABLE 6

	all syllable-final contexts	stem-finally	word-finally
a	−	−	−
b	−	−	+
c	−	+	+
d	+	+	+
*e	−	+	−
*f	+	+	−
*g	+	−	−
*h	+	−	+

TABLE 7

	Gon-çález Holguín	Anon, *Usca Paucar* (Sahua-raura)	Anon, *Ollan-tay* (Sahua-raura)	Anon, *Ollan-tay* (Justi-niani)	modern dialects	
(x) w > y (suf)	–	–	+	+	+	+
(x) w > y (stem-final)	–	–	%	+	+	+
(x) w > y (stem)	–	–	–	%	%	+

(suf) = in suffixes;
(stem) = in stems;
+ = regularly attested;
% = variably attested;
– = not attested

derivational suffix *-wsi-* > *-ysi-* 'to assist to VERB' prior to its spread into stems, where there is still dialectal variation in the modern language (see Table 7). The shift has been completed in final position in stems, as in *pʔunčaw* > *pʔunčay* (invariably) 'day(light)', but not stem-medially, where the older form *wawqi* varies with a newer *wayqi* 'brother of a male'. The two *Ollantay* codices—which reflect similar but not identical states of the language—provide a useful comparison. In the Sahuaraura text *-wsi-* > *-ysi-* is complete, but both *punčau* and *punčai* appear for 'day(light)'. In the Justiniani manuscript it has gone to completion stem-finally.

Notice that (xiii), the phonologically motivated condition on sound change, accounts for the relationship between the stem-final and stem-medial environments, but does not correctly account for the initiation of the change in suffixes. The *-wsi-* > *-ysi-* shift precedes any change in stem-final position, even though it occurs word-medially. Were the expansion of the sound change motivated entirely on phonological grounds, we would expect rather that the stem-final change (with concomitant leveling of the variant forms to the newer one) precede the word-medial change in the suffix system. Moreover, these data are consistent with others in the textual and dialectological data sets, and with the application of synchronic phonological processes. Consider sound change (viii), in which syllable-final labials spirantize and merge with the uvular (uvularization; see Table 8). There are three instances in which the appropriate structural descrip-

Table 8

	Centeno	Anon, Usca Paucar (Sahua- raura)	Anon, Ollan- tay (Sahua- raura)	Anon, Ollan- tay (Justi- niani)	modern dialects	
(vi) p > ø (suf)	–	%	%	+	+	+
(vi) p > ø (stem)	–	–	–	%	+	+
(viii) ø > χ (suf)	–	%	%	+	+	+
(viii) ø > χ (stem)	–	–	–	–	–	%

(suf) = in suffixes;
(stem) = in stems;
+ = regularly attested;
% = variably attested;
− = not attested

tion is met: in the postvocalic alternant of the genitive, -p-; in the switch-reference subordinator -pti-; and in numerous stems (for example, hapt?ay 'handful' or q?apnuy 'to dent'). The syllable-final bilabial merged with the uvular spirant first in the genitive, then in the switch-reference subordinator (both in the eighteenth century) and is currently shifting in stems. (The extant textual data show uvularization together with spirantization in the suffixes, but as independent of one another in stems. Dialectological evidence supports their separateness in stems.) Uvularization of the genitive is complete in the Sahuaraura codex of *Ollantay,* but switch-reference uvularization is variable, and there is none in stems. By the time of the Justiniani codex of *Ollantay,* uvularization was complete in the suffixes. At the present time, uvularization in stems is a major dialectological variable in the Department of Cuzco.

The weakening of syllable-final palatals (sound change i) resulted in a š : s contrast in that position. Syllable-final š in turn conditioned aspiration on the following stop, provided that the context met other restrictions on aspiration, namely that it can only occur in stems, and on the first oral stop in a word (sound change ii). The š : s contrast has since been eliminated in suffixes by sound change (iii), in which š > s. The change has spread to stems in Cuzco and the area north and east of the Vilcanota River, where aspiration (from sound change ii) is the only remaining trace of the former contrast between palatal and nonpalatal sibilants. (The only syllable-*initial* š is in the durative suffix as a result of other changes. But in the Urubamba valley the š > s merger is in the process of being generalized to eliminate the unique syllable-initial š as well.) To the area south and west of the Vilcanota River, the merger of final sibilants (iii) is restricted to suffixes, leaving the š : s contrast intact in stems. The contrast is reinforced by syllable-*initial* variable palatalization, s > š, before front vowels and (in loan-words) before palatal glides. The š : s contrast is one of the principle parameters of dialectal variation in modern-day Cuzco-Collao Quechua. In the historical texts, š > s is first attested in Aguilar's *Arte,* where it had taken place in suffixes. It is complete in stems in Centeno and in the two dramatic poems recorded by Sahuaraura (see Table 9). The dramatic poems evidently belong to the dialect area that includes the city of Cuzco and the area to its north and east. The association of the dramatic poem *Ollantay* with the village of Tinta (southwest of Cuzco; Markham 1912:90, Lewin 1943), is not supported for either the Sahuaraura or the Justiniani manuscripts of *Ollantay.*

The morpho-syntactic condition on the syllable-final changes is stated in (xiv). It is a condition on the output of changes and is not restricted to sound changes. Thus, the restructuring of preterite -*rqa*- > -*ra*-, an inflectional suffix, which is currently a dialectal variable, is a precondition for a comparable restructuring of the "urgency" (derivational) suffix, -*rqu*- ~ -*rqa*- > -*ru*- ~ -*ra*-.

TABLE 9

	Gon-çález Holguín	Aguilar	Centeno	Anon, *Usca Paucar* (Sahua-raura)	Anon, *Ollantay* (Sahua-raura)	Anon, *Ollantay* (Justi-niani)
(iii) š > s (suf)	−	+	+	+	+	+
(iii) š > s (stem)	−	−	+	+	+	+

(suf) = in suffixes;
(stem) = in stems;
+ = regularly attested;
% = variably attested;
− = not attested

TABLE 10

	stem	derivation	inflection/ discourse
a	−	−	−
b	−	−	+
c	−	+	+
d	+	+	+
*e	−	+	−
*f	+	+	−
*g	+	−	−
*h	+	−	+

(xiv)

If a change takes place in stems, then it takes place in derivational formatives; if in derivational formatives, then in inflectional and discourse-level formatives,[14] provided that the structural description of the change is met.

The implicational hierarchy in (xiv) is consistent with the cases summarized in rows a–d of Table 10, but not consistent with e–h.

Conditions (xiii) and (xiv) are constraints on the expansion of the changes. Thus (xiii) does not stipulate that sound changes must expand from the word-final environment to the syllable-final, but rather that it can only expand consistent with the condition. Simultaneous actualization of the change throughout the word, for example, would be consistent with case d of Table 6. Nor does (xiv) stipulate that a sound change in the suffix system must precede the same change in the stem. Condition (xiii) countenances the cases listed in rows a–d of Table 6 and rules out those starred in e–h, as (xiv) does those in Table 10.

But there is a violation of these conditions in the philological corpus. Centeno's drama *El pobre más rico* shows completed lenition of syllable-final palatals except for the postvocalic alternant of the dubitative *-ča* which regularly appears as *-č*. Worse still, *-ča* ~ *-č* is always the last suffix in the word. It contradicts both conditions (xiii) and (xiv) by realizing case f of Tables 6 and 10. The motivation for the retention of the *-č* form is clear. The postconsonantal long form of the dubitative *-ča* provides a model for restoration of the stop in the postvocalic short form *-č*. The alternation was parallel to *-mi* ~ *-m* 'scope of affirmation, witness' and

-si ~ *-s* 'scope of affirmation, reported'. We must therefore weaken conditions (xiii) and (xiv) with a third condition, (xv), which allows conditions (xiii) and (xiv) to be overridden in the event that a morpheme alternation in a regular paradigm provides a model for restoring the final stop.

(xv)

The expansion of sound change may be retarded for a formative which otherwise meets the structural description if it is involved in a phonologically determined alternation from which the original form can be reconstituted.

Final *č* was restored in the *-č* suffix, which alternated with a longer *-ča* form. In the sequence *-ču* + *č,* in which it never alternated, it was not restored; the resulting *-ču* + *s* was reanalyzed as a single formative. By the time of the Sahuaraura manuscript of *Usca Paucar,* the *-ča* suffix had been reassigned from the class of alternating enclitics to the nonalternating class. It invariably appears there as *-ča,* just as it does in the modern language.

Motivating the Conditions

The first part of condition (xiii) has a clear phonological motivation. The sound system of language is organized into a hierarchy of nested constituents. Below the level of the word there are features nested into segments, segments nested into syllabic onset and rhyme, onset and rhyme nested into syllables, syllables nested into feet, and feet nested into words. The weakenings and mergers occur at the level of the syllabic rhyme. Rhymes are defined by their role in the organization of the syllable. In Southern Peruvian Quechua, a rhyme consists of a vocalic nucleus followed by a consonantal adjunct. The next larger constituent, the foot, plays a role in the distribution of stress in Southern Peruvian Quechua, but does not seem to be relevant at all to the weakenings and mergers. Finally, there is the word, which is composed of an integral number of syllables and feet. Both "word" and "syllable" are relevant contexts for the changes. Any sound change that takes place at the ends of syllables perforce takes place at the ends of words, *but not vice versa.* If __ $, then __ # (see clause 1 of xiii). The second clause of condition (xiii) and condition (xv) appear to be consequences of the strong orientation of Southern Peruvian Quechua to agglutinative, transparent morphology, in other words, to a condition in which every formative has one and only one surface manifestation. Southern Peruvian Quechua has few morphological alternations and very few obvious morphophonemic processes. There are exceptions, but they are relatively rare. Thus in the case of the second clause of condition (xiii), word-medial but stem-final consonants are leveled to word-final alternants. Conversely, in the case accounted for by (xv), an alternation was used to restore the older phonetic form and prevent allomorphy, at least until another mechanism for preventing allomorphy won out.

Condition (xiv) is another matter; it allows for the spread of sound changes from discourse and inflectional formatives to derivational formatives to word-stems. The neogrammarian position that "sound-laws, inasmuch as they are mechanical, hold without exception," has been so productive (Hockett 1965 is correct in referring to it as one of the few "great discoveries" in linguistics) that we are often loath to accept the possibility of nonphonological conditioning of what are otherwise regular sound changes. This is not to say that all phonological changes are sound laws (*lautgesetze*). The neogrammarians recognized analogy and contamination (secondary sound symbolism; sound association) as valid mechanisms of phonological change; Whitney (1875 [1971]:106) and Meillet (1924 [1967]:14), among others, recognized primary sound symbolism (onomatopoeia) works in other ways, and Wang, Chen, and Labov (also among others) have shown the importance of phonetically defined word classes to the phonological histories of Middle Chinese and Modern American English. But the syllable-final weakenings and mergers are garden variety "sound-laws," *lautgesetze,* exactly the kind of change to which the neogrammarian axiom applies. And condition (xiv) *does* hold for these changes, as well as other, more properly morphological innovations. Nor is it an isolated set of "co-incidences." Cerrón-Palomino (1974) observed similar conditioning of sound change in Wanka, a Central Quechua language. He suggested that (xiv) is a type of conditioning of sound change that is characteristic of the Quechua family. Inflectional lead in sound change has also been observed in Indo-European by Turner (1927, 1937; for Indic) and Malkiel (1968; for Romance); and in Uto-Aztecan by Lastra and Horcasitas (1978; for Mexicano [Nahuatl]).

The conditions on phonological change provide a restrictive account of the relationships that may hold between any two successive—dialectal or historical—grammars. As such, they are testable against two kinds of data, contemporary dialectal variation and philologically attested historical systems, which is to say, diachronic variation. Together with the motivated relative chronology of the sound changes (e.g., the role of relative gravity in determining the sequence) they establish both a set of consistent (or "lawful") variant phonological systems and a partial diachronic ordering (or relative chronology) among them. They draw attention to a significant type of covariation between form and meaning in Southern Peruvian Quechua, in which the relative domains of the synchronic reflexes of the changes reflect the internal structure of the word. And in doing so, they shed light on the nature of form/meaning covariation in language. The observations by Cerrón-Palomino, Lastra and Horcasitas, Malkiel, and Turner demonstrate that the Southern Peruvian Quechua conditions on phonological change are instances of a phenomenon of more general applicability, and demonstrate the need for a general theoretical account of these principles.

If we restrict comparative reconstruction to statements of correspondences, the syllable-final lenitions and mergers appear to be a single, uniform change, of local interest—useful as a statement of correspondences between Southern Peruvian Quechua and the other languages in the family. In this chapter, I have demonstrated that it is otherwise: The changes in question took place as individual innovations over several centuries. The itinerary that the changes followed has been more variable than it first appeared, as we saw with the cases in which formal determinants delayed otherwise regular sound changes (the temporary retention of final -č) or left them incomplete (the maintenance of syllable-final φ in dialects in which an initial φ segment has appeared). On the other hand, the internal logic of the changes is far more regular than first appeared, and closely fits the morphosyntactic pattern of the language. The fine-grained control over historical detail that we achieve by enriching comparative genetic reconstruction with dialectal and philological evidence involves both a loss and a gain, then. Though we are forced to surrender otherwise neat generalizations, we gain in the degree of precision with which we can come to terms with the internal logic of the changes. No compromise is necessary between the demands placed on historical linguistics: that we attend to the particular history of *a* language and to the general nature of language change.

NOTES

1. The research reported here was supported in part by grants from the Organization of American States, the National Science Foundation, the Wenner-Gren Foundation for Anthropological Research, and the Horace Rackham School of Graduate Studies, University of Michigan. I am grateful to Janise Hurtig for comments on an earlier draft.

In order to make this article more accessible for comparative purposes, I use a technical orthography, rather than the standard Southern Peruvian alphabet which I follow in other publications. The differences between the technical orthography and the official alphabet (Republic of Peru, *Resolución ministerial* 4023-75-ED, 16-x-75; *Resolución ministerial* 1218-85-ED, 18-xi-85) are as follows: [č] = *ch*, palatal stop; [š] = *sh*, palatal spirant; [λ] = *ll*, palatal lateral; [ʰ] = *h*, aspiration; and [ʔ] = ', glottalization.

In addition, I use the following special symbols: [φ] bilabial spirant; [s] dorsal sibilant; [ş] apical sibilant; [x] velar spirant; [χ] uvular spirant; [ſ] retracted tap *r*; [ɹ] retracted spirant *r*; [aʷ] labialized *a*; [ŋ] velar nasal; [ɛ] lax, front, mid vowel; [ɩ] lax, front, high vowel; $ syllable boundary; and { } orthographic unit.

For all citations of written sources, I use the author's orthography without any modification.

2. For two dissenting positions, see Trubetzkoy (1939) and Hymes (1973 : 62f.).

3. Parker and Chávez gloss the "toad" cognate as "to walk with difficulty."

4. Most of the rest of Ancash-Huailas Quechua is part of an *h* > ø *sprachbund*.

5. Gonçález Holguín (1607, 1608) devised special symbols to account for the uvulars with a Spanish-based orthography. He used both {cc} and {k} at the ends of syllables. It is unclear whether his orthographic variation can be interpreted as evidence of a variable spirantization process (in which {cc} = [q] and {k} = [χ], or is simply an orthographic quirk. But is is worthy of note that orthographic {g} does not appear, and by the early seventeenth century it is the expected representation of a final [χ].

6. Two problematic exceptions are *qquiñua* [qiñ$ua] 'cinchona tree' and *quinua* 'quinoa (a grain)' (both citations, Gonçález Holguín 1608 : 309). Both have etymological syllable-final *ñ* prior to a labial glide. The former has since undergone metathesis of the ñw sequence, and is currently [qewña] (see Cusihuamán 1976b : 114 and Lira 1944 : 457). The latter has a number of currently attested variants: In addition to a form that is parallel to the first [kiwña], [kinwa] is common. (It was possibly back-borrowed from Spanish.) Two variant forms have unique epenthetic vowels (raised in the phonetic transcriptions) which do not form syllabic domains for the purposes of stress assignment: [kinᵘwa] and [kiwⁱna] (attested by Lira 1944 : 326 as *kíwina*). The first might be treated as having an underlying /ñᵘ/. There is no independent evidence for this analysis, though. The epenthetic vowel in the second is clearly a reflex of the palatal property of the nasal and appears to be a variant of the [kiwña] pronunciation. I am indebted to Peter Landerman for pointing out the problem.

7. For more detailed discussion of the formal properties of these texts see Rivet and Créqui-Montfort (1951) and Mannheim (1988).

8. This is an effect of the word structure constraint that restricts ejectives and aspirates to the first stop in a word. The comparatively few occurrences of the durative immediately following a stem with no stops would presumably have been leveled out.

9. *mutki-* is attested by Gonçález Holguín (1608 : 608) as *mutquini; mitka-* in Anonymous-Ollantay (Sahuaraura codex), 114 as *mitcasccaita;* and *utqay* in

Anonymous-Ollantay (Sahuaraura codex), 114 as *utccaitan*. The sources of aspiration and glottalization, and the time of their acquisition, are not known.

10. Andahuaylillas was the parish of Juan Pérez Bocanegra, who wrote a Quechua-language priest's manual based on his experiences there in the early seventeenth century.

11. In addition, the accusative case was leveled from *-kta* (/V__) ~ *-ta* (/C__) to *-ta*. The change appeared variably in Aguilar's *Arte* and was completed by the time of Centeno.

12. Compare Lastra and Horcasitas (1978) on word-final "lead" of sound change over word-medial in Nahuatl.

13. Exceptions to this generalization all involve reduplication. For example, *haqay* 'there (deictic)' / *Haχ-haχ-haqay* 'over there! (as a warning)'; *wičʔis* 'pig cry' / *wičʔičičiy* 'to cry sharply' (Cusihuamán 1976a : 217).

14. By "discourse level formative" I refer to a class of suffixes that notionally indicate the epistemic and evidential status of the utterance as well as question /negation /affirmation and their respective discourse scopes.

References

Aguilar M., Juan de

    1691   *Arte de la lengua quichua general de Indios del Perú*. Facsimile of holo-
    [1939]   graphic manuscript. Tucumán: Instituto de Antropología, Universidad Nacional de Tucumán.

Anonymous

    1586   *Arte y vocabulario en la lengua general del Peru llamada Quichua y en*
    [1951]   *la lengua Española*. Lima: Antonio Ricardo. G. Escobar R. editor. *Vocabulario y phrasis en la lengua general de los Indios del Perú, llamada Quichua,* Lima: Universidad Nacional de San Marcos.

Anonymous—Huarochirí

    (late 16th, early 17th century)   *Runa ynᵒ niscap machoncuna ñaupa pacha . . . ,*
    [1942]   manuscript 3169, ff. 64R-114R, Biblioteca Nacional, Madrid. Published *De priscorum huaruchiriensium origene et institutis,* ed. H. Galante (transcription, Latin translation, photocopy of most of the manuscript), Madrid: Instituto Gonzalo Fernández de Oviedo.

Anonymous—*Usca Paucar*

    n.d.   *Auto sacramental, El Patrocinio de Nuestra Señora María Santicima en Copacabana.* (Sahuaraura codex), Biblioteca Nacional del Perú.

Anonymous—*Ollantay*

    n.d.a   Justiniani: *Tragicomedia del Apu Ollantay y Cusi Coyllur. Rigores de*
    [1938]   *un padre, y generosidad de un Rey.* Facsimile edition, *Ollantay,* ed. H. Galante. Lima: Universidad Nacional de San Marcos.

Anonymous—*Ollantay*

    n.d.b   Sahuaraura: *Comedia trágica que intitula los rigores de un Padre y ge-*
    [1938]   *nerosidad de un Rey.* Published in *Ollantay,* ed. H. Galante. Lima: Universidad Nacional de San Marcos.

Centeno, Gabriel
 n.d. *El pobre más rico,* ed. José M.B. Farfán and Humberto Suárez Alvarez. Lima: (1939) including a facsimile of the manuscript.
Cerrón-Palomino, Rodolfo
 1974 "Morphologically conditioned changes in Wanka-Quechua." *Studies in the Linguistic Sciences* 42:40—75.
Chen, Matthew Y.
 1972 "The time dimension: Contribution toward a theory of sound change." *Foundations of Language* 8:457—98.
Chen, Matthew Y. and William S.-Y. Wang
 1975 "Sound change: actuation and implementation." *Language* 51: 255—81.
Cusihuamán Gutiérrez, Antonio
 1976a *Gramática Quechua: Cuzco-Collao.* Lima: Instituto de Estudios Peruanos.
 1976b *Diccionario Quechua: Cuzco-Collao.* Lima: Instituto de Estudios Peruanos.
Gonçález Holguín, Diego de
 1607 *Gramática y arte nueva de la lengua general de todo el Perú llamada lengua Qquichua o del Inca.* Los Reyes: del Canto.
 1608 *Vocabulario de la lengua general de todo el Perú llamada lengua Qquichua o del Inca.* Los Reyes: del Canto.
Guaman Poma de Ayala, Felipe
 c. 1615 *El primer nveva corónica i bvē gobierno.* Facsimile edition, 1936. Paris: Institut d'Ethnologie.
Hockett, Charles F.
 1965 "Sound change." *Language* 41:185—204.
Hymes, Dell
 1973 "Speech and language: On the origins and foundations of inequality among speakers." *Daedelus* 102. 3:59—86.
Krishnamurti, Bh.
 1978 "Areal and lexical diffusion of sound change." *Language* 54:1—20.
Labov, William A.
 1981 "Resolving the neo-grammarian controversy." *Language* 57:267—308.
Landerman, Peter
 1983 "Las sibilantes castellanas, quechua y aimaras en el siglo xvi: Un enigma tridimensional. In *Aula quechua,* ed. Rodolfo Cerrón-Palomino, pp. 203—34. Lima: Ediciones Signo.
Lastra de Suárez, Yolanda and Fernando Horcasitas
 1978 "El Náhuatl en el norte y el occidente del Estado de México." *Anales de Antropología* 15:185—250.
Lewin, Boleslow
 1943 *La rebelión de Túpac Amaru,* Third edition, 1967. Buenos Aires: Sociedad Editora Latino Americana.
Lira, Jorge A.
 1944 *Diccionario Kkéchuwa-Español.* Tucumán (Argentina): Universidad Nacional de Tucumán.

Malkiel, Yakov
    1968   "The inflectional paradigm as an occasional determinant of sound change." ed. Winfred P. Lehmann and Yakov Malkiel, pp. 21–64. In *Directions for Historical Linguistics.* Austin: University of Texas Press.

Mannheim, Bruce
    1982   "Person, number and inclusivity in two Andean languages." *Acta Linguistica Hafniensia* 17:138–54.
    1984   "'Una nación acorralada': Southern Peruvian Quechua language planning and politics in historical perspective." *Language in Society* 13.3:291–309.
    1985a   "Southern Peruvian Quechua." In *South American Indian Languages, Retrospect and Prospect,* ed. Harriet E. Manelis Klein and Louisa R. Stark, pp. 481–515. Austin: University of Texas Press.
    1985b   "Contact and Quechua-external genetic relationships." In *South American Indian Languages, Retrospect and Prospect,* ed. Harriet E. Manelis Klein and Louisa R. Stark, pp. 644–88.
    1988   "On the sibilants of Colonial Southern Peruvian Quechua." *International Journal of American Linguistics* 54.2:168–208.

Mannheim, Bruce and Madeleine Newfield
    1982   "Iconicity in phonological change." In *Papers from the Fifth International Conference of Historical Linguistics,* ed. Anders Ahlqvist, pp. 211–22. Amsterdam: John Benjamins B.V.

Markham, Clements
    1912   *The Incas of Peru.* London: Trübner.

Meillet, Antoine
    1924   *La méthode comparative en linguistique historique.* Oslo: Aschehoug.
    [1967]   Translated by G. B. Ford as *The Comparative Method in Historical Linguistics.* Paris: Champion.

Molina, Cristóbal de
    c. 1575   *Relación de las fabulas y ritos de los Yngas.* . . . Biblioteca Nacional de Madrid, Manuscript 3169, ff. 2–36. Reprinted in Carlos A. Romero and Horacio Urteaga (1916), *Colección de libros y documentos referentes a la historia del Perú,* (series 1, volume 1). Lima.

Parker, Gary J.
    1963   "La clasificación genética de los dialectos quechuas." *Revista del Museo Nacional* 32:241–52.
    1969–71   "Comparative Quechua phonology and grammar." *University of Hawaii Working Papers in Linguistics* I: 1.1:65–88; II: 1.2:123–47; III: 1.4:1–61; IV: 1.9:149–204; V: 3.3:45–109.
    1969b   *Ayacucho Quechua Grammar and Dictionary.* The Hague: Mouton.

Parker, Gary J., and A. Chávez Reyes
    1976   *Diccionario Quechua: Ancash-Huailas.* Lima: Ministerio de Educación and Instituto de Estudios Peruanos.

Pérez [de] Bocanegra, Juan de
    1631   *Ritual formulario e institución de Curas para administrar a los naturales de este Reyno los Santos Sacramentos . . . por el Bachiller J. P. B., presbiterio, en la lengua Quechua general.* Lima.

Rivet, Paul and Georges de Créqui-Montfort
    1951   *Bibliographie des langues aymará et kičua* (vol. 1). Paris: Institut d'Ethnologie.
Rowe, John Howland
    1950   "Sound patterns in three Inca dialects." *International Journal of American Linguistics* 16:137–48.
Santa Cruz Pachacuti Yamqui, Juan de
    c. 1615   *Relacion de antigüedades deste reyno del Piru,* manuscript 3169, ff. 132–169, Biblioteca Nacional, Madrid.
Santo Tomás, Domingo de
    1560a   *Grammatica o arte de la lengua general de los indios de los reynos del*
    [1951]   *Peru.* Valladolid: Fernández de Cordova. Facsimile edition. Lima: Universidad Nacional de San Marcos.
    1560b   *Lexicon o vocabulario de la lengua general.* Valladolid: Fernández de
    [1951]   Cordova. Facsimile edition. Lima: Universidad Nacional de San Marcos.
Soto Ruíz, Clodoaldo
    1976   *Diccionario quechua: Ayacucho-Chanca.* Lima: Instituto de Estudios Peruanos.
Stark, Louisa R.
    1975   "A reconsideration of proto-Quechua phonology." *Actas del 39 Congreso Internacional de Americanistas* 5:209–19. Lima.
Tercer Concilio Limense
    1584   *Doctrina Christiana y catecismo para instrucción de los Indios, y las demás personas que han de ser enseñados en nuestra sancta Fé.* Lima: Antonio Ricardo.
    1585   *Tercer catecismo y exposición de la doctrina Christiana por sermones . . .*
    [1773]   *Conforme a lo que se proveyó en el Sancto Concilio Provincial de Lima el año pasado de 1583.* Lima: Antonio Ricardo.
Torero Fernández de Cordova, Alfredo
    1964   "Los dialectos quechuas." *Anales Científicos de la Universidad Agraria* 2:446–78.
Trubetzkoy, N. S.
    1939   "Gedanken über das Indogermanenproblem." *Acta Linguistica Hafniensia* 1:81–89.
Turner, R. L.
    1927   "The phonetic weakness of terminational elements in Indo-Aryan." *Journal of the Royal Asiatic Society* 2:227–39.
    1937   "Anticipation of normal sound changes in Indo-Aryan." *Transactions of the Philological Society:* 1–14.
Wang, William S.-Y.
    1969   "Competing changes as a cause of residue." *Language* 45:9–25.
Whitney, William Dwight
    1875   "Φυσει or Θέσει—Natural of conventional?" *Transactions of the*
    [1971]   *American Philological Association for 1874*: 95–116. Reprinted in *Whitney on Language,* ed. Michael Silverstein, pp. 111–323. Cambridge: MIT Press.

IV

Grammatical Matters

Stephen H. Levinsohn

Variations in Tense-Aspect Markers Among Inga (Quechuan) Dialects

ABSTRACT

Inga storytellers typically employ two or three "past" tense-aspect markers in their narratives to distinguish between foregrounded and types of backgrounded information. The functions of the individual markers vary from dialect to dialect. Correspondences in the functions of two of the markers (*rca* and morphological ø/*n*) enable the dialects to be divided into two groups, confirming Inga traditions of at least two distinct migrations into southwest Colombia. Variations in the function of the third marker (*sca*) may suggest a subdivision of one of the groups.[1]

Introduction

This chapter concerns variations in the use of the Inga tense-aspect markers *rca, sca,* and morphological ø/*n* in the three mountain dialects of Aponte (Department of Nariño, S.W. Colombia), Santiago (Putumayo), including Colón, and San Andrés (Putumayo), and in the lowland dialects of Puerto Guayuyaco and of Yunguillo (including Condagua). (See Figure 1.) The next section describes patterns in the way *rca* and ø/*n* are used, which indicate that the dialects fall into two groups in line with oral traditions concerning migrations of Ingas: Aponte-Santiago and San Andrés–Lowland Inga. Variations in the function of *sca* (*shca/shka* in other Quechuan dialects) between Puerto Guayuyaco and the remaining communities, identified in the final section, may suggest a further subgrouping of the dialects.

The phonemes of Inga are:[2]

vowels: /a i u/

consonants: /b c č d g h k l lʸ m n ñ p r s š t w y/.

(In Yunguillo, the /lʸ/ and /y/ phonemes are combined as /y/.)

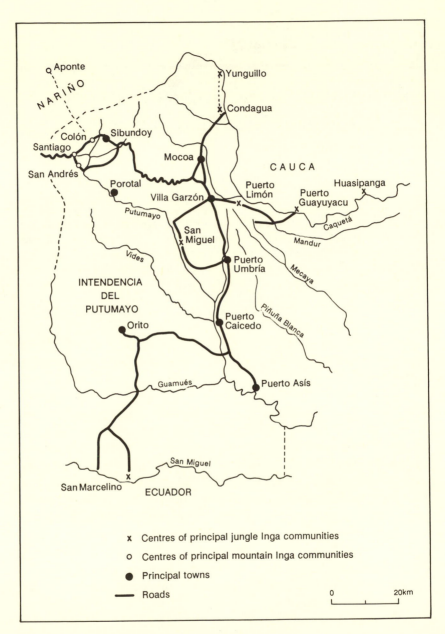

Figure 1. Inga (Quechuan) speaking area of Colombia.

The above set of phonemes closely parallels that given by Orr and Longacre for their representative Ecuadorian Quichua (EcQ) dialects "Q (Quito) and T (Tena)." In particular, Inga manifests with EcQ "certain unique shared innovations . . . : (1) Voiced allophones of stops and affricates, which occur in Proto-Quechua only after nasals, have become phonemic. (2) Velar and postvelar stops have merged." The authors, who refer to Inga as "P (Putumayo, Colombia)," were not aware that b, d, g (and š) are distinct phonemes, not only in EcQ, but also in Inga (Orr and Longacre 1968: 530, 531, 542).

Inga oral traditions have the Santiago people arriving in the region by the time of the Spanish conquest in the early sixteenth century and later establishing an outpost in Aponte, several hours' walk across the mountains, by 1700. The San Andrés Ingas, who live only two miles from Santiago, are reputed to have come from the lowland region to the south of Mocoa after the Santiago people were well established (Levinsohn and Avendaño 1982a:1–31).[3]

The Ingas themselves often describe their dialectical differences in terms of the pronunciation of /r/. For example, the Santiago Ingas often wish to write rolled [ř] as rr, to distinguish their pronunciation from that of the San Andrés Ingas. The latter dialect uses a retroflexed flap with a voiced sibilant on- or off-glide [ᶻř řᶻ]. When preceding a voiceless consonant, however, it is often manifested as a voiceless retroflexed alveopalatal stop [č]; see Levinsohn (1976:24f). In turn, speakers from Aponte and the lowlands use a simple flap except that, preceding a voiceless consonant, Aponte speakers employ [š].

Dialectical differences appear in what Muysken (1977:43) calls the "past" conjugation of the verb, the singular of which is as follows (employing the root ni, 'say'):

Person	Aponte	Santiago	San Andrés/ Lowlands	Meaning
1	ni-sha-ni	ni-rca-ni	ni-rca-ni	'I said'
2	ni-sha-ngui	ni-rsha-ngui	ni-rca-ngui	'you said'
3	ni-sh(a)	ni-rca	ni-rca	'he/she said'
1 to 2	ni-sha-iqui	ni-rsha-iqui	ni-rca-iqui	'I said to you'

In other words, the "past" marker most commonly has the form rca; however, it is rsha in Santiago when the second person is involved in the action, and *sha* in Aponte, the final vowel commonly being dropped before silence.

Ingas can also produce a list of words that vary according to the dialect. The following table gives a few of these. (It is common when two forms exist, as in the last item, for the one used in Aponte or in the lowland region to differ from that of the remaining dialects.)

Meaning	Aponte	Santiago	San Andrés	Yunguillo	Guayuyaco
'still'	chara	chara	chaira	chira	chira
'100'	patsa	patsa	pátsag	pásag	pásag
'walking stick'	tahuina	tahuina	taugna	tanua	tanua
'pass'	llalli-	yali-	yalli-	yayi-	yalli-
'bend down'	cumuri-	cumuri-	pagchari-	pagchari-	cumuri-
'ear'	ringri	rinri	rinri	ringri	ringri
'Let's go!'	acuichi	acushi	acuichi	acuichi/acú	acuichi/acú
'hole'	utcu	utcu	utcu	jutcu	jutcu
'become angry with each other'	huarbuñi-	piñachiri-	piñachiri-	piñachiri-	piñachiri-

A number of authors have observed that, in Quechua folktales and other stories in which the narrator was not a witness, two if not three basic tense-aspect markers are employed with independent verbs. Muysken, for example, states (1977:43) that the tenses of EcQ are "present or unmarked ø; past or preterite *rka;* sudden discovery *shka.*" He later comments (p. 60): "In EcQ it [/-shka/] occurs typically in legends, stories, etc., as the suffix used in the first few sentences of narratives, at various intermediate points, and at the end. Often the actions in the story are marked with the /-rka/ past or are unmarked for tense." Ross (1963:79) makes a similar observation: "Some districts favor begining a story with the *-shca* form for several verbs, then switching over to the present, or the past with *-rca.*"

It is significant that Ross speaks of "some districts," because EcQ dialects display considerable variation in the employment of these markers. Chimborazo texts published by Guacho and Burns (1975:27), for example, employ *rka* ("pretérito narrativo") for the body of the narrative, with *shka* ("pretérito descriptivo") reserved mainly for the opening sentences. In Cañar texts collected by Howard-Malverde (1981:312), the speaker "JMT" from Quinoa Pota consistently uses *shka* for the body of the narrative. Muysken (1977:60) is faced with the same problem, for, after quoting various definitions of the function of *shka,* he concludes, "The resulting definitions turn out to be contradictory and implausible."

An examination of Inga dialects displays a similar phenomenon. The three basic tense-aspect markers discussed by Muysken (see above) are found in all the dialects. However, the functions of *rca* and the "present or unmarked" morphological ø/*n* form in the dialects of Aponte and Santiago are reversed in the dialects of San Andrés and Yunguillo (see discussion below). In all these dialects *sca* is employed only as an indicator of "sudden discovery," whereas in Guayuyaco it is also used frequently in connection with the events of the narrative.

rca and Morphological ø/*n* in the Mountain Inga Dialects and Yunguillo

In his article on aspect and foregrounding, Hopper (1979:213ff.) discusses evidence for a distinction between background information and the main events or foreground of a narrative, based on the distribution of independent verb forms in various languages (see also Givón 1984:287ff.). Different authors have recognised this distinction as underlying the distribution of the Quechuan tense-aspect markers in narrative material. Thus, Gaucho and Burns (1975:27) talk of a descriptive versus a narrative preterite. Larsen (1974:424) recognises that, in Ancash Quechua, the full form of the verb ending *-naq,* which characterises legendary narrative, is used in connection with background information. Weber (1983:108) observes that the narrative past marker in Huanuco Quechua is used "to mark these events as of less importance to the text (i.e., push them into background) relative to what follows." Zahn (n.d.:1) explains the distribution of *-rka* and *-shka* in Pastaza Quechua in terms of "background information" and "main line events." In 1978 I used a similar analysis of *rca* and morphological ø/*n* in the dialects of Santiago and San Andrés. Rather than repeat the arguments of the works cited above, the present comparative study *assumes* that the background-foreground distinction underlies the distribution of the tense-aspect markers.

In all the Inga dialects except that of Guayuyaco (see below), the background-foreground distinction readily explains the distribution of *rca* and morphological ø/*n*. What is remarkable is that, whereas in San Andrés and Yunguillo background information is presented using *rca* while the main events of the narrative employ the ø/*n* form, in Aponte and Santiago the functions are reversed.

In general terms, the background information expressed in independent clauses in Inga may be divided into three categories:

(a) Events and states which are *preliminary* to the main events of the story, including that which did not take place (when followed by what did) and a rhetorical usage, immediately preceding the climax or "peak" (Longacre 1976 : 212ff.).

(b) *Comments* on and expansions of a previously stated main event of the story.

(c) Events and states which take place away from the scene of the main events of the story. These include that which is perceived, discovered, or otherwise *not performed* by the character central to that part of the story. (The location of the central character is then treated as the scene of the main events.)

These categories are illustrated in the following four stories, one from each dialect. (Only the independent verbs are given in Inga, the relevant marker being italicized. The markers are not attached to verbs of subordinate clauses. See the appendix for the Inga text and a word-by-word translation of Story 1.)

Story 1 is in the Santiago dialect. The main events are marked by *rca*. Background information (indented) is morphologically unmarked (ø) preceding silence, and marked by *n* preceding other suffixes. A brief commentary follows the story.

STORY 1 "THE GOSSIP" (CHASOY 1982A : 4–6)

(Preliminary Incident:)

1. A boy who was a gossip used to tell (huillacu*n*si)[4] everyone who arrived, "We are collecting bean pods, to go to heaven."
2. His parents said (ni*n*cunasi), "There will not be enough for everyone. Just a few of us are going to go to heaven. So why are you telling everybody who arrives about this?"
3. The boy said (ni*n*si), "They are not serious when they tell me off. We are going to heaven, to heaven."
4. And he used to dance around (bailaricuø) on one leg like a dove.
5. "Be quiet, boy! Don't be telling everybody!" his parents said (ni*n*cunasi). "We have already told you 'No!' You are going to be staying behind for being such a gossip."
6. The boy did not listen (uyáø) at all.

(Main Events:)

7. The father collected (mira*rca*) bean pods until the house was full of them.

8. When the time arrived to go to heaven, he said (ni*rca*) to the child, "Go and bring water! There is none in heaven."

9. He sent (cacha*rca*) him with an open-weave basket to bring the water.

10. Running, he filled (jundachi*rca*) it in a flash.

11. Like the wind he arrived (chayagri*rca*), carrying it.

(12–17. The child is sent twice more for water, first with a sifter, then with a sieve. *rca* is attached to each verb.)

18. "You lack water for yourself." He sent (cacha*rca*) him with a woven bag.

(Comments on the previous events:)

19. It was not known (yacharø) how to delay him.

20. He used to go around (muyucuø) in no time, like the wind.

21. That trip with the woven bag delayed (unaya*rca*) him twice.

(22–27 describe the problems the boy had and how he overcame them; *rca* is attached to each verb.)

28. He arrived (chayagri*rca*) running.

(Observation by boy [central character]:)

29. But when he looked, there was (tia*n*cuna) only the water he had brought.

30. "Gracious!" he said (ní*rca*si). "They were sending me for water, just to leave me behind."

31. He pushed (tangachi*rca*) the bean pods into the midst of the fire.

32. Jumping, he rose (sica*rca*) upwards in the smoke.

(Observation by boy:)

33. His parents were visible (cahuarinacúø) like flies, up on high.

(Preliminary event: new setting:)

34. Now he too was nearly reaching (alcansacugriø) heaven.

35. He was lacking (pisicu*rca*) just two lengths (20 feet) to secure himself to heaven.

(Preliminary to 37 [climax]: away from and not performed by boy:)

36. Then the bean pod smoke completely failed (pisigriø).

37. He came (samu*rca*) right down from there.

38. He came and fell (urmagsamu*rca*) unconscious.

39. About two hours later, he woke up (rigcharigsamu*rca*), turned into a bird.

(Expansion on 39: what sort of bird:)
40. It used to cry (yacháø caparicunga),[5] "Gossip, gossip, gossip" . . .
41. And that is how the gossip, becoming a gossip bird, remained (quida*rca*) in this world.

The first events of the above story, which describe the boy's behaviour prior to the time to go to heaven and explain why his parents would wish to leave him behind (sentences 1–6), are treated as background information. They form a separate incident from the main events of the story (compare Story 3, sentences 1–4). The main events themselves consist of the completion of the preparations (sentence 7) plus the events of the great day itself (sentences 8ff.).

Once into the body of the story, just a few sentences are treated as background. Sentences 19–20 give background information because they do not describe a new event, but rather explain the problem that the father was trying to solve by sending the boy for water with leaky containers. Sentences 29 and 33 are treated not as events but as observations made by the boy, who has been performing all the actions of this section of the story (21–32). Then, as the climax of the story approaches, the treatment of sentence 34 as background information suggests a change of setting for the main events, away from earth to the proximity of heaven. This is confirmed by the treatment of sentence 36 as background; although clearly a key event of the story, it is neither performed by the boy nor does it take place near him. Finally, sentence 40 does not describe a new event, but rather identifies the bird mentioned in sentence 39.

*   *   *

Story 2 is in the Aponte dialect. As in Santiago, background information (indented) is morphologically unmarked (ø) preceding silence, and marked by *n* preceding other suffixes. The main events are marked by *sha*, which corresponds to *rca* in the other dialects.

One difference with Santiago is that introductory statements, such as sentences 1 and 2, which employ the construction *yacha-* 'know' plus a future infinitive (terminating in *nga*) with the meaning "reputed to . . . ," carry the *sha* marker. Contrast sentence 1 with the opening sentence of a Santiago story (Tandioy T. and Levinsohn 1985:14). This sentence also introduces its central character and reads, "Once there was reputed to be (tiángasi yacháø) a man called Carlos Tamabioy."

STORY 2 "THE YOUTH WHO WENT TO BATHE DURING HOLY WEEK"
(LEVINSOHN 1983A:55)

1. Once there was reputed to be (yachá*sha*si tianga) a young man.
2. Not at all is he reputed to have feared (yacha*sha* manchanga) God.
   (Preliminary events to speech 8:)
   3. In defiance he went (ri*ø*) to bathe in the big river.
   4. While he was bathing, on the other side he saw (cahua*n*si) a black mule which was drinking water.
   5. He did not become afraid (manchari*ø*).
   6. Then a man drew near (caillayagsamú*ø*), saying, "Why are you bathing at such a time as this?"
   7. The youth replied (aini*n*si), "Because I want to! Who is there to see what I do?"
8. On hearing this, the man said (ní*sha*si), "As you have that attitude, something may happen to you."
9. Having said this, he went away (rí*sha*si), without saying anything else.
10. The youth remained (quida*sha*), thinking, "What was this man trying to say to me? Will something happen to me?"
11. Having thought that, he just continued bathing (armacu*shá*llasi).
    (Preliminary to 13 [climax]:)
    12. When he had now finished and went to put on his clothing, he didn't find (tari*ø*) it.
13. When he looked to the other side, he hid (pacacu*sha*) his face in his hands, exclaiming "Good God!" to see the wretched mule with his clothes placed on it.

In contrast with Story 1, the preliminary events that are treated as background information (sentences 3–7) for the main events of the above story (sentences 8ff.) are part of the same incident as the main events themselves. However, they may be viewed simply as setting the scene for the key speech of sentence 8 and its consequences. For example, the attitude of the youth, as expressed in his speech of sentence 7, may be seen as an illustration of the statement of sentence 2 that he did not fear God.

As in Story 1 (sentence 36), the climax (sentence 13) is immediately preceded by a sentence presented as background information. See also Story 3, sentence 7.

*   *   *

Story 3 is in the San Andrés dialect. In contrast with stories in the other mountain dialects, the main events are morphologically unmarked (ø; *n* preceding certain suffixes). Background information (indented) is marked by *rca*.

STORY 3 "SUN WATER LAKE" (BY LÁZARO MOJOMBOY P.)
(LEVINSOHN AND AVENDAÑO 1982B : 7)

(Preliminary Incident [see Story 1, sentences 1–6]:)
1. In Sun Water Lake, an evil serpent with seven heads and seven tails used to emerge (llugsicu*rca*).
2. It used to wait (suyacu*rca*) each Sunday at the edge of the lake for a person to be given to it.
3. They used to send (cachanacu*rca*) someone who didn't go to Mass, to be handed over to the evil serpent.
4. It was eating (micucu*rca*) so many that the people living there became very few.
(Main Events:)
5. Then they sent (cacha*n*cuna) a youth to be handed over.
6. He went (riø) with a large machete.
   (Preliminary to 8 [climax]: not performed by the youth:)
   7. It came and churned up (timbugsamu*rca*) the water, to swallow the boy.
8. Then he, cutting off its neck with his machete, killed (huañuchiø) it.

*   *   *

Story 4 is in the lowland dialect of Yunguillo. As in San Andrés, background information (indented) is marked by *rca*. The main events are characterised throughout by the presence of *n*. (On the function of *sca* in sentences 11 and 19, see below.)

STORY 4 "THE OLD BACHELOR" (LEVINSOHN 1983B : 36–37)

(Preliminary States:)
1. An old bachelor was wanting (munacu*rca*) to marry the woman he loved.
2. For him she was (capú*rca*si) a good-looking girl.
3. So he told (huillá*n*) his mother, "I am going to get married this coming festival, when the priest comes."

4. His mother would not let (lisinsiá*n*) him.
5. In those days, he got (tucú*n*) diarrhoea.
6. He began (cayarí*n*) to take long walks.
7. On one walk he saw (cahuari*n*si)
   (Observation:)
   8. His beloved was coming toward him (samupucu*rca*).
9. So he said to himself (nirí*n*), "My coming is a disaster; I stink with the diarrhoea."
10. While he was thinking this, he went and met (tuparigri*n*) her.
    11. She turned out to be (cádusi ca*sca*) a devil.
12. She took (apa*n*si) the man a long way off into a cave.
13. He went and saw (cahuagri*n*si) many devils in a fire.
14. Then the one who had brought him said (ni*n*), "Return home again!"
    (Preliminary Event: new setting:)
    15. He arrived (chaya*rca*) at the house.
16. He sat down (tiari*n*si) at the table.
17. He asked (maña*n*si) his mother for some corn-brew.
18. When she went to pass it to him, she saw (cahua*n*si).
    19. Already he had died (huañu*sca*) just at the table.

In the above account, sentences 1–2 set the scene for the events of the story, as does sentence 15 for the climax. As in Story 1, observations and discoveries (sentence 8; see also 11 and 19) are not treated as main events.

*   *   *

To summarise, then, the following distribution of tense-aspect markers is found in the Inga dialects examined to date:

	Aponte	Santiago	San Andrés	Yunguillo
background information	ø/n	ø/n	rca	rca
main events	sha	rca	ø/n	n

The dialects of Santiago and Aponte thus employ their tense-aspect markers in basically the same way, the only significant difference being in the marking of introductory "reputed to" statements that employ the "know" verb construction. Similarly, the San Andrés and Yunguillo dialects employ their tense-aspect markers in essentially the same way.

It is noteworthy that a speaker is not obliged to use the background information marker in a story. In a particular narrative, he may choose to present all the sentences as main events (e.g., Levinsohn and Avendaño 1982b:15–16 [San Andrés]). In such narratives, in the San Andrés and Yunguillo dialects, all the independent verbs have the morphological ø/*n* tense marker, whereas the tense-aspect marker is *rca/sha* in Santiago and Aponte.

sca and the Puerto Guayuyaco Dialect

In folktales in the Guayuyaco dialect, the morphological ø/*n* tense-aspect marker is used in connection with the main events of the story, as in San Andrés and Yunguillo. However, many background sentences employ not *rca* but *sca*.

All the Inga dialects employ *sca* as a nominaliser of past events (see Muysken 1977:65), e.g., chayagri*sca*cunata huillacunsi (those-who-had-arrived he-used-to-tell) "He used to tell those who had arrived" (Chasoy 1982a:4). It is used also "like the past participle in Spanish" (Stark et al. 1973:230), for example, yapa cuiya*sca* carca (very loved he-was) "He was [the one who was] much loved" (Tandioy T. and Levinsohn 1985:11). *sca* also occurs verbally as a perfective. Concerning this usage, Ross writes (1963:79), "It specifies events having taken place while the speaker was in a state of ignorance, which has now been remedied by a discovery of the true state of affairs." Consequently, Muysken calls /-shka/ the marker of a "sudden discovery tense" (1977:60).

This use of *sca* is exemplified in Story 4 (Yunguillo), sentence 11 (see also sentence 19):

EXCERPT FROM STORY 4

10. While he was thinking this, he went and met her.
    11. She turned out to be (cádusi ca*sca*) a devil (and he hadn't known it until then).

This usage of *sca* is found in Guayuyaco (see excerpt 6 below). However, the vast majority of examples of *sca* in Guayuyaco narratives present preliminary *events*. *rca* is restricted to the presentation of preliminary *non-*

events, states that are perceived or discovered by the central character of that part of the story, and comments on a previously stated event of the story.

✳   ✳   ✳

Story 5 illustrates many of these points. *rca* is restricted to the opening nonevents of the story (sentences 1–3) and to the nonevents discovered by the monkey (sentences 39–40). *sca* is used in connection with events that build up to each set of main events. The main events themselves, as in the dialects of San Andrés and Yunguillo, are in the morphologically un-marked form (ø; *n* preceding certain suffixes).

STORY 5 "THE TREE WHICH DARKENED THIS WORLD" (JAMIOY Y. 1985:15–19)

(Nonevents:)
1. After God made this world, it was (ca*rca*) not like it is now: proper days.
2. The sun used not to appear (cahuadiru ca*rca*).
3. At that time there was (tiá*rca*si) a very wise medicine man.

(Buildup to 5:)
4. He said (ni*sca*), "We are not enjoying proper days, because there is a great tree which is darkening the whole world. If we could cut down that tree, there would be good days, because there is something to give us light, called 'sun.'"
5. Then everyone, meeting together, asked each other (tapunacúø) what could be done to cut down that tree.

(Buildup to 8:)
6. Then he answered (aini*sca*), "Up to now it is not known what to do to cut it down."
7. After that all the medicine men, meeting together, drank (upia*sca*cuna) (a hallucinatory drug).
8. Then they said (ni*n*cúnasi), "It will be possible to cut down that tree, just by drinking the drug and chanting."

(Buildup to 10:)
9. Then they asked (tapu*sca*cuna) which medicine man could chant like that until the tree fell.
10. And he answered (aini*n*si), "The great owl will be able to."

(Buildup to 12ff.:)

11. Having said that and having asked him, they took (pusa*sca*cuna) him (to the tree).

12. Then, standing beside it, he began (callari*n*si) to chant, . . .

13. While he was chanting, in truth the tree began (callariø) to bend.

14. It became (tucúø) as though about to fall.

15. And then breath failed (pisigriø) the chanter.

16. With that, the tree again became upright (dirichariø).

(17–34. Further attempts to make the tree fall also fail. *sca* and ø/*n* are employed. Finally:)

(Buildup to 41ff.:)

35. Then the wise men, again meeting together drank (upia*sca*cuna).

36. And they said (ni*sca*cúnasi), "We see that a vine is holding the tree up from above. When someone cuts it, it will fall."

37. Having said that, they asked (rua*sca*cúnasi) the *coto* monkey to go and cut the vine.

38. He, having gone up the tree, found (tarigri*sca*)

(The nonevents he discovered:)

39. The tree had (yuca*rca*) ripe fruit.

40. It was (cár*ca*si) good to eat.

41. Then the monkey, filling his stomach, lying down up in the tree, was resting (siricuø), warming himself in the sun.

42. And he didn't remember (yuyariø) why he had gone there.

43. Those on the ground were waiting (suyanacu*n*si) to see when the tree would fall.

(Buildup to 46:)

44. Because it wasn't falling, they asked (rua*sca*cuna) the squirrel, "Go and see why the tree isn't falling!"

45. Then the squirrel, having gone to see, said (ni*sca*), "The monkey hasn't cut the vine. He's living there without a care in the world."

46. Then they asked (rua*n*cuna) the squirrel himself to go and cut the vine.

(Buildup to 48:)

47. He went and cut (trusagri*sca*) the vine.

48. Then the tree fell (urmáø).

*   *   *

The following excerpt from another Guayuyaco text illustrates the use both of *rca,* in connection with an explanatory comment, and of *sca,* in connection with what was perceived, with Muysken's "sudden discovery" meaning.

1. The youth, telling the old man off, ordered (mandáø), "Fill the bag quickly, so that we can return!"
   (Explanation of 1:)
   2. That wise youth wanted (munárcasi) to see, when he bent down, whether it really was his father since, if it was a devil, in his neck would be a second mouth with great teeth like a tiger's.
   (What was perceived by the youth:)
   3. When the old man bent down and he looked, it turned out to have been (cáscasi) a devil, with all those terrifying teeth.
4. Then the youth said (ninsi), "Bend down quickly and gather them up!"
5. As soon as the devil bent down, he speared (pasachiø) him with his fish lance, right through to the ribs.

The "sudden discovery" function of *sca* in sentence 3 of the above excerpt is readily distinguishable from its more common usage in narrative, in that the information is a nonevent which the young man observed (usually marked by *rca*).

*   *   *

In his work on Proto-Quechua, Parker (1969:141) labels *š + qA as an indicator of "quotative tense," in contrast with *r + qA, which simply indicates "past tense." Certainly in Inga, whether used for "sudden discoveries" or in connection with the preliminary events of a story, *sca* is restricted to occasions in which the narrator is not a witness to the events. As soon as the narrator is a witness, *rca* replaces *sca* in Guayuyaco as the marker of such events.

This is illustrated by the following excerpt from a history of how Ingas came to live in Puerto Guayuyaco (Jamioy Y. 1985:1–14). The events that took place before the author was born or in her absence are presented using the ø/*n* or the *sca* forms (e.g., sentence 1). As soon as the author is a witness to the events, *rca* is employed instead of *sca*.

EXCERPT 7 (JAIMOY Y. 1985:12–13)

1. The colonists said (ni*sca*cuna). "This business of electing an Indian governor is pointless. It's enough to have just a sheriff for everybody."
2. Here also for two years there was (tira*rca*) no governor.
3. Then the past governors, meeting together, said (ni*rca*cuna), "It is because we believed the colonists that we are now suffering all these calamities. . . .
4. Then, because no-one was willing to agree to be governor, they commanded (manda*rca*cuna) Baltazar Peña (the author's husband) to be governor.
5. The next year, they reelected (riligi*n*cuna) him, and again for a third year.

The distribution of the tense-aspect markers in narratives in the different Inga dialects may therefore be summarised as follows:

	Aponte	Santiago	San Andrés	Yun- guillo	Gua- yuyaco
Background information					
nonevents and comments	ø/n	ø/n	rca	rca	rca
preliminary events	ø/n	ø/n	rca	rca	sca (*rca* if witnessed)
"sudden discovery"	sca	sca	sca	sca	sca
Main events	sha	rca	ø/n	n	ø/n

From the above table, it is clear that the distribution of *rca* and *ø/n* divides the dialects into two groups: Aponte-Santiago and San Andrés-Yunguillo-Guayuyaco.

As for *sca,* Muysken states (1977:60), "Narrative /-shka/ and sudden discovery /-shka/ have enough in common to be considered one tense; they will be considered the central meaning of /-shka/, and the use of /-shka/ as a generalised past tense marker will be considered a secondary, though significant, development." If Muysken's conclusion is right, then the use of *sca* in Guayauyaco would correspond with his central meaning, and its function in the other Inga dialects would represent a significant restriction in its use.

Alternatively, the variation in the function of *sca* may suggest that, in spite of the tradition that the San Andrés Ingas migrated from the region to the south rather than the north of Mocoa, the San Andrés and Yunguillo dialects should be associated together, over against the Guayuyaco dialect. Possible confirmation for this hypothesis is found in the traditional stories common to San Andrés and Yunguillo, but not generally known in Guayuyaco. Asked for a story often told by the old people, for instance, Ingas from both the mountain dialects and Yunguillo responded with the Inga equivalent of "Hansel and Gretel" (Cuatindioy C. 1972; Garreta 1985: 9–14) and the rivalry between the Rabbit and the Bear (Chasoy 1982b:1–16; Garreta 1985:1–8)!

Appendix

INGA TEXT AND WORD-BY-WORD TRANSLATION OF STORY I, *CHANCUALA*, "THE GOSSIP," BY JOSÉ CHASOY DE SINJINDIOY (SANTIAGO)

1. *Chancuala huambra maicán chayagriscacunata huillacunsi, "Purutu cara mirachinacunchi, nucanchi sug luarma ringapa."*
   Gossip boy anyone to-those-who-went-and arrived 3[rd person]-is-telling, "Bean pod we-are-collecting, we other to-place to-go."
2. *Chihura atuncuna nincunasi, "Tucuítac manima pusangapa canchu. Nucanchi cuintadúllami ringapa canchi cieluma. Camcarí ímata ña maicanpas yaicuscacunata parlacungapaglla?"*
   That-time big-ones 3-say, "To-all not to-take 3-is. We just-few to-go we-are to-heaven. You-in-contrast what now anyone-whatever to-those-who-arrived to-just-be-telling?"
3. *Chi huámbrac ninsi, "Nucanchita yángami piñanacú. Nucánchic cieluma cieluma ringapa canchi."*
   That child 3-says. "Us in-vain 3-are-rebuking. We to-heaven to-heaven to-go we-are."
4. *Paluma bailadur ca: chásasi sug chaquillahua huarcuspa, caima y chima bailaricu.*
   Dove dancer 3-is: thus one with-just-leg hanging, to-here and to-there 3-is-dancing-around.
5. *"Upalla cay, huambritu. Pítapas mana parlacuy," atuncuna nincunasi. "Ña nucanchi parlangapa 'Mana' ninchi. Parlunmándami quidangapa cangui."*

"Quiet be, boy. To-anyone-at-all don't be-telling," big-ones 3-say. "Now we to-talk 'don't' we-say. For-gossip to-remain you-are."

6. *Ñi ímapassi mana uyá.*
   Not anything-at-all not 3-hears.

7. *Sutípasi huasi junda purutu cara mirarca.*
   Truly house full bean pod 3-collected.

8. *Ña cieluma ringapa hura chayahúrac, chi huambrátac nirca, "Apagriy yacu. Cielupi manima tianchu."*
   Now to-heaven to-go hour when-arrived, that to-child 3-said, "Go-and-bring water. In-heaven not there-is."

9. *Saparuhua cacharca, yacu apangapa.*
   With-basket 3-sent, water to-take.

10. *Calpáspac, man'unailla jundachirca.*
    Running, not-long-at-all 3-filled.

11. *Huáiralla aparispa chayagrirca. . . .*
    Just-wind carrying 3-went-and-arrived. . . .

18. *"Cam quinmándami pisicu." Quiquinmanda jígrasic cacharca.*
    "You for-self 3-is-lacking." For-self bag 3-sent.

19. *Mánasi yacharí imasa paita unayachinga.*
    Not 3-is-known how him to-delay.

20. *Paic man'unailla huáirallasi muyucu.*
    He not-long-at-all just-wind 3-is-going-round.

21. *Chícar jígrahua párissic unayarca. . . .*
    That with-bag twice 3-delayed. . . .

28. *Calpa chayagrirca.*
    Running 3-went-and-arrived.

29. *Cahuagrihúrac, chasállasi tiancuna astáscac.*
    When-went-and-saw, just-thus there-are what-had-carried.

30. *"Caramba!" nircasi. "Caicúnac saquihuangamanda, nucata mandahuanacú."*
    "Gracious!" 3-said. "These for-to-leave-me, me 3-are-sending-me."

31. *Purutu caracunátac chaugpi nínasi tangachirca.*
    Bean pods middle fire 3-pushed.

32. *Saltaspa, huíchay cusnipi sicarca.*
    Jumping, upwards in-smoke 3-rose.

33. *Atuncúnac chuspisinállasi ahuapi cahuarinacú.*
    Big-ones just-like-fly on-high 3-are-appearing.

34. *Chihúrac ñalla paipas alcansacugri.*
    That-time nearly he-also 3-goes-and-is-reaching.

35. *Iscay tupusinalla pisicurca, cieluma piarigringapa.*
    Two just-like-length 3-was-lacking, to-heaven to-go-and-grasp.
36. *Chihúrac purutu cara cúsnic impas pisigrí.*
    That-time bean pod smoke completely 3-goes-and-fails.
37. *Chimandata samurca impas.*
    Right-from-there 3-came completely.
38. *Ña sug rigcha yuyachi urmagsamurca.*
    Now other likeness caused-feeling 3-came-and-fell.
39. *Unaipi, sug íscay hurapisina, rigcharigsamurca, piscu tucuspa.*
    After-while, other two like-after-hour, 3-came-and-awoke, bird
    becoming.
40. *Chicarí, "Chancuala chancuala chancuala" . . . yachá caparicunga.*
    That, "Gossip gossip gossip" . . . 3-knows to-be-crying.
41. *Chásasi parlunca, chancuala piscu tucuspa, cay mundupi aicha quidarca.*
    Thus gossip, gossip bird becoming, this in-world flesh 3-became.

NOTES

1. The texts were gathered during field trips made between 1968 and 1985. The work itself is based on an analysis of more than seventy narratives, some given orally and recorded, others dictated, and some written by the Inga storyteller.

All the narratives quoted in the chapter are published in monolingual (Inga) or bilingual (Inga-Spanish) textbooks for schools supervised by Educación Nacional Contratada (Vicariato Apostólico de Sibundoy). Copies of the texts in microfiche form may be obtained from the author (58 Hithercroft Road, High Wycombe, HP13 5RH, England).

2. The Spanish alphabet is used for all the Inga examples cited, /š/ being written *sh* and /c/ *ts*. See Levinsohn (1976:19–29) and Tandioy J. and Levinsohn (forthcoming) for descriptions of the phonology of Inga.

3. The Guayuyaco people used to live in Puerto Limón (Jamioy Y. 1985:1). I have encountered no clear tradition concerning migrations of the Yunguillo or Condagua people from other areas.

Personal conversations with Ingas from San Miguel suggest that they speak the same dialect as the Guayuyaco people. They say that they lived close to Mocoa earlier in this century.

4. The reportative enclitic *si* is optionally attached to the main verb phrase of the sentence, or to any phrase preceding the verb that is given prominence (see Levinsohn 1975:14ff. for a detailed discussion of this point). The equivalent enclitic for events to which the author is a witness is *mi*.

5. In the Santiago dialect, this "habitual" construction differs from the "reputed to" construction (see Story 2), in that the verb *yacha-* 'know' almost always precedes the infinitive and often is not contiguous to it. In the "reputed to" construction, the infinitive immediately precedes *yacha-*. In Aponte, the distinction

between the two constructions appears to have been lost, as *yacha-* always precedes the infinitive.

REFERENCES

Cuatindioy C., Miguel
  1972   *Iscay Huajchu* (*Los Dos Huérfanos*). Lomalinda: Instituto Lingüístico de Verano.

Chasoy Sijindioy, José
  1982a   *Sachucu caugsagcuna tucuscamanda parlocuna* (*Cuentos en que las personas se convierten en animales*). Sibundoy: Educación Nacional Contratada.
  1982b   *Conejomanda y Gurguntillumanda parlocuna* (*El Conejo y el Oso; Bordoncillo*). Sibundoy: Educación Nacional Contratada.

Garreta, Jacinto
  1985   *Condaguamanda antihua parlucuna* (*Tradiciones de Condagua*). Sibundoy: Educación Nacional Contratada. Manuscript.

Givón, T.
  1984   *Syntax: A Functional-Typological Introduction.* Amsterdam: John Benjamins.

Guacho, Juan Naula and Donald H. Burns
  1975   *Bosquejo gramatical del quichua de Chimborazo.* Quito.

Hopper, Paul J.
  1979   "Aspect and foregrounding in discourse." In *Syntax and Semantics Vol. 12, Discourse and Syntax,* ed. T. Givón, 213–41. London: Academic Press.

Howard-Malverde, Rosaleen
  1981   "Dioses y diablos: Tradición oral de Cañar Ecuador." *Amerindia* número special 1. Paris.

Jamioy Y. de Peña, Otilia
  1985   *Antihua pacay ginticunapa parlucuna* (*Tradiciones de los inganos pacayes*). Sibundoy: Educación Nacional Contratada.

Larsen, Helen
  1974   "Some grammatical features of legendary narrative in Ancash Quechua." In *Advances in Tagmemics,* ed. Ruth M. Brend, 419–40. Amsterdam: North-Holland.

Levinsohn, Stephen H.
  1975   "Functional sentence perspective in Inga." *Journal of Linguistics* 11:13–37.
  1976   *The Inga* (*Quechuan*) *Language.* The Hague: Mouton.
  1978   "¿Tiempo pretérito, o acción de fondo? Una diferencia dialectal en inga," *Courrier du Sud* 11:53–61. Pasto.
  1983a   (ed.) *Nucanchipa Rimay* (*Lenguaje Inga*). Sibundoy: Educación Nacional Contratada.
  1983b   (ed.) *Nucanchipa Simi Rimay* (*Lenguaje Inga*). Sibundoy: Educación Nacional Contratada.

Levinsohn, Stephen H. and Luis Francisco Avendaño, eds.
    1982a   *San Andresmanda gentecuna imasa costumbre y parlo yucascacuna (Leyendas y Costumbres de San Andrés)*. Sibundoy: Educación Nacional Contratada.
    1982b   *Parlocuna leesunchi (Cartilla inga 2)*. Sibundoy: Educación Nacional Contratada.
Longacre, Robert E.
    1976   *An Anatomy of Speech Notions*. Lisse: Peter de Ridder Press.
Muysken, Pieter
    1977   *Syntactic Developments in the Verb Phrase of Ecuadorian Quechua*. Lisse: Peter de Ridder Press.
Orr, Carolyn and Robert E. Longacre
    1968   "Proto-Quechumaran." *Language* 44.3 (September): 528–55.
Parker, Gary J.
    1969   "Comparative Quechua phonology and grammar II. Proto-Quechuan phonology and morphology." *University of Hawaii Working Papers in Linguistics*, Vol. 1, No. 1.
Ross, Eileen
    1963   *Introduction to Ecuador Highland Quichua*. Quito: Instituto Lingüístico de Verano.
Stark, Louisa R. et al.
    1973   *El Quichua de Imbabura: una gramática pedagógica*. Otavalo: Instituto Interandino de Desarrollo.
Tandioy J., Francisco and Stephen H. Levinsohn
    forthcoming   "Fonologia comparativa de los dialectos del inga."
Tandioy T., Luis Manuel and Stephen H. Levinsohn, eds.
    1985   *Santiagomanda gentecuna imasa parlo yucascacuna (Tradiciones de Santiago)*. Sibundoy: Educación Nacional Contratada. Manuscript.
Weber, David John
    1983   *A Grammar of Huallaga (Huanuco) Quechua*. Ph.D. dissertation, University of California, Los Angeles. Available from University Microfilm, Ann Arbor, Mich.
Zahn, Charlotte
    n.d.   *Tense Sequence in Pastaza Quechua Text Structure*. Lima: Instituto Lingüístico de Verano, Manuscript.

Adalberto Salas

The Minimal Finite Verbal Paradigm in Mapuche or Araucanian at the End of the Sixteenth Century

ABSTRACT

This chapter presents the core of the Mapuche verbal paradigm (i.e., the system of mode, person, and number markers) toward the end of the sixteenth century, and contrasts it with that of the present-day language. It is discovered that after 400 years, the system remains the same in both the phonological surface and the deep morphological structure. This high degree of resistance to change may be seen as an overall, prominent feature of the Mapuche language.

Introduction

The first complete Mapuche or Araucanian grammar was published in Lima in 1606, under the title of *Arte y Gramatica General de la Lengva que corre en todo el Reyno de Chile.* . . . It was written by the Jesuit missionary Luis de Valdivia (Valdivia 1606 [1887]).[1] In this article I present the minimal verbal paradigm known at the end of the sixteenth century, as described by Father Valdivia, and contrast it with that of the modern language in order to gain some insight into change/permanence in this language during the almost four hundred years that have passed since Father Valdivia's *Arte*.

The Mapuche finite verbal forms are those obligatorily inflected by mode and focal person[2] or by mode, focal person, and number. They are structurally and functionally opposite to nonfinite verbal forms, grossly corresponding to the infinitive mode of Latin traditional grammars (infinitive, gerund, participle, and so forth).

The Mapuche finite verbal forms consist minimally of a verb stem (in the simplest construction it is a single root) and a finite verbal inflection, manifested by a suffix or suffix cluster carrying the meaning of mode, focal person, and number. When, in a given verbal form, only the stem and the finite inflection are manifested, the verbal form is minimal. When one or more optional suffixes are manifested (such as negation, tense, perfective, locatives, satellite person[3]), the verbal form is nonminimal or expanded. The total set of forms involving only a given verb stem and its finite inflection is the minimal finite verbal paradigm.[4] Thus, the minimal finite verbal paradigm includes, for a given verb stem, forms contrasting only by mode and focal person or by mode, focal person, and number. On the other hand, every verbal form that does not present these contrasts is nonfinite.

Old Mapuche

Father Valdivia's *Arte* is modeled after the traditional grammars of Latin. Therefore, the Mapuche verb is presented by reference to Latin verbal conjugation and its typical categories (voice, mode, aspect, tense, person, and number). In the active voice (*Arte,* Chapters IIII–V, folios 11–18) there are five modes: (1) indicative, (2) imperative, (3) optative, (4) subjunctive, and (5) infinitive. The last mode does not contain finite forms. The optative is not a true mode because it does not have specific forms; rather, the optative meaning is expressed by means of the so-called mixed tenses of the indicative, by the imperative, or by some tenses of the subjunctive (Chapter III, folios 13–14).

Both indicative and subjunctive have eight tenses each. Four of them are called "principal": (1) present, (2) imperfect, (3) first future (imperfect future), (4) first mixed tense (future-in-the-past). The other four tenses are: (1) perfect, (2) pluperfect, (3) second future (perfect future), and (4) second mixed tense (perfect-future-in-the-past). The imperative has one tense only, called present (Chapter IIII, folio 13). There are three persons (1st, 2nd, 3rd) in each tense and three numbers in each person (singular, dual, and plural).

In the active voice, the minimal present forms are: indicative, imperative, and subjunctive. The other tenses are nonminimal because they are formed by means of optional markers of tense and/or of perfective, placed between the stem and the finite suffixes.

The forms of the present indicative are:

SINGULAR

I	elun	[e·'lun]	I give[5]
II	eluymi	[e·'lui̯·mi]	you give
III	eluy	[e·'lui̯]	he/she gives

DUAL

I	eluyu	[e·'lu·yu]	both of us give
II	eluymu	[e·'lui̯·mu]	both of you give
III	eluyḡu	[e·'lui̯·ŋu]	both of them give

PLURAL

I	eluiñ	[e·'lu·iñ]	we give
II	eluymn	[e·'lui̯·mən]	you give
III	eluyḡn	[e·'lui̯·ŋən]	they give

(See Chapter IIII, folio 12.) The root *elu* 'to give' and the following suffixes and suffix clusters may be isolated:

	SINGULAR	DUAL	PLURAL
I	-n	-yu	-iñ
II	-ymi	-ymu	-ymn
III	-y	-yḡu	-yḡn

The forms of the present imperative are:

SINGULAR

I	eluchi	[e·'lu·či]	may I give!
II	eluḡe	[e·lu·'ŋe]	you give!
III	elupe	[e·lu·'pe]	may he/she give!

DUAL

I	eluyu	[e·'lu·yu]	let us give (both of us)!
II	elumu	[e·'lu·mu]	both of you give!
III	elupe or elupe (e)ḡu	[e·lu·'pe·ŋu]	may both of them give!

PLURAL

I	eluyñ	[e·'lu·iñ]	let us give!
II	elumn	[e·lu·'mən]	you give!
III	elupe or elupe (e)ḡn	[e·lu·'pe·ŋən]	may they give!

(See Chapter IIII, folio 13.) The suffixes and suffix clusters are:

	SINGULAR	DUAL	PLURAL
I	-chi	-yu	-yñ[6]
II	-ḡe	-mu	-mn
III	-pe	-pe(e)ḡu	-pe(e)ḡn

It may be noted that the inflection of 1st person dual and plural is the same as the corresponding indicative.

The forms of the present subjunctive are:

SINGULAR

I	eluli	[e·'lu·li]	when I give or if I give
II	elulmi	[e·'lul·mi]	when you give, etc.
III	elule	[e·'lu·le]	when he/she gives, etc.

DUAL

I	elulyu	[e·'lu·lyu]	without glosses in Valdivia
II	elulmu	[e·'lul·mu]	
III	elulḡu	[e·'lul·ŋu]	

PLURAL

I	eluliñ	[e·'lu·liñ]	without glosses in Valdivia
II	elulmn	[e·'lul·mən]	
III	elulḡn	[e·'lul·ŋən]	

(See Chapter IIII, folio 14.) The suffixes and suffix clusters are:

	SINGULAR	DUAL	PLURAL
I	-li	-lyu	-liñ
II	-lmi	-lmu	-lmn
III	-le	-l(e e)ḡu	-l(e e)ḡn

Father Valdivia observes that sometimes 3rd person dual or plural subjects agree with 3rd person singular verbs (Chapter XV, folio 39). This observation permits us to assume that there was only one form of 3rd person, the so-called singular:

INDICATIVE	IMPERATIVE	SUBJUNCTIVE
eluy	elupe	elule

and that the apparent forms of 3rd person dual and plural:

	INDICATIVE	IMPERATIVE	SUBJUNCTIVE
DUAL	eluyḡu	elupe (e)ḡu	elul(e e)ḡu
PLURAL	eluyḡn	elupe (e)ḡn	elul(e e)ḡn

contain optional markers of dual (eḡu ~ ḡu) and plural (eḡn ~ ḡn). Father Valdivia's examples:

(1) aldúpuche kúpay
    [al·'θï·pu·če kə·'pai̯]
    many Indians come
(2) aukapuche vfchiduamlay
    [aw·'ka·pu·če uf·či·θwam·'lai̯]
    the braves do not like peace

suggest that the optional markers of number do not occur when duality/ plurality is expressed by lexical means in the subject (in the examples, the segment -pu- in *aldúpuche* and *aukapuche* is a pluralizer of nouns).

Father Valdivia includes two other voices: impersonal voice (in two variants) and passive voice. The first variant of impersonal voice (Chapter VII, folio 20) contains verbal forms of undetermined agent and undetermined patient, as in *eluam* 'it is given'. This variant is marked by the suffix *-am* [am], which does not present the typical contrasts of finite verbal forms (mode, focal person, number). The second variant (Chapter VII, folios 21–22) contains forms of undetermined agent and determined patient. It is formed by means of the verbal root *g̃e* [ŋe], meaning 'to be,' directly added to the stem. The verb *g̃e* follows the normal inflection of the language (Chapter VI, folios 19–20). In the context of *g̃e* the focal person has the semantic value of patient:

| eluymi | [e·ˈluᵢ·mi] | you give |
| eluǧeymi | [e·lu·ˈŋeᵢ·mi] | you are given |

elu is the root for 'to give' and *ǧeymi* is the 2nd-person singular of the present indicative of *ǧe* 'to be.' This 2nd person corresponds to patient, and agent remains undetermined.

Passive verbal forms are marked by the participial suffix *-el* [el] which does not present the typical contrasts of finite verbal forms (Chapter VIII, folios 22–23). Since it does not carry personal markers at all, agent and patient are expressed at the clause level.

To summarize, in the stage of language at Father Valdivia's time, the minimal finite forms are those of (1) active indicative present, (2) active imperative present, and (3) active subjunctive present. There are three persons in each one of these three series. The 1st and 2nd person are obligatorily marked by number (singular, dual, plural). There is only one form for 3rd person, since it does not present obligatory number contrasts at word level. Imperative 1st person dual and plural are the same as the corresponding indicative. Therefore, the minimal verbal paradigm contains nineteen different forms.

Modern Mapuche

There are three modes in the modern Mapuche language: (1) real (indicative), (2) volitive (imperative), and (3) hypothetical (subjunctive). There are three focal persons (1st, 2nd, 3rd) and three numbers (singular, dual, and plural). There is only one form in 3rd person, since it does not carry (obligatory at word level) number contrasts. Volitive mode lacks 1st person dual and plural.

There are three optional tense suffixes and one optional perfective suffix. A form in real mode without tense or perfective markers has a vague semantic value going from nonremote past to present, depending on the meaning of the verbal stem. A form in hypothetical mode without tense or perfective markers is a present. In volitive mode, tense or perfective markers do not occur.[7]

Thus, the forms of present/nonremote past of the real mode, those of the present of the hypothetical mode, and those of the volitive mode are minimal finite. Therefore, in the modern language, the minimal finite verbal paradigm contains the following nineteen different forms:

(A) REAL (INDICATIVE)

SINGULAR

I	[e·'lun]	I give[8]
II	[e·'luį·mi]	you give

DUAL

I	[e·'lu·yu]	both of us give
II	[e·'luį·mu]	both of you give

PLURAL

I	[e·lu·'iñ]	we give
II	[e·'luį·mən]	you give

WITHOUT NUMBER DENOTATION

III	[e·'luį]	he/she gives, they give

(B) VOLITIVE (IMPERATIVE)

SINGULAR

I	[e·'lu·či]	may I give! or let me give!
II	[e·'lu·ŋe]	you give!

DUAL

II	[e·'lu·mu]	both of you give!

PLURAL

II	[e·'lu·mən]	you give!

WITHOUT NUMBER DENOTATION

III	[e·'lu·pe]	may he give! or may they give!

(C) HYPOTHETICAL (SUBJUNCTIVE)

SINGULAR

I	[e·'lu·li]	if I give
II	[e·'lul·mi]	if you give

DUAL

I	[e·'lu·lyu]	if both of us give
II	[e·'lul·mu]	if both of you give

PLURAL

I	[e·lu·'liñ]	if we give
II	[e·'lul·mən]	if you give

WITHOUT NUMBER DENOTATION

III	[e·'lu·le]	if he/she gives or if they give

The modern language has two free morphemes: {eŋu} (ŋu ~ eŋu) and {eŋïn} (ŋən ~ eŋən), meaning, respectively, dual and plural of 3rd person. They are optional and occur at the clause level when the subject does not carry lexical expression of number. When they are contiguous to the verb they tend to occur in the short (enclitic) forms (ŋu and ŋən).[9]

The first variant of Father Valdivia's impersonal voice (*eluam* 'it is given') remains today only in the fossilized form [pi·'am] 'it is said' (from the root [pi] 'to say'), frequently used as a parenthetical expression in folktales.

In modern Mapuche, there is a satellite person suffix -[ŋe] 'undetermined agent' in which context the focal person expresses the patient. For example:

(1) lelin
    {leli 'to look'; -n 'real mode, focal person 1st singular' (agent)}
    I looked

(2) leliŋen
    {leli 'to look'; -ŋe 'undetermined agent'; -n 'real mode, focal person 1st singular patient'}
    I was looked at

This suffix accounts for the second variant of Father Valdivia's impersonal voice, that containing verbal forms of undetermined agent and determined patient.

Comparisons

Simple inspection shows that the minimal verbal paradigm has not changed for some four hundred years. The system of finite verbal suffixes remains the same, in the phonological surface as well as in the abstract morphological structure.

Configuration of finite inflection in terms of its slots and slot fillers is the same in both stages of language. This system contains four types of morphemic strings:

(1) one slot of mode and focal person:

finite inflection
mode and person
-pe   volitive, 3rd

16TH CENTURY	20TH CENTURY	MORPHEMIC STRING
[e·lu·'pe]	[e·'lu·pe]	{elu-pe}

(2) two slots, one of mode and one of focal person:

finite inflection	
mode	person
-i real	ø 3rd
-l hypothetical	-e 3rd

16TH CENTURY	20TH CENTURY	MORPHEMIC STRING
[e·'luɨ]	[e·'luɨ]	{elu-i-ø}
[e·'lu·le]	[e·'lu·le]	{elu-l-e}

(3) consisting of three slots: one of mode, one of focal person, and one of number:

finite inflection
mode, person, and number
-n   real, 1st singular
-či   volitive, 1st singular
-ŋe   volitive, 2nd singular

16TH CENTURY	20TH CENTURY	MORPHEMIC STRING
[e·ˈlun]	[e·ˈlun]	{elu-n}
[e·ˈlu·či]	[e·ˈlu·či]	{elu-či}
[e·lu·ˈŋe]	[e·ˈlu·ŋe]	{elu-ŋe}

(4) three slots, one of mode, one of focal person, and one of number:

finite inflection

mode	person	number
(-i 'real')	-i '1st'	-u 'dual' -ñ 'plural'
-i 'real'	-m '2nd'	-i 'singular' -u 'dual' -ən 'plural'
ø 'volitive'	-m '2nd'	-u 'dual' -ən 'plural'
-l 'hypothetical'	-i '1st'	-ø 'singular' -u 'dual' -ñ 'plural'
	-m '2nd'	-i 'singular' -u 'dual' -ən 'plural'

16TH CENTURY	20TH CENTURY	MORPHEMIC STRING
[e·ˈlu·yu]	[e·ˈlu·yu]	{elu-(i)-i-u}
[e·ˈlu·iñ]	[e·lu·ˈiñ]	{elu-(i)-i-ñ}
[e·ˈlui̯·mi]	[e·ˈlui̯·mi]	{elu-i-m-i}
[e·ˈlui̯·mu]	[e·ˈlui̯·mu]	{elu-i-m-u}
[e·ˈlui̯·mən]	[e·ˈlui̯·mən]	{elu-i-m-ən}
[e·ˈlu·mu]	[e·ˈlu·mu]	{elu-ø-m-u}
[e·ˈlu·mən]	[e·ˈlu·mən]	{elu-ø-m-ən}
[e·ˈlu·li]	[e·ˈlu·li]	{elu-l-i-ø}
[e·ˈlu·lyu]	[e·ˈlu·lyu]	{elu-l-i-u}
[e·ˈlu·liñ]	[e·lu·ˈliñ]	{elu-l-i-ñ}
[e·ˈlul·mi]	[e·ˈlul·mi]	{elu-l-m-i}
[e·ˈlul·mu]	[e·ˈlul·mu]	{elu-l-m-u}
[e·ˈlul·mən]	[e·ˈlul·mən]	{elu-l-m-ən}

Conclusion

Comparison between Mapuche at the end of the sixteenth century and contemporary Mapuche shows very clearly that the nucleus of the verbal conjugation, the system of finite suffixes, has not changed except for the placement of the accent, which is nonphonemic in both stages of the language. After a careful reading of Father Valdivia's *Arte,* I have the impression that this high degree of resistance to temporal change may be found throughout the core of the grammar and vocabulary of this language.

NOTES

1. Luis de Valdivia (born in Granada, Spain, 1561–died in Valladolid, Spain, 1642) wrote his Mapuche grammar in Chile, between March 1605 and April 1606. He learned the Mapuche language during his first trip to the country, between 1593 and 1602 (Campos Menchaca 1972, chapters V–VI).

2. On the notion of focal and satellite person, see Salas (1978).

3. See note 2. An overview of modern Mapuche verbal structure is found in Salas (1984 : 17–18, 32–42).

4. See Elson and Pickett (1962 : 76n).

5. Father Valdivia's orthography is given first, followed by a broad phonetic transcription based on the information contained in Chapter I (De la Pronunciacion y Ortographia, folios 7–8) and Chapter 28 (Final del Acento, folio 55).

6. Note that the corresponding indicative form is written *-iñ.* The orthographic difference *i* versus *y* does not have phonological relevance. In Mapuche as well as in Spanish, Father Valdivia vacillates between the two letters, even in the same item; for example, *reyno* ~ *reino.*

7. A detailed presentation of tense suffixes is found in Croese (1984). See also Fernández Garay (1981).

8. The verbal root *elu* 'to give' is marked by agent (person who gives) and patient (person who receives). The given thing is expressed beyond the verb, at the clause level. The modern Mapuche items are transcribed in a broad phonetic transcription; details can be found in Salas (1984 : 14–17).

9. A detailed discussion can be found in Salas (1979).

REFERENCES

Campos Menchaca, S.J., Mariano José
    1972   *Nahuelbuta.* Buenos Aires: Editorial Francisco de Aguirre.
Croese, Robert A.
    1984   "Tiempo verbal en mapudungun." *Actas: Jornadas de Lengua y Literatura Mapuche.* Temuco, Chile: Universidad de la Frontera-Instituto Lingüístico de Verano, 64–76.
Elson, Benjamin and Velma Pickett
    1962   *An Introduction to Morphology and Syntax.* Santa Ana, Calif.: Summer Institute of Linguistics.

Fernández Garay, Ana V.

1981   "Algunos sufijos verbales mapuches." *Revista Latinoamericana de Estudios Etnolingüísticos* 1 : 5–25. Lima.

Salas, Adalberto

1978   "Terminaciones y transiciones en el verbo mapuche: Crítica y bases para una nueva interpretación." *RLA. Revista de Lingüística Teórica y Aplicada* 16 : 167–79. Concepción, Chile.

1979   "¿Hay marcas de número en la 3a. persona de los verbos mapuches? Una discusión sobre *engu* y *engün*." *Estudios generales* 1 : 225–40.

1984   *Textos orales en Mapuche o Araucano del centro-sur de Chile*. Concepción, Chile: Editorial de la Universidad de Concepción.

Valdivia, P. Luis de

1606   *Arte y Gramatica General de la Lengva que corre en todo el Reyno de*
[1887] *Chile, con un Vocabulario y Confessonario, compuestos por el Padre Luys de Valdivia de la Compañia de Iesus en la Prouincia del Piru . . .* En Lima por Francisco del Canto. Año 1606. Facsimile edition prepared by Julio Platzmann. *Arte, Vocabulario y Confesionario de la Lengua de Chile, compuestos por Luiz de Valdivia*. Edición Facsimilar. Leipzig: B.G. Teubner.

V

Ethnolinguistics

Gustavo Rodríguez

The Talátur: Ceremonial Chant
of the Atacama People

ABSTRACT

The purpose of this work is to present two versions of the "Talátur," a ceremonial chant of the Atacama people whose language ceased to be spoken at
the end of the last century. This presentation of the texts aims at giving a
testimonial to the extinct language of the "Likan Antai" (Atacameños) rather
than to reconstruct the language or to represent historical process, since the
evidence is scant, heterogeneous, and multiform.

The Talátur is a ceremonial chant sung (even today) during the so-called
limpia de canales (cleaning of canals or channels) by the mountain people in
northern Chile, in the so-called II Region, who inhabit the same geographic
area as the Atacama did.

In 1976 we collected the last version of this chant and we attempt here to
unravel some of its meaning. The notes provide some scant data about a text
which is written, supposedly, in "Cunza" (= Kunza), the language of the
Atacameños, wherein some elements of the grammatical structure of this
dead language may be glimpsed.

Introduction

This text contains the last remnants of the extinct Cunza language of the
Atacameños or "Likan Antai." I have verified from my two field trips (in
which I traveled to San Pedro de Atacama, Toconao, Talabre, Camar, Socaire, and Peine) that there are no speakers of Cunza at present.

This ceremonial song was collected in Socaire in northern Chile,
85 km from San Pedro de Atacama. The population of Socaire is about 345
inhabitants. The houses are made of stone and straw with small doors and
windows to minimize effects from the cold and windy weather. The
weather is very harsh due to the altitude: the temperature drops below
freezing at night, even in the summer. At present, the town has a modern

clinic, a school, and one telephone. It also has electric power at certain hours.

Goatherders formerly slept near the main arroyo (*quebrada*) of the town. Circular building remains have Atacameñan names such as *sícher, cuno, Toronal, Achal, Quisuna*.

Background

Documents dealing with the Cunza language such as the "Glosario" by Vaïsse, Hoyos, and Echeverría (1895); "Noticias" by Echeverría y Reyes (1890); "La lengua cunza" by San Román (1890); and some notes about Cunza by Mostny (1954) have been used for this work.

The mountain range of northern Chile forms a border zone with Peru, Bolivia, and Argentina. There is an exchange of educational, social, and other cultural elements in this part of Chile.

Tarapacá and Antofagasta form a vast territory: Antofagasta is about 126,000 km², and Tarapaca is 50,000 km². These two areas were inhabited by many Indian groups in the past. Testing by the radiocarbon process has demonstrated that settlements can be traced back to ten thousand years in some coastal areas of Tarapacá. Inhabitants of these towns became known as "Changos" during the colonial period.

The Puquinas, another group that lived in northern Chile, left their traces in the toponymy. Another group, the Uros, lived in the north coastal region of Tarapacá. They mixed with the Changos, colonies of fishermen brought from Lake Titicaca during the period of Inca conquest. The Aymaras lived, and are still living, in the prerange and interior plateau of Atacama. According to one hypothesis, Aymaras descend from an Arawak family from the continental Carib; they settled later along the coastal Pacific Ocean, where they divided into families and branches that evolved separately, among them the Uros, the Puquinas, the Quechuas, the Chingay, and others. Slow shifts of these groups peopled parts of Peru, southern Bolivia, and northern Chile and Argentina. The Incas conquered them around the fifteenth century and incorporated them into their empire. The conquerors named these regions "Colla." The tracks of these people are recognized by the abundant toponymy found in the range and interior plateau of Tarapaca.

The Atacameños inhabit the Andes range of northern Chile, but their origins are not known exactly. The rich civilization of the Atacameños, whose cultural and linguistic features differ from those of the Aymaras, the Quechuas, and other groups of the area, left traces in southern Peru, southwest Bolivia, northwest Argentina, and the coast of the I and II regions of Chile. The core of this culture was located in the region of San Pedro de Atacama, and it expanded from this point to other areas. Atacameña culture reached its maximum development in the ninth century, but a subsequent contraction process led them to live in the hydrographic region of Atacama, where they were conquered by the Incas prior to the arrival of the Spaniards. The Atacameña language, Cunza (also, "Kunza" and "Cunsa," a possessive meaning "ours") was lost at the end of the nineteenth century. Written information about the characteristics of this language is scarce.

There is little information on the Inca presence in the area, since little archaeological evidence has been uncovered to date. Some historians such as Garcilaso de la Vega and Bibar, have some data that allow us to calculate that Inca dominance over the Atacameños was brief, amounting to approximately fifty to seventy years (Echeverría y Reyes 1890:93).

Spanish reports of 1840 indicate that the region of the plateau and the Chilean prerange was widely populated by farmers, who founded other villages and towns, giving rise to an increasing population. In 1581 Pedro Lozano M., the first person to report information on the Indian population (Lehnert 1978:10), calculated the population of Atacama at about 2,000 persons. D'Orbigny in 1839 reported the following figures: 5,046 Indians and 1,200 mestizos for Tarapacá; 1,942 Indians and 970 mestizos for Atacama. And by 1884 Bertrand found that there were 4,000 Indians for the Puna of Atacama (Echeverría y Reyes 1890:90).

Method of Inquiry

The objectives of my field trips were to find out (1) what elements of Cunza are still found in the language spoken today; and (2) what knowledge or awareness the speakers have with regard to these words or forms.

With the help of existing literature, a 300-item questionnaire was devised concerning activities typical to the region, for example, activities related to agriculture, cattle breeding, and animals and plants of the zone. In this way, we were able to show that some words are still used by the people of Atacama whereas others are not. The work was carried out at the lexical level only (Rodríguez 1980–82:419–27).

During the interviews we learned that the following words are still known:

(1) Three terms related to *weaving*.

(2) Four terms related to the *human body*.

(3) Nine terms for *zoology* (out of 62 terms in the literature).

(4) Six *plant* names.

(5) One term for *clothing*.

(6) Three terms related to *colors*.

(7) Seven terms for other referents.

In brief, only a small vocabulary of 33 words bear testimony to the extinct language of the Atacameños.

Feasts, Rites, and Customs

Several celebrations have, for the present inhabitants of the Atacama region, a deep mythical meaning that is manifested in a series of traditional activities performed by the Atacameños on specific occasions. For instance, certain rites such as *el convido,* "ofrenda" (offering), which are extremely ancient and penetrating, involve Nature, or Mother Earth, who receives the name *pachamama,* or simply, *la pacha.* She represents the source that provides the means of daily subsistence, thus when an individual drinks or eats, he or she takes a little bit of the portion and pours it upon the earth as a sign of an offering. Nonrealization of this ritual implies future family problems or the death and destruction of crops or animals.

In the *floramiento* (or *enfloramiento*) 'flowering' ceremony, the ears of animals are marked or decorated with flowers, ribbons, or multicolor pom-poms in the *estancia* or *puesto*—a stone room and corral located on the slopes of a hill or volcano. These ceremonies are accompanied by music and dancing, after which the flock, *la tropa* (*rebaño*), is left *afloriada* 'enflowered'.

The festival known as the *Talátur, talato,* or "cleaning of channels," is performed as a water cult and has also been preserved with great vitality. This festivity is normally observed once a year; its observance is marked by dancing, which proceeds as the community works collectively. The feast ends with a great banquet and much imbibing. The person who directs the Talátur is called *capataz* or *capitán* 'foreman' or 'captain'. The word *talátur* is of Cunza origin and means "dance"; it is also the name for the final chanting at the end of the process of cleaning the channels. The dance related to sowing is called *tuscalo,* which possibly derives from *tusckantur* (*escarbar* 'dig a hole'). The Talátur feasts are traditionally celebrated on 24 October in Socaire.

The Talátur

Several factors justify the presentation of this analysis, mainly the fact that documents about this lost language of northern Chile contain serious linguistic limitations that make their use in a rough reconstruction of Cunza problematic. These limitations involve:

(1) The heterogeneity of the collected materials.

(2) The fact that many of the papers include small vocabularies of doubtful accuracy.

(3) The fact that some of the people who gathered information about the Atacameños were not prepared linguistically.

This is not to say that the earlier work was not important for the sketch we have of Cunza today. From the bibliography, it can be seem that few texts exist in Cunza: two versions of the *Pater noster* given by Tschudi; the Talátur version collected by Grete Mostny; and the version we present in this chapter. Mostny's version was obtained from a local inhabitant from Peine who had it written down in a notebook (Mostny et al., 1954:162):

> This text was copied from that of Socaire, to which it is identical, except for some expressions. Thus, the Talátur from Peine begins with *wilti* (or *wilte*) which is the name for a spring [= well] in that locality, while the Socaire text begins with *muya,* the name of the spring from there.

The Mostny Version
The version below is that of Grete Mostny et al. (1954:162–63). The numbering of the stanzas is maintained in accordance with the original.

TALATUR

I

Wilti puri yuyo sai
quepe puri pachata
awai   awai   awai.

2

Solar puri yuyo talu sai
tami puri pachata
awai   awai   awai.

3

Echar sacta cheresner
Saque acta colcaina colcaina
awai   awai   awai.

4

Yuro tucor nace colcoinar
sake tucor nace colcoinar
awai   awai   awai

5

Laus saisa carar monte colcoinar
Chile saisa carau saire y sairina
saire sairina y yentes lulayne yentes
carar y yentes illauca saflu islilla.

6

Tumi saisa monte colcoinar
Chile sisa carau sare y sairina
saire sairina y yentes lulayne y yentes
carar y yentes illauca saflu islilla.

7

Quimal sisa carar monte colcoina
Chile saira y yentes lulayne y yentes
curar y yentes iyauca saflu islilla.

(NOTA: aquí empieza el "zapateo")

8

Calal tanti sayno
islamas tanti sayno

isay pani y ques capana
isay San Antonio

9

Ayil tanti sayno
katur tanti sayno
isay pani y ques caspana
isay San Antonio

10

Tarar chusli sayno
pauma chusli sayno
isay kone islujlina
isay San Antonio

11

Lipis chusli isayno
koiway chusli sayno
y say kone y esluslina
y sai San Antonio

12

Uway leyer licau simainuna
y pauna licau simanuna
y kaper licau simanuna
y eya techaynita
y eya katalur ya qui
y yai y yale y yai iyawe
iyawe yolasquita.

Textual observations made by Mostny refer to the incorporation of some Hispanic elements (*monte,* San Antonio, Quimal, etc.). She also points out that this ceremonial chant is no longer understood; it is only repeated by rote by the *capataz/capitán* (foreman or captain) who directs the ceremony of the cleaning of the channels. Mostny recognizes that her version of the chant may have been modified in relation to the original form because of the oral character of the tradition. In addition to her other conclusions about the supposed meaning of several words or forms, Mostny summarizes (p. 165):

In other words—and making it explicit that this is only an attempt at translation—we believe that the Talátur is danced at the beginning of the precolumbian agricultural cycle and before the planting process, and that it invokes the different springs so that they may flow abundantly from the rocks to all the surroundings so that these may be covered by clouds and so the maize and potatos may sprout satisfactorily and yield rich harvests. Children and grown-ups are invited to celebrate and to revel.

The Rodríguez version

The text presented here was collected during my fieldwork in 1976 in Socaire; the informant was Don Andrés Ramos, who was then seventy-eight years old. This version differs from Mostny's, and it is important to remember that she said her version was a faithful copy of the one obtained in Socaire. We have phonetically transcribed the recording of the text so that some of these differences may be observed.

Observations

Comparing the two versions reveals three types of forms (or should we speak of "words"?):

Forms of Hispanic origin. Those of marked Hispanic origin, such as *San Antonio* (patron of these communities); Chile; *yentes* (*gentes*) 'people'; *montei* (*monte*) 'hill'; and *Quimal* (perhaps Quechua?), the name of a mountain to the west of San Pedro de Atacama, on whose peak may be found traces of sanctuaries dedicated to the cult of that divinity (some authors indicate that this was the sacred mountain of the Atacameños). Other forms appearing in the text also seem to be of Hispanic origin: *tʰalú* (*salud*) 'health'; *solar, nasé* (*nace*) 'born'; *islilla* (*isla*); *kʰantéi* (*cantar*) 'sing'.

Variants of a single form.

yuyo, yullo:	This form is explained in the "Glosario" as a variety of quínoa.
pure, puri:	*Agua* 'water'. Water has always been the fundamental element for the subsistence and development of Atacameño culture. Hence the form *pure, -i* combines in other terms of Cunza origin: *purilari* 'agua colorada' (colored water); *puritama* 'agua caliente' (hot water); *purikujter* 'agua salobre' (brackish water); *purichari* 'agua overa' (muddy water); and so forth. Many toponyms include the element *puri*.
pechar, echar:	Of unknown origin. It is not recorded in any of the glossaries. Possibly, 'echar'?

TALÁTUR
Andrés Ramos

I

[ʔiyáj purí yuʌó:
tʰalú tʰayú tʰɔxmí:
purí: pačáta
  awár ʹ awár jawáj ʹ

II

solár puré yuyó:
tʰalú saí pasą́w ʹ
ʔų̃ndrį́ŋ kajná čatáj ʹ
  awár ʹ awár jawáj ʹ

III

ʔečár saxtáj čeresnį̇́r ʹčeresnį̇́r ʹ
čokí jaʂtáj kʰokʰɔjná kʰokʰɔjnąɭ ʹ
hawáj awáj ʹ

IV

yurúa tukų́r
nasé jokɔjnár ʹ
śakí tukų́r
nasé jokɔjnár ʹ
hawáj awáj ʹ

V

lą́ws sajsáj kʰarą́w
mɔ̃ntéj kʰokʰɔjnár ʹ
čile siséj kʰarą́w
sajrí ʹsajriná: sajrí ʹsajrína
sajrí ʹsajrį̇n ʹ
jḛntés lulajnḛ́n
jḛntéjs kʰarár ʹ
jḛntés iʌąwká:j ʹsaʃlú:isliʌa ʹ

VI

tomí sajsáj kʰarą́w ʹ
mɔ̃nté kʰokʰɔjnár ʹ
čile sajsáj ʹkʰarą́w ʹsajrí ʹsajriná
sajrí ʹsajrína ʹsajrí ʹsajrį̇n ʹ

jḛntés lulajnḛ́ ʹjḛntes kʰarár
jḛntés iʌąwkʰá: ʔi saʃlú ʔiʌą́w ʹ

VII

kʰimąl sisáj kʰarą́w
mɔ̃nté ʹkʰɔlkʰɔjnąɭ ʹ
čile sajsáj kʰarą́w ʹ
sajrį̇n ʹsajrína ʹsajrį̇n ʹsajrína ʹ
sajrį̇n ʹsajrį̇n ʹ
jḛntés lulajnḛ́: jḛntés kʰarár ʹ
jḛntés iʌąwká ʹšaʃluš ʹʔiʌą́w ʹ

VIII

tarár tą̃ntéj sajnó
jeslamáj tą̃ntéj sajnó ʹ
ʔisajpą́ne jeskarpáma
ʔi jáj san ą̃ntónjo ʹ

IX

ʔayíl kʰą̃ntéj sajnó ʹ
jeskʰatʰejl kʰą̃ntéj sajnó ʹ
ʔisajpą́ne jeskarpáma
ʔi jáj san ą̃ntonjo ʹ
tarár čy̨šléj sajnó
jespą́wma čy̨šléj sajnó ʹ
ʔisáj kɔ̃nné jesly̨šlima ʹ
ʔi jáj san ą̃ntónjo

X

lípe čy̨šléj sajnó
nį̇škɔjváj čy̨šléj sajnó ʹ
ʔisáj kʰɔ̃nné jesly̨šlima ʹ
ʔi jáj san ą̃ntónjo ʹ

XI

ʔuváj leyáj likąw semájnu
jespą́wnaj likąw semájnu ʹ
ʔi kʰapér likąw semájnu ʹ
ʔi jeyáj tečaxnita ʹ
ʔi jéya kʰatálo yakʰé ʹ
ʔi ya: yá le ʹʔi yá: yále ʹ
ʔi yále yolaskʰíta]

Figure 1. Text of Talátur by Don Andrés Ramos.

saxtái, sakta: Of unknown origin. We might suppose by the sig-
                   nifier that it is from the Spanish *santa.*
cheresñir, cheresner: According to Mostny (p. 164) it is an opening in
                   the rock through which water flows, *vertiente*
                   'spring'.
cocoina, colcoina: A very old concept supposed to derive from the
                   Cunza form *ckolckol* (*rótula*) 'knee-cap' and from
                   ckolekitur (*embarazo*) 'pregnancy'.
túcor, túcur: According to the "Glosario," this form derives from
                   tuckor 'buho' (owl), even though its relation to
                   the content of the rest of the stanzas is not clearly
                   seen.
yuro, yurúa: Undocumented form.
saque, saqui: This form might derive from *sacka* 'también' (by si-
                   militude of the signifier) and by the position in
                   which it appears in stanza IV.
saisa, saisai: It seems that this form corresponds with that of
                   saire, sairina. Compare the fifth stanza in both
                   versions, where it means 'lluvia' (rain).
carar, carau: According to Mostny, 'nubes' (clouds).
tumi, tomi: According to Mostny, it is the name of a hill in
                   Peine. During our fieldwork, an informant gave
                   us several references as to the toponymy of the
                   zone. One of them refers to a mountain known
                   as *Tumisa.* (Remember that the Talátur is an in-
                   vocation to the hills, 'montañas, nubes, y agua'
                   [mountains, clouds, and water].)
islamas, ieslamái: Possibly a hybrid of *isla* + a Cunza morpheme?
isay pani, pisaipane: Undocumented form.
y quescapana, "iescarpana":   Undocumented form.
ayil, payil: 'Corn', according to the "Glosario," p. 534.
chušli, chušléi: 'Potatoes', according to Mostny.
lipis, lipe: Undocumented form.
leyer, leyai: 'Far', according to Mostny.
simainuna, semainu: This could possibly be related to *sima* 'man' because
                   it appears together with *licau* 'woman'.
katabur, katalo: Undocumented form.

Differing forms. Forms absolutely different that appear in both versions in the same verses and stanzas, but, it seems, with an altogether
different sense. Some of these include:

(a) Version 1, stanza 1, begins with *wilti* 'name of the Peine spring',
    according to Mostny. Version 2 begins with *piyai.* We have not
    found this form in any glossary. It might refer to a spring in
    Socaire.

(b) In version 2, stanza 1, the form tʰalú (instead of quepe—possibly derived from *ckepi* 'ojo' (eye)—in version 1); and thoxmí (of unknown meaning) recorded in version 1.

(c) The forms iawái/awai and awár (versions 1 and 2, respectively) represent two variants appearing in both texts at the end of the first four stanzas. Mostny ventures the hypothesis that they might be related to the form *aiawalte,* which is an invitation made by the *mingueros* when they come to work (Mostny 1954:164).

Conclusion

To conclude, we observe that it is impossible to reconstruct this text in its original sense, as was explained above. We believe that the explanations Mostny offered in her attempt at translation are acceptable, owing to the fact that the documentary and testimonial backgrounds—scant as they are—allow for only a fragmentary vision of the Atacameños.

The people that today inhabit the region that belonged to their ancestors maintain their rites, customs, and idiosyncracies vigorously. They are the living testimony of an already vanished culture.

REFERENCES

Buchwald, Otto von
    1922   "Análisis de una gramática atacameña." *Boletín de la Academia Nacional de Historia* 5.12–14:292–301. Quito.
Echeverría y Reyes, Aníbal
    1890   "Noticias sobre la lengua atacameña." Santiago: Imprenta Nacional, pp. 1–16. Reprinted (1966) in *Ancora* 3:89–100.
Lehnert, Roberto
    1976   "La lengua kunza y sus textos." Universidad de Chile, Antofagasta, *Cuadernos de Filología* 5:71–80.
    1978   "Acerca de las minorías étnicas de los Andes de la I y II Región." Universidad de Chile, Antofagasta, *Documentos de Trabajo* 1:1–45.
Mostny, Grete, Fidel Jeldes, Raúl González, and F. Oberhauser
    1954   *Peine, un pueblo atacameño,* Universidad de Chile, Santiago, *Publicación del Instituto de Geografía* 4:139–70.
d'Orbigny, Alcides
    1839   *L'homme américain (de l'Amérique méridionale) considéré sous ses rapports physiologiques et moraux.* Paris.
Rodríguez, Gustavo
    1980–82 "Efectos del sustrato en el español atacameño." Universidad de Chile, *Boletín de Filología* 31.1:419–27.

Rodríguez, Gustavo, Orieta Véliz, and Angel Araya
    1980   "Particularidades lingüísticas del español atacameño" (I). Valdivia,
            Estudios Filológicos 15:51—77.
San Román, Francisco J.
    1890   "La lengua cunza de los naturales de Atacama." *Ancora* 3:76—88. San-
            tiago, Universidad Técnica del Estado.
Tschudi, Johann Jakob von
    1869   "La lengua kunza." Translation and notes by Leopoldo Sáez Godoy,
    [1971]   Valparaíso, *Signos* 5.1:15—20.
Vaïsse, Emilio, Félix Hoyos, and Aníbal Echeverría
    1895   "Glosario de la lengua atacameña," Santiago, *Anales de la Universidad*
            de Chile 91:527—56.

VI

Distant Relationships

Julian Granberry

Amazonian Origins and Affiliations of the Timucua Language

ABSTRACT

The structural and lexical characteristics and components of the seventeenth-century Timucua language of Florida are examined and compared with those of other native American languages of both hemispheres. Correlation of such comparisons with archaeological data from the southeastern United States, the northern South American littoral, and Amazonia indicates a probable Amazonian origin and point of dispersion for both the Timucua language and the Timucua people.

Introduction

At the time of Spanish contact and the colonization of Florida in the middle and late 1500s, speakers of the Timucua language occupied the Atlantic coast of the United States from an as yet indeterminate position on the Georgia coast between the mouths of the Altamaha and Satilla Rivers—probably closer to the latter—south to the Daytona region on the north-central coast of Florida. They certainly occupied southeastern Georgia as far inland as the Okefenokee Swamp and the whole of the northern section of the Florida peninsula, from the Atlantic as far west as Florida's Withlacoochee River and the adjacent coastal lowlands along the Gulf of Mexico in central Florida. The lowland regions themselves, from the mouth of the Withlacoochee River northwest along the Gulf coast to an as yet undetermined location near the Aucilla River, were probably not a part of the Timucua realm. They seem, rather, to have been populated by tribal groups of probable Muskogean affiliation, stretching from the Apalachee homelands in the Tallahassee–Big Bend area, down the coastal periphery to, and including, Calusa country in far south Florida. South and west of a line from the sources of the Withlacoochee, through southern Orange County to Lake Harney—just inland and slightly north of Cape Canaveral—there seems to have been only sparse, if any, Timucua

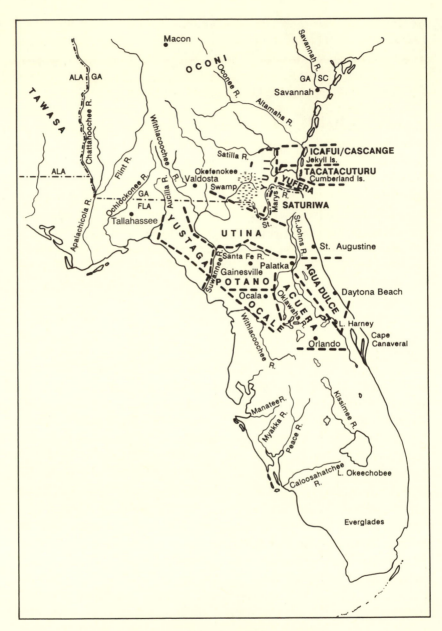

Figure 1. Timucua political and dialect boundaries (ca. 1600).

settlement. The east-coast peoples from the cape south to the Keys were probably Muskogean-speaking and seem to have been related to the dominant south Florida Calusa.

To the north in Georgia were the little-known Oconi, presumably from near the coast in the Altamaha River region, on inland as far as the Oconee River, or perhaps distributed *along* those river systems, with Muskogean-speaking Guale between. It is not totally unreasonable to suggest that the Oconi may have occupied the riverine environments of north Georgia as far as the Savannah River and the present Georgia—South Carolina border, though considerably more archaeological, linguistic, and ethnographic data would have to be summoned to support this suggestion in full. The Oconi were definitely Timucuan in speech, but their precise linguistic affiliations with the other Timucua tribes to the south is quite unclear. They were also found in the mid-1600s as far west and south as the confluence of the Flint, Chattahoochee, and Apalachicola Rivers. In the 1700s they settled on the Alachua Prairies of north-central Florida, retrenching, as all the remnant Timucua tribes did, toward Spanish protection in St. Augustine and against increasing Muskogean and Anglo-American pressures from the north.

Yet farther west, in the region between Montgomery, Alabama, and the Chattahoochee-Apalachicola confluence, with extensions as far west and south as the Mobile area, were the Tawasa. Like the Oconi, their distribution seems to have been riverine, embedded in essentially Muskogean territory. Also clearly Timucuan, they are as elusive and shadowy in affiliation as the Oconi.

While we have no information on the organization of either the Oconi or the Tawasa at the time of initial French and Spanish colonization, the Timucua of southeast Georgia and Florida were organized into tribal-political entities, some apparently very loose-jointed and others with a considerable degree of formalization. The approximate geographical boundaries of these entities are shown on Figure 1, solid lines indicate relatively certain boundaries and dashed lines indicate probable boundaries. These tribal units have been ably defined and discussed by Milanich (1978) and Deagan (1978) and can be summarized as follows:

Tribal unit	Political status	Location
Yustaga	Independent	East of the Aucilla River and west of the Suwanne River (Madison & N. Taylor counties).

Tribal unit	Political status	Location
Utina	Independent	North of the Santa Fe River into south Georgia, and from the east bank of the Suwannee River probably to the west bank of the St. Johns River.
Potano	Independent	Alachua County.
Ocale	?	Marion County, north-east of the Withlacoochee River, east to the Ocala National Forest, and south to the central Florida lake region.
Icafui/Cascange	?	Georgia coast opposite Jekyll Island west to the Satilla River.
Yui	Independent	West of the Satilla and St. Mary's Rivers west to the Okefenokee Swamp.
Yufera	Independent	Between the Satilla River and the north bank of the St. Mary's Rivers, opposite Cumberland Island.
Tacatacuru	Independent	Cumberland Island.
Saturiwa	Independent	From the Atlantic, west to the east banks of the St. Mary's and St. Johns Rivers, from the south bank of the St. Mary's River in the north to south of St. Augustine in the south.
Agua Dulce	Semi-independent (?)	From the Atlantic coast, west to the east bank of the St. Johns River, from just south of St. Augustine in the north to the vicinity of Lake Harney and the cape in the south.
Acuera	Semi-independent (?)	Between the St. Johns and Oklawaha Rivers, from the Ocala National Forest region in the north to just south of Orlando in the south.

In addition to the above tribal-political entities, Pareja (1627:f.37) refers to the Tucururu, presumably somewhere in southeastern Georgia. This, however, is the sole mention, as far as I am aware, of this Timucua-speaking group, and we cannot make even an intelligent guess regarding its identity or affiliation.

Laudonnière and Le Moyne (Lorant 1946) refer to the Onatheaqua, located immediately to the east of the Aucilla River on the East/West Florida boundary, but there is no other mention of this group in the literature of the times. Onatheaqua does not have a Timucua ring to it. It is possibly Muskogean, and the diagraph ⟨th⟩ represents the Muskogean voiceless [ɫ].

The Tocobaga, Oçita (= Pohoy?), and Mocoço, encountered by the de Soto expedition in the Tampa Bay region and considered by Swanton (1946) as Timucua, were very probably not Timucuan, to judge from both archaeological and ethnographic evidence. Rather, the affiliations seem to be with the clearly Muskogean peoples of northwest Florida and/or the probably Muskogean Calusa to the south (Bullen 1978).

Lastly, two bogus terms, Yustega and Mocamo, have inadvertently crept into the literature in Florida archaeology since the late 1950s. Neither spelling occurs in any original source, or, for that matter, in any secondary source, from the late sixteenth century through the mid-twentieth century. Mocamo, in fact, is morphologically impossible in Timucua, and these mistakes should be corrected to Yustaga and Mocama, as they uniformly occur in the sources of the times.

While Florida was known to the Spanish from the very early 1500s, it was not until Juan Ponce de León's first voyage in 1513 that the area and its inhabitants began to attract notice. Even then it was not until Hernando de Soto's epochal expedition of May 1530–September 1543 that intimate contact was made with any of the Timucua-speaking peoples. We have some helpful ethnographic information in the interesting narrative of the de Soto expedition left by the Gentleman of Elvas, but we have to wait until the arrival of Jean Ribault and the French in 1562 and his successor René de Laudonnière in 1564 before we have any substantive ethnographic data (Lorant 1946), supplemented by the famous drawings of Jacques Le Moyne, the artist who accompanied the expedition (Lorant 1946, Le Moyne 1875).

From a linguistic point of view, the French accounts give us little more than isolated words, and, while the spellings are of interest from a phonological view, they provide little in the way of helpful information. Full linguistic and ethnographic information is not available until Fr. Francisco Pareja began his service in Florida in 1595. This Franciscan missionary was stationed at the mission of San Juan del Puerto on Ft. George Island, near the mouth of the St. Johns River. He quickly became the leading, and, for a time, the only scholar of the Timucua language. He wrote five volumes, including a Timucua grammar, from which we gain the bulk of what we know today about both the Timucua language and the ethnography of the Timucua peoples. The latter information is usually quite inadvertent, enmeshed in Christian polemics on the evils of Indian lifeways (Milanich and Sturtevant 1972). Although he displays all the expected prejudices of a cleric of his times, Pareja was nonetheless an unselfish, dedicated, and literate man. He spent thirty-three years living among the Timucua. Sometime after 1626, he left Florida for Mexico, where, we are relatively certain, he died in 1628. A full listing of his works is given in Granberry (1987a: 7–8).

From the First Spanish Period in Florida (1565–1763), we have almost no additional data on the Timucua. There is, of course, ample clerical and historical information, but that is all. When the Spanish left Florida for Cuba in 1763, most of the remaining Timucua, long since thoroughly Christianized and Hispanicized, went with them to form the nucleus of the little town of San Agustín Nueva near Habana, called then as now by the Timucua name Ceibamocha (Ceiba = 'silk-cotton tree' + *mo* 'speak' + *-ča* 'place of' = 'Speaking Place of the Ceiba Tree'. Cf. *Utinamochara* = 'Speaking Place of the Lord of the Land', *-moča* being a typical manner of naming primary towns). Tawasa speakers lasted until at least the end of the century—we have a 1797 word list—but they, too, few in number, were ultimately absorbed by their neighbors, the Muskogean-speaking Alabama.

While dialect differences within Timucua seem to have been slight, it is nevertheless the case that dialect boundaries, as indicated by Pareja, seem to have coincided very closely with tribal-political boundaries. This is probably just another way of saying that tribal-political entities were defined largely along dialect lines. The only dialect we are unable to correlate with a political entity is the Tucururu dialect, which, as pointed out earlier, is only mentioned once. The Tawasa are first heard of in the 1540 reports of the de Soto expedition as the Toasi, located on the Tallapoosa or upper Alabama River, the same area they occupied 250 years later (Swanton 1929). They are not mentioned by Pareja. Swanton (1929) showed conclusively, however, that Tawasa was a Timucua dialect.

Pareja mentions ten Timucua dialects: Acuera, Agua Fresca, Agua Salada, Itafi, Mocama, Oconi, Potano, Timucua, Tucururu, and Yufera

(Pareja 1627). With Tawasa this makes a total of eleven known Timucua dialects. The lexical material on dialects other than Mocama is scanty, and we have no specifically grammatical statements on them at all. It is, therefore, impossible to make any but the most general of statements on dialect differences. Pareja does state that the Mocama and Timucua dialects were the major forms of the language, reflecting our current archaeological definition of eastern versus western Timucua cultural differences (Milanich 1978, Deagan 1978).

Dialects and tribal-political entities may be correlated as shown in the table.

Dialect	Tribal-political unit
Timucua	Utina
Potano	Yustaga, Potano, Ocale (?)
Itafi	Icafui/Cascange, Yui (Ibi)
Yufera	Yufera
Mocama	Tacatacuru, Saturiwa
Tucururu	?
Agua Fresca (= Agua Dulce)	Agua Dulce
Agua Salada	Coastal Saturiwa
Acuera	Acuera
Oconi	Oconi (not a political unit?)
Tawasa	Tawasa (not a political unit?)

This writer's earlier statements on Timucua dialects (Granberry 1956) were both incomplete and inaccurate and should not be followed.

Archaeological Correlates

The late John Goggin made the first attempt to correlate the then-known linguistic, ethnographic, and archaeological data on the Timucua (Goggin 1953). His insights still hold together remarkably well after a period of thirty-five years of increasingly intensive archaeological work in all the Timucua areas.

The most recent summaries of archaeological correlates of Timucua tribal/linguistic units are those of Milanich (1978) for the Western Timucua and Deagan (1978) for the Eastern Timucua. Both are careful, well written accounts which build on Goggin's earlier base. The primary alteration of Goggin's data is the elimination of his Southern Timucua group (Tocobaga, Oçita, Mocoço), largely on the basis of data acquired since the time Goggin wrote, which would suggest that these Tampa Bay tribes were likely Muskogean in language and wider cultural affiliation (Bullen 1978).

Essentially, the Eastern Timucua (Yui, Icafui/Cascange, Yufera, Tacatacuru, Saturiwa, Agua Dulce, and Acuera) are represented archaeologically by the long St. Johns Tradition in Florida and this tradition, together with the Wilmington-Savannah, on the Georgia coast. The Western Timucua (Yustaga, Utina, Potano, Ocale) participate in the Alachua Tradition and the Fort Walton/Leon-Jefferson Traditions. The picture in the western region is considerably more complex than that in the eastern region, however, inasmuch as the north-central and northwestern parts of Florida were from earliest times a mixing-ground for peoples (?) and traits, both indigenous and foreign, from the west, north, and east.

In both the eastern and western regions there is clear cultural continuity from at least a thousand years before the historic period to that time-marker (Milanich 1978:61). In the eastern region, in fact, there is rather clear continuity from Mt. Taylor times (ca. 4000–2000 B.C.) through St. Johns IIc times (A.D. 1513–65). Such material culture continuity, while also implying a considerable degree of continuity in nonmaterial culture traits and possible in situ population as well, does not necessarily imply that the Timucua language was indigenous to either the eastern (especially) or western Timucua regions. We will look at the latter statement in considerable detail later.

It may be pointed out, as Gatschet first noted in 1880 (p. 465), that the lexical base of the Timucua language is not genetically related to any language "spoken in the neighborhood of its native soil." A thorough examination of the vocabularies of not only neighboring languages but also of all documented North American languages, stocks, and phyla shows no convincing relationship nor even large-scale borrowing of lexical forms. There are, as would be expected, a small number of Muskogean borrowings, some from probable Proto-Muskogean times (ca. 2000–1500 B.C.), most from later times. There is no broader Gulf, Algonquian, Siouan, Iroquoian, Coahuiltecan, or other affiliation, either lexically or grammatically. From a native North American point of view, Timucua is a linguistic anomaly.

It is of some interest to note that there is also a very important archaeological anomaly at approximately the 2500–1500 B.C. time level in what Goggin, Milanich, and Deagan have called the Eastern Timucua region. This is the rather sudden appearance of ceramic wares in a Late

Archaic context in the St. Johns and Savannah River areas. The wares, the earliest known in North America, while showing some similarity in shape and function to earlier steatite wares, show, as James Ford (1969) has pointed out, difficult-to-explain detailed trait similarities and near-identities to wares from the northwestern Caribbean coast of Colombia. As Ford indicates, it is hard to rationalize the independent invention of such a complex artifactual system on the Archaic base of the southeastern United States, particularly since no gradual developmental sequence from that base to the subsequent ceramic base has so far been discovered. It may not appear completely "full-blown," but the archaeological impression is close to that.

I am, obviously, implying that the two anomalous systems—the Timucua language and the archaeologically defined Orange/Stallings Island cultures—may have more in common than meets the eye. Radiocarbon dates and the time of arrival of Timucua speech in North America, as indicated by the few Proto-Muskogean words in the language, both point to the 2000–1500 B.C. time line. Such problems of origin have been studiously avoided in all recent summaries and detailed statements on Florida archaeology, almost as though they were not problems (Milanich and Fairbanks 1980, for example). While we fully agree that origin problems are always difficult of solution, it is nonetheless now possible to form an intelligent, testable hypothesis in the light of our current linguistic and archaeological data. Such a hypothesis will be suggested in the last section of this chapter.

Linguistic Components of Timucua and Their Origins

Background
Crawford has summarized the history of the linguistic investigation of Timucua from Brinton (1858) to the time of his own writing (Crawford 1979). As he points out, attempts have been made to connect Timucua genetically to a wide range of North and South American languages, all to no avail.

Even a cursory examination of Timucua language data makes it abundantly clear that one is dealing with an unusual system. Lexically an isolate, it nonetheless contains a fairly large number of forms stemming from several quite readily discernible sources. Grammatically, it fits a well-known areal model in a single particular part of the Americas and conforms especially well to one segment of that model still in existence today. Yet no one source can explain the totality of the system. There is no known dominant contributor.

The language has all the expectations of what anthropologists and linguists refer to as a *creolized* system, and it is probably for this reason that attempts to find *the* source of Timucua linguistically have been fruitless. To put it another way, the lack of success in assigning Timucua to a single genetic source is a piece of positive data in itself. The language has no single provenience, in either space or time. One must, rather, talk of the process of ethnic and linguistic formation. The sources of Timucua are clearly multiple, as we shall see. They are partly definable, partly not. Our problem is to identify the sources and estimate the frequency and importance of each component's contribution to the overall system. We may then be able to arrange the components in some kind of logical temporal and spatial framework.

If we have difficulty in finding a dominant lexical contributor to Timucua, we have less trouble in finding a primary grammatical contributor. The basic patterns of Timucua grammar conform rather closely to Macro-Chibchan. The closest similarities are, on the one hand, to the Warao isolate of the Orinoco Delta in far western Venezuela, tentatively assigned by Greenberg to the Paezan stock within Macro-Chibchan (Greenberg 1960), and, on the other hand, to Cuna, a member of the Chibchan stock proper within the macrophylum. The specific similarities will be examined in detail later in this chapter.

There are also individual morphemes and lexemes that bear striking resemblances to modern Warao, as well as an even larger number of lexemes with equally striking resemblances to languages of the Vaupés-Caquetá-Inírida-Guaviare branch of Northern Maipuran Arawakan. The number and close correspondence of nominal and verbal prefix and suffix morphemes with those of Warao is noteworthy—44 percent of Warao noun suffixes and 17 percent of Warao verb suffixes have Timucua parallels or identities.

Floyd Lounsbury (Rouse 1986:121) has suggested that the similarities, particularly to Warao, "are neither numerous nor strong enough to eliminate independent invention or the transmission of linguistic norms from one local population to another through trade or other means of intercommunication." While it is certainly the case that the number of resemblances is small, certain peculiarities of the morphemic structure and semological usage would, in my opinion, mitigate Lounsbury's suggestion of independent invention. The peculiarities are shared only by seventeenth-century Timucua and modern Warao; they do not occur in other neighboring languages in either the southeast or Venezuela, nor, for that matter, in any other native South or North American language. To attribute such a situation to independent invention is, I think, greatly stretching a point. On the other hand, attribution of such similarities to borrowing as a result of various kinds of intercommunication, particularly if the common elements are not dominant in one of the languages, is not only feasible but quite likely.

The picture is not a simple one, but the multiple sources of Timucua lexicon and grammar point to a long process of creolization. Such a process can, of course, take many forms. When one culture and language is politically dominant, one usually sees large-scale relexification, as in the case of Anglo-Saxon after the Norman Conquest in 1066. If total military subjugation and fragmentation of the nondominant population is involved, as was the case in the Atlantic slave trade, almost total relexification and large-scale grammatical restructuring of the nondominant language(s) usually occurs, the Caribbean Creoles serving as the classic case. If contact between cultures is largely economic, without extensive military or political domination on the part of one of the participants, as in the case of the development of Swahili, the basic lexicon of the less dominant language tends to remain largely intact but with lexical, morphemic, and syntactic borrowings from the more dominant participant.

Timucua would seem to be an example of the last sort—peaceable economic contact over a long period of time leading to incorporation of lexical and grammatical structures from nonnative sources. While the nonnative contact source for the Bantu peoples of East Africa was largely unitary—the Perso-Arabic dialects of southern Arabia—the contact sources for Timucua seem to have been multiple: at least one or more Waroid languages, Northwestern Chibchan, Northern Maipuran Arawakan, and Muskogean, the latter through a 3,000-year time period.

The uniqueness of Timucua is that no single dominant source for the language can be identified. A primary lexical source of unknown origin, clearly not Waroid, is countered by a primarily Waroid grammatical source. None of the lexical contributors can be considered dominant in any sense. The only similar case of which I am aware is that of the Mbugu language of northern Tanzania (Goodman 1971). Mbugu, too, has a primary lexical source of unknown origin, though its grammar is essentially Bantu. There are contributing lexical and grammatical elements from both Sudanic and Hamitic languages, neither of them dominant.

The Timucua case is perhaps more amenable to solution than that of Mbugu, however, for we have considerable archaeological data with which to work, both in the Southeastern United States and in the Amazonia–Northwestern South America regions; some of it is quite enlightening with regard to the possible formation of the Timucua language.

STRUCTURE

The most striking accord between Timucua and Warao is that found in the morphemic structure of nouns. In both languages, a lexeme has nominal usage syntactically and semologically if the root morpheme, usually a free-form, is capable of taking the noun-pluralizing suffix *-tooma* (Timucua): *-tuma* (Warao). There are six additional affixes which either designate a lexeme as a noun or derive a structural noun of some particular type from another noun or other part of speech. The list here exhausts the noun-designating/deriving machinery of Timucua and represents six of a total of seventeen such affixes for Warao (see Osborn 1967b:254). There is one additional member of this group of affixes which shows a similarity between the two languages. 'Long' occurs in Warao as the noun-deriving suffix *-wari*. In Timucua 'long' is indicated by the bimorphemic lexeme *ihi-riwa*. Metathesis might explain W. *-wari*: T. *-riwa*. That is, eight, or 44 percent, of Warao noun-designating/deriving affixes are mirrored by similar or identical forms in Timucua, accounting for 100 percent of the noun-designating/deriving machinery of that language.

Timucua		*Warao*	
na-	nominalizer	-na	nominalizer
-si[1]	reflexive goal-marker	-si	goal-marker
-ma[2]	definite goal-marker	-ma	goal-marker
-ko	augmentative	-ka	diminutive
-siwa	quantitative	-sebe	quantitative
-ma[3]	plural agent	-mo	plural agent

The possessive affixes of both languages are also similar. Timucua 3S optionally, but with high frequency, adds the goal-deriving suffix *-ma²*, essentially a definite article. Homophonous *-ma¹* and *-ma²* behave according to different rules of phonological alteration and are therefore considered separate morphotactic entities, indicated by the superscript notation. Both Timucua *-ma*[1] and Warao *a-* indicate 3S unless otherwise specified, but they may be used with any specified person, as in Timucua *heka pahama* 'our house' (*heka* 'we'), Warao *oko amōkō* 'our hand(s)'. They are both general possession markers. As Osborn points out (his N = noun), "unless the person is otherwise specified *a-* + N may be glossed *the-N* or *third-person's N*" (Osborn 1967b: 258), indicating an identical semological function for Timucua *-ma*[1] (± *-ma*[2]) and Warao *a-*.

	Timucua	*Warao*
1S	-na	ma-
2S	-ya ~ -ye	hia- ~ hi-
3S	-ø ~ -ma[1] (+ -ma[2] > -mima)	ø- ~ a-
1P	-na + ka > -nika	ka-
2P	-ya + -ka/-ke > -yaka/-yake	yatu-
3P	-ma[1] + -ka + -re + -ma[2] > -mikarema	—

The *-ka* pluralizer of Timucua is also frequently used as a general noun pluralizer. When it is so used, it is normally followed by lexeme-final suffix *-re*, which has no counterpart in Warao. A *-re* suffix, however, does occur widely in Arawakan languages to indicate a possessed noun, a noun in "combining form," or a stative when affixed to nouns (Matteson 1972: 164). In Timucua, *-re* is used as a noun combining-form with both singular and plural possessive affixes on plural nouns only, as in *pahana* 'my house', *pahanikare* 'my houses' (*-na* + *-ka* > *-nika*), *pahaye* 'your (sg.) house', *pahayekare* 'your (sg.) houses', *pahama* or *pahamima* 'his house', *pahamikare* 'his houses' (*-ma*[1] + *-ka* > *-mika*). With plural possessive affixes, the same principle occurs: *pahanika* 'our house', *pahanikakare* 'our houses', *pahayake* 'your (pl.) house', *pahayakekare* 'your (pl.) houses', *pahamikarema* 'their house', *pahamikaremakare* 'their houses'. In actual practice, however, special stative verbal structures are more usually used to identify a plural possessive plural noun: *heka pahamilekare* 'our houses' (= '3P pronoun + they are possessed houses'), *pahamitilakare* 'their houses' (= 'they are 3P-possessed houses'). Morpheme *-re* is rarely used to indicate morpheme combination except with nouns, always in the plural, the sole noted exception being its use in the 3P pronominal affix group *-mikarema* 'their'.

The structure of lexical verbs in Timucua and Warao is also intriguingly similar. Of a total of fifty-nine Warao designative and derivational verbal affixes, ten, or 17 percent, occur in identical or very similar form and semological function in Timucua. In both languages, the verb is structurally defined by the presence or potential presence of the verb-pluralizing suffix -*wo* (Timucua): -*bu* (Warao). Other forms showing similarity are listed. As in the case of the nominal affixes, the verbal affixes and their semological descriptions have been taken from Osborn (1968:46–47, 62).

Timucua		Warao	
-hero	optative	-mehere	desire, command
-he	potential	-buhu	potential
-ku	subjunctive	-ku ~ -kuna	subjunctive
-ke	optative	-ko	optative
-ta ~ -te	durative	-ta	occurrence-momentaneous
		-ti	occurrence-durative
-no	infinitive	-ne	gerundive
-ko	conditional	-kore	conditional, simultaneous
ya	negative	-yana	negative
-o	intensive	-u	intensive

The -*si* nominal suffix, a goal-marker in both languages, also occurs with lexemic verbs in both languages to indicate "reflexive/reciprocal."

Of a total of 32 verb-designative/derivative affixes in Timucua, 11, including -*si,* are similar to Warao forms—35 percent of the Timucua total.

In addition to the morphemic similarities between sixteenth-century Timucua and twentieth-century Warao, there are striking resemblances in patterns of phonological vowel harmony. The concept itself is totally alien to the native languages of the American Southeast, but it is very prevalent in Amazonian languages, regardless of phylum affiliation. The specific patterns seen in Timucua and Warao are so similar both to one another and to those generally found in most Macro-Chibchan languages that they cannot be ignored. I hasten to add that it is of course realized that phonological processes may be similar or even identical in widely divergent languages without the slightest implication of genetic relatedness, and it is also recognized that we are here comparing two languages four hundred years apart in time. The resemblances are *still* striking.

In both Timucua and modern Warao, the process of vowel harmony is morpheme specific. In Warao it affects directional prefixes of CV- shape when they occur immediately before a base. In Timucua it affects a finite number of bases, usually kin terms, when they occur with immediately following pronominal suffixes and also with pronominal suffixes when they are followed by any other suffix. In both languages the change is regressive, affecting the first morpheme in the set only. In both languages it is only the last vowel of the first morpheme that changes. The change is conditioned by the nature of the vowel in the second morpheme of the set, whether or not consonants intervene. These *regressive substitutions* may be summarized by saying that, in the circumstances just described, a low vowel as the last vowel of the first morpheme may not occur before a low vowel as the first (or frequently only) vowel of the second morpheme.

Both Timucua and Warao have five vowel systems, but the arrangement differs in the two languages. In both languages /i/, /a/, and /u/ are high-front, low-central, and high-back vowels, respectively. Vowels /e/ and /o/ in Warao are phonetically [E] and [o] ~ [ɔ], [o] predominating statistically. In Timucua, the patterns of vowel harmony suggest that /e/ was [ɛ] or [æ] and /o/ was [ɔ] or [ω]. The latter allophonic structure of /e/ and /o/ is typical of many Chibchan languages (such as Cuna; cf. Holmer 1946 : 185).

In both languages, morpheme-final /e/ in the first of such a morpheme-set is raised to /i/, with the exception that in Timucua /e/ before /e/ > /a/, as in *itaye* 'your father' (*ite* 'father' > *ita* + *-ye* 'your [sg.]'). In Warao, this rule means that *Ce-* directional prefixes become *Ci-* before bases with /a/ as their first vowel, as in *sewiri* 'to arrive by canoe' (*se-* + *wiri* + 'to paddle'), *sinaka* 'to fall down' (*se-* > *si-* + *naka* 'to fall'), *temoi* 'to blow on' (*te-* + *moi* 'to blow'), and *tiahi* 'to cut on' (*te-* > *ti-* + *ahi* 'to cut'). In Timucua, the process affects only base + pronominal suffix sets, since there are no pronominal suffixes except variant *-ye* of *-ya* 'your (sg.)' which contain /e/ before /e/, /a/, or /o/; for example, *itina* 'my father' (*ite* > *iti* + *-na* 'my'). The latter may be contrasted with a non-kin base, such as *paha* 'house', as in *pahana* 'my house'. In the sole instance in which the /e/–/e/ combination occurs in Timucua, *itaye* 'your father' (*ite* > *ita* + *-ye* 'your [sg.]'), /e/ > /a/, as indicated earlier.

In Timucua, low vowel /a/ is also replaced by /i/ before another low vowel, as in *itimile* 'it is his father' (*ite* > *iti* + *-ma²* > *-mi* 'his, the' + *-le* 'it is'), *pahanikare* 'my houses' (*paha* + *-na* > *-ni* 'my' + *-ka* 'plural' + *-re* 'noun combining-form suffix'), and *pahamino* 'it is his house' (*paha* + *-ma²* > *-mi* 'his, the' + *-no* 'it is').

There are no other kin-term bases nor pronominal suffixes that end in /o/ so it is impossible to say what /o/–/e/, /o/–/a/, /o/–/o/ would have become in Timucua.

It is, for both languages, tempting to postulate an earlier period in which specific kinds of morpheme sets containing a low vowel as the last vowel of the first member of such sets altered before any second morpheme that also contained a low vowel as its initial vowel, regardless of whether there were intervening consonants. The normal substitution was to raise the initial morpheme's final low vowel to /i/ except in combinations of /e/–/e/, where in Timucua, at least, the first /e/ becomes /a/. The suggestion is unarguably circular in that we have defined Timucua phonetic vowels to accommodate the system—/e/: [ɛ] ~ [æ], /o/: [ɔ] ~ [ω]. However, such an accommodation yields regular predictions and also has precedent in Cuna and other Chibchan languages.

There are also structural similarities between Timucua and non-Waroid Macro-Chibchan languages. By far, the greatest degree of similarity is with Cuna, a Chibchan language of Panama.

Noun and verb-pluralizing suffixes containing a bilabial stop, nasal, spirant, or semivowel—/p/, /b/, /m/, /ƀ/, /ƥ/, or /w/—followed by central /a/ or back /o/ or /u/ are quite frequent in Chibchan and Paezan languages (Wheeler 1972). Cuna, for example, uses *-(r)pa(a)*, *-ma* (with verbal suffix *-la*), and *-pi(i)* to indicate plurality in both verbs and nouns, as in *uce* 'hot' and *ucepa(a)* 'much heat', *uamala* 'there are many fish' (*ua* 'fish' + *-ma* + *-la* 'there are'), *sanpi(i)* 'all meat', *penamala* 'you all are going' (*pe-* 'you' + *-na-* 'go' + *-ma* + *-la* 'verbalizer'). This usage is quite congruent with Timucua *-wo* and *-ma³* verb pluralizers, described earlier.

Timucua has a lexeme *pukʷa* (morphemically *pu-* + *-kʷa* 'intensifier') indicating "much, many," similar in usage to the Cuna form *-(r)pa(a)*. Both languages, like Warao, have a *-ka* plural. In Timucua, this is normally combined with *-re*, in Cuna with *-na,* as in Cuna *niiskana* 'stars', Timucua *čuwowokare* 'stars'.

Cuna uses *-la* with nouns to indicate the result of a verbal action and *-le* with verbs to indicate a passive participle. Timucua uses both suffixes with nouns to indicate verbalization, as in *itinile* 'he is my father' (*ite* > *iti* 'father' + *-na* > *-ni* 'my' + *-le* 'it is'). With verbs, Timucua *-la*/*-le* indicates 'immediate action,' as in *hontala* 'I am' (*ho-* 'I' + *-ini-* > *-n-* 'be' + *-ta* 'durative' + *-la* 'immediate action'), paralleling Cuna *uamala* 'there are many fish' and *penamala* 'you all are going'.

We have earlier referred to the *-ma* morpheme and indicated that it fills three tactical slots: *-ma¹* '3S', *-ma²* 'definite goal-marker, the', and *-ma³* '3P verbal subject'. The semological functions of *-ma¹* and *-ma²* are shared with Warao; the semological function of *-ma³* is shared with Cuna.

Cuna *-ti* derives verbs from nouns, as in *soke* 'to say', *soketi* 'the act of saying'. A suffix *-tae* indicates "habitual action." Timucua uses *-ta* to derive nouns from verbs, as in *hewa* 'speak', *hewata* 'the act of speaking'. It uses *-ta/-te* as an indicator of "durative action" with verbs, as in the example *hontala* 'I am' used above. Perfect action in Cuna is indicated by *-ča*, in Timucua by *-ču*. Present time is indicated in Cuna with *-na, -la,* or *-ya;* Timucua uses *-la/-le,* as pointed out earlier, to show 'immediate action.'

In addition to the phonological similarity in the allophonic definition of the /e/ and /o/ phonemes in Timucua and Cuna, it is also of interest to note that Cuna form-initial, postjunctural vowels are preaspirated. Pareja's orthography for Timucua shows many pairs of lexeme variants in which an initial /h/ sometimes is used and sometimes is not, as in *eka* or *heka* 'wind', *hiwa* or *iwa* 'rain'.

There are several structural similarities between Timucua and the Misumalpan Chibchan languages of Central America. Twahka, for example, uses pluralizing suffixes *-rau* and *-pak,* both meaning "abundance" (Conzemius 1929:79). Timucua uses independent lexemes *ara* and *pukʷa* with the same meaning. In Twahka, the morphemes in question are used largely with bases designating plants, while in Timucua *ara* and *pukʷa* are generally used only with bases designating plants or animals (but not humans).

Timucua has some structural resemblances to Panoan languages. Greenberg (1960) assigned these languages to a Gê-Panoan-Cariban phylum, unrelated to Macro-Chibchan or Andean-Equatorial, but no regular sound correspondences link them to either Gê or Cariban (Rodrigues 1985:397). Key (1968) has shown a definite genetic relationship between Panoan and Tacanan. Though largely limited today to two regions—the Andean foothills and an area in northwestern Bolivia—with Brazilian/ Venezuelan Yanomama as a possible northeastern extension (Migliazza 1978; 1985:29), the Panoan tribes seem not to have had any great migratory tendencies at any time in their history (Lathrap 1970:81). They seem to have occupied their present areas throughout the past, the discontinuities between the two major Panoan-speaking regions representing Arawak migratory intrusion into the pre-Andine regions of far western Amazonia.

The system of grammatical affixation of Chacobo (Ch.) shows the following similarities with Timucua (T.): T. *-wo* '1P/2P verb subject' : Ch. *-bo* 'noun plural'; T. *-weta* 'for, with' : Ch. *-büta* 'with'; T. *očo* 'behind' : Ch. *-čo* 'behind'; T. *ka* 'here' : Ch. *-ka(ya)* 'here'; T. *-ke* 'optative' : Ch. *-ki* 'conditional'; T. *-na²* 'durative' : Ch. *-na-* 'to become'; T. *-no¹* 'active' : Ch. *-noʔo* 'locative intransitive'; T. *-no* + *-so* 'active transitive' : Ch. *-noʔšo* 'locative transitive'; T. *-so* 'transitive' : Ch. *-šo* 'transitive'. The base morpheme glossed as 'black' in both languages is also similar: T. *čuku* : Ch. *čükï*. Chacobo data are from Prost (1962).

There are, lastly, four Timucua affixes with structural parallels in Northern Maipuran Arawakan. All are monosyllabic affixes, and the similarities may therefore be fortuitous. They are: T. *ha* 'be in the future': Goajiro *-he* 'future time'; T. *na-* 'V > N': Island Carib *-ni* ~ *-ne* 'V > N'; T. *ni-*/*na-* 'first person': Island Carib *n-*/*-na* 'first person'; and the form cited earlier, T. *-re* 'noun combining-form' : general Northern Maipuran *-re* 'noun combining-form'. We have already noted that Timucua *na-* 'V > N' is paralleled by Warao *-na* with the same semological function. It is also possible that Timucua *ha* 'be in the future' is paralleled by Warao *ha-* 'must, have to, will' with the same function as the Timucua form (Osborn 1968 : 54). That is, the similarities may simply reflect broadly generalized pan-Amazonian/pan-Chibchan patterns rather than specific Arawakan sources.

There is only one structural similarity between Timucua and any of the Muskogean languages—Timucua *ha* 'be in the future' and Choctaw *-he* 'future time'. Again, the monosyllabicity of the form renders comparison rather meaningless in and of itself.

Vocabulary

In contrast to this overwhelmingly Macro-Chibchan/Waroid grammar is the non-Waroid, non-Chibchan basic vocabulary, only a small percentage of which can be traced unambiguously to any source.

Numbers and pronouns are often taken as indicators of the extent of outside influence on a language, since they are normally resistant to change. Both systems tend to maintain an overall patterning inherited from genetic forebears, and intrusive borrowings are generally very obvious, as in the case of English independent pronoun borrowings from Scandinavian. A determination, therefore, of resemblances between the number or pronominal systems of several languages is likely to tell us something about genetic relatedness and borrowing.

The number system of Timucua is particularly informative in this regard. Timucua cardinal numbers are: *yaha* ~ *yakfa* '1', *yuča* ~ *yuksa* '2', *hapu* '3', *čeketa* '4', *marua* '5', *mareka* '6', *pikiča* '7', *pikinahu* '8', *pekečeketa* '9', *tuma* '10', *čupi* '100'. *Čupi* is certainly a borrowing from Muskogean *čokpi-* '100' (Alabama, Koasati, Creek), related to *čõ·pi* 'large'. *Tuma* '10' is related to the pluralizing morpheme *-tooma*, used also as a free lexeme with the meaning "all, total, complete." *Hapu* '3' is similar to Pre-Andine Maipuran *hepü* '2' (Canamarí), though *pa* occurs as a component of many numbers in a large range of Arawakan languages. *Čeketa* '4' bears a resemblance to Muskogean *ošta·ka* '4' (Alabama, Koasati). 'Five' *marua* is similar to Paezan Chocó *mare* '5' in *kʷī mare* '4' (= '1 from 5'), though the *mare* form itself is not presently used for '5' in Chocó (Loewen 1963:366). A possible etymology for Timucua *marua* is -*mir*- 'all, complete' as in *amiro, mirika* 'all' plus *hue* ~ *we* 'hand' > *mir-hue* > *marua* 'complete hand = 5'.

The same -*mir*- > *mar*- element is found in *mareka* '6', which might be taken to mean 'all + 1'. If this is the case, then one would expect that '7' should be 'all + 2', something like *maruča* or *maruksa*, which, however, do not occur. *Pikiča,* the form for '7', though, does have the final syllable -*ča,* which could well be the -*ča* of *yuča* '2'. The possible morpheme *piki*- ~ *peke*- in that case, needs an explanation. It is presumably the same *piki*- that occurs in *pikinahu* '8' and *pekečeketa* '9'. *Pekečeketa* certainly contains *peke*- plus *čeketa* '4', leading one to assume that *piki*- ~ *peke*- means '5' or 'hand' or some similar concept. *Pikinahu* then, should mean '5 + 3' or 'hand + 3', -*nahu* an aberrant but not impossible variant of *hapu*. *Pikiča* '7' should mean '5 + 2', which, as suggested earlier, is indeed possible. This somewhat circuitous etymologizing would lead us to assume a meaning of '5' or "hand" for the putative morpheme *piki*- ~ *peke*-, occurring as a bound form only in these three numerals.

The overall pattern of the Timucua cardinal number system is one in which there are separate morphemes for 1–4, a term for 5 meaning 'complete hand' or something similar, and, for numbers 6–9, words meaning 'hand + 1, 2, 3, 4'. 'Ten' in such systems is often, as in Timucua, a term meaning "total." The 'hand + ' system is not used in Arawakan nor in the native languages of the southeastern United States. It does, however, occur with frequency in the Chibchan and Paezan languages, particularly those of the Colombia-Panama border region. The Cuna cardinal numerals, for example, are: *kʷena* '1', *po(o)* '2', *pa(a)* '3', *pakke* '4', *attale* '5', *nerkʷa* (*lel* > *ner* 'head' + *kʷa* '1' = 'head + 1') '6', *kukle* '7', *paapakka* '8', *pakke-pakka* '9', *ampeki* '10'. Ordinals are formed by adding -*kʷa* '1' to the cardinals, as in *paakʷa* 'third'.

The Cuna term for '5', *attale,* means "hand on head"—*atta* 'hand' + *le(l)* 'head'—a typical Chibchan '5'-term, found also in the Misumalpan languages of Central America, as in Miskito *matalal/matasip* '5': *mata* 'hand' + *lal* 'head' or *mata* + *sip* 'complete'. In Ulua *tin* 'hand' = '5'. In the Cuna instance '6' is 'head + 1', as indicated above. 'Seven', *kukle,* is *kuk*- '2' + 'head'. In '8' and '9', however, we see exactly the system used in Timucua: '8' = '3 + *pakka*', '9' = '4 + *pakka*'. Just as in Timucua the ordinary form for '5', *marua,* is not compounded to form higher numbers, so in Cuna *attale* is not used for that purpose. Instead a morpheme with obscure meaning, *pakka,* is used in such compounds. Just as we hypothesized a relic morpheme *piki- ~ peke-* '5/hand' in Timucua, so we can hypothesize a relic morpheme *pakka* '5/hand' in Cuna. In the Cuna system '8' = '3 + 5/hand' and '9' = '4 + 5/hand'. 'Ten', *ampeki,* means, like Timucua *tuma,* "complete, whole."

While, in short, the phonological form and content of the Timucua cardinal numbers 1–4 shows no lexical similarity to any other native language of North or South America, the overall system shows remarkable similarities to that of Colombian-Panamanian Chibchan and Paezan, with extensions of that system well into Central America. The two Timucua '5' bases, *mar-* and *piki- ~ peke-,* show close phonological correspondence as well as identical semological function and syntactic usage to Paezan Chocó *mare* '5' and Chibchan Cuna *pakka,* respectively.

Timucua independent pronouns show no similarity to any other specific language or language group except for the infrequently used 3S form *oke,* which is reminiscent of Arawakan, as in Campa *oka* 'this', and the 2P form *yake,* which is similar to modern Warao *yatu.* For comparative purposes, both the independent pronouns and the verbal pronoun affixes of Timucua are given in the table.

	Independent pronouns	Verbal pronouns
1S	ho-ni-he	ho-, ni-
2S	ho-či-e	či-
3S	ø, oke	ø-
1P	he-ka, ni-he-ka	ni- + STEM + -wo
2P	yake, či-he-ka	či- + STEM + -wo
3P	ø, oke-ka-re	ø- + STEM + -ma³

The remainder of the Timucua lexicon shows forms similar to Warao (or some earlier Warao-related language), Chibchan-Paezan, Tucanoan, Gê, Panoan, and the Muskogean languages. In a total surviving lexicon of approximately 1,500 roots, only 189 are sufficiently similar to be tentatively considered borrowings. Ninety-two percent of the Timucua lexicon, that is, shows no convincing relationship to any other native American language at the present stage of research. Each of these possible connections will be discussed in turn.

It is difficult to assess the resemblances between Timucua and modern

Warao inasmuch as we are comparing forms from languages almost four hundred years apart. We are as yet unfortunately unable to reconstruct an earlier stage of Warao, even from internal evidence, and the equivalences we are suggesting are open to criticism. We do know, however, from toponymic data that Warao-like languages were at one time spoken from an indeterminate position on the Caribbean coast of Colombia-Venezuela between Lake Maracaibo and the Magdalena, east through the Orinoco Delta (Wilbert 1957:11–18). Speakers of these languages occupied the northern segment of South America as far south as the Amazonian rain forest and the confluence of the Rio Vaupés and the Rio Negro. It is, of course, clear that Timucua did not borrow directly from Warao or its immediate ancestors, to judge from the lack of regular phonological correspondences. Nonetheless, the similarities seem close enough to warrant discussion.

The following Timucua-Warao resemblances are particularly noteworthy. They are given with the Timucua first:

(1) *itori* : *ruru-ruru* ([duru-duru]) 'alligator'

(2) *yuriko* : *oriki* 'anger'

(3) *atulu* : *atabu* 'arrow'

(4) *utasi* : *ataihase* 'attack'

(5) *aruk^wi* : *araka* 'child : younger brother'

(6) *na-* : *nao-* 'come'

(7) *kuk^we* : *kuku-* 'cover'

(8) *hio* : *hoa* 'curse'

(9) *miso* : *misi-* 'devil'

(10) *ipa(ru)* : *hobi* 'drink'

(11) *uti* : *hota* 'earth : high land/mountain'

(12) *ho* : *ho-* 'eat'

(13) *eka* : *eku* 'enter/in'

(14) *eka* : *mon-uka* 'equal'

(15) *asu-rupa* : *so* 'excrement'

(16) *muku* : *mu* 'eye'

(17) *amara* : *emoera* 'fat : to be soft'

(18) *wara* : *yiwara* 'finish'

(19) *taka* : *rokia* ([dokia]) 'fire : flame'

(20) *yawi* : *yaba-* 'fishhook : to fish'

(21) *hawe* : *ohia* 'fox'

(22) *awara* : *ari* 'harvest' (see also no. 18 'finish')

(23) *ha-* : *ha* - 'have'

(24) *okoto* : *noko* 'hear'

(25) *kume* : *kobe* 'heart/breast'

(26) *hono* : *nōhō* 'hunger'

(27) *ho-ni-he* : *ine* 'I'

(28) *nihi* : *na-* 'kill'

(29) *nahiawo* : *nahobo* 'know/understand'

(30) *karo* : *o-kera* 'light'

(31) *hani* : *hahinai* 'lose'

(32) *howa/huwa* : *obo-* 'love'

(33) *wiro* : *arao* 'man : people'

(34) *sowa* : *toma* 'meat'

(35) *aku* : *waniku* 'moon'

(36) *nariwa* : *nibora* 'old man : man'

(37) *awi* : *aba* 'put on : put'

(38) *hono-sta* : *hunu* 'shellfish : shrimp'

(39) *hewa* : *ehewere* 'sing : sing/cradle song'

(40) *weni* : *abani* 'slow'

(41) *yorowa* : *ni-hara-baka* 'snake : cayman'

(42) *hani* : *ha-* 'stop'

(43) *tari* : *taera* 'strong'

(44) *aka/haka* : *haka* 'wind'

(45) *ak^wera* : *ak^weru* 'name of the southernmost Timucua border province : border/coast'

There are also lexical resemblances with Chibchan and Paezan languages:

(1) *itori* : Chocó *kore* 'alligator'
(2) *čulufi* : Timote, Cuica *ču* 'bird'
(3) *marua* : Chocó *mare* 'five'
(4) *na(ta)* : Cuna *naa-* (< *na-*) 'go'
(5) *hue/we* : Chocó *hua* 'hand'
(6) *ta-pola* : Chocó *pe*, Chibcha *aba*, Manare *epa* 'maize'
(7) *wiro* : Yanomamo *waro/waru* 'man'

(8) *aku* : Chocó *(h)edexo*, Sumu *waiku*, Cacaopera *aiku*, Matagalpa *aiko* 'moon' (also Chocó Saixa dialect *axo-nihino* 'sun' : Timucua *akunihino* 'fiery moon')
(9) *nipita* : Chocó *itae* 'mouth'
(10) *hiwa* : Cuna *iya* 'rain'
(11) *ču-wo(wo)* : Yaruro *boé* 'star'
(12) *itu-kʷa* : Sumu, Ulua *tuke*, Brunca *-kʷa*, Cuna *wa-*, Chibcha *p-kʷa*, Manare *kʷa* 'tongue'
(13) *iwi(ne)* : Yaruro *wi*, Esmeralda *wivi* 'water'

There are six interesting free-base parallels between Timucua and Proto-Tucanoan as reconstructed by Waltz and Wheeler (1972:119–48). Tucanoan languages are neither Macro-Chibchan nor Andean-Equatorial in Greenberg's classification. They were and are centered in the Rio Vaupés–Rio Negro confluence region of Venezuela, Colombia, and Brazil. The forms in question are:

(1) *itori* : **iSo(-ri)* (S = /s/∼ /h/∼/y/∼ /d/) 'alligator/cayman/crocodile' (*-ri* is a frequent Amazonian noun-designating affix)
(2) *isi* : **zie* 'blood'
(3) *uku* : **ūkū* 'drink'
(4) *napona* : **poa* 'hair'
(5) *hue/we* : **wā* 'hand'
(6) *kečela* : **kasero/katsero* 'skin/bark'

There is a single Timucua form—*yaraha/hiyarawa* 'panther'—that has possible parallels in the Gê languages. In Remokamekran "jaguar" is *orobo*, in Aponegikran *oropa*, in Kayapó *rop*. Eastern Gê (Xavante) uses an alternate stem *hu* ∼ *ru*. One is tempted to postulate a Timucua form utilizing both stems, *hu-orop/ba* > *(hi)yarah/wa*. The very ingenuity of the etymology, however, gives one reason to pause. There is also, it should be pointed out, a Pre-Andine Maipuran **hi-yVra-ta* form meaning 'kill', which is interestingly similar (Matteson 1972:179), and a Tupinambá form *yawar* 'jaguar' (Rodrigues 1985:391).

Resemblances between Timucua and Arawakan have been noticed for many years. Swadesh (1964:548) has presented a tentative listing of such forms, though unfortunately his data were both inadequate and inaccurate, for he presents a fair number of erroneous forms for both Timucua and the Arawakan languages. Nonetheless, his insight was correct, as the following list of resemblances indicates:

(1) *kume* : Proto-Pre-Andine **tsomi*, Canamarí *tsuma* ('back'), Culino *tsuhuri* 'breast/chest/heart'

(2) *čokolo* : Chamicuro *tulu*, Lokono *óloa* 'heart'

(3) *ike* : Culino *tsiki* 'earth'

(4) *paha* : Apolista *pi-*, Yamamadí *ube*, general Eastern Maipuran *pa-*, Goajiro *pe-*, Guahibo *po-*, Lokono *báhɨ* 'house'

(5) *nekero* : *ikubuti* 'kneel'

(6) *wiro* : Taino *-eri*, Piapoco *-ali* 'man'

(7) *pira* : Paumarí *puru* 'red : black (?)'

(8) *čokori* : Culino *kara-* 'strong'

(9) *aye* : Culina *awa*, Lokono *ada* 'tree'

(10) *yuwa* : Canamarí *tsuma* (see also no. 1 above) 'back'

(11) *ičikosa* : general Pre-Andine Maipuran *kači-* 'cold'

(12) *uku* : general Pre-Andine Maipuran *-ika* 'drink : eat'

(13) *taka* : general Pre-Andine Maipuran *titi*, *tak* ('sun'), general Eastern Maipuran *tike* 'fire'

(14) *hue/we* : Ipuriná. Apolista *wa-*, Piro *we-*, Lokono *we-*, Baré *wa-*, Achagua *-he* 'hand'

(15) *ilaki* : Piro *ilačinu* 'night'

(16) *-ti* : Campa *-te* 'not'

(17) *ka/oka* : Campa *oka* 'this'

(18) *ora* : Campa *ora* 'that'

(19) *hapu* : Canamarí *hepü* '3 : 2'

(20) *itori* : **(iy)akare* 'alligator/cayman/crocodile'

(21) *ičiko* : Baré *nika* 'bite : eat'

(22) *isi* : Catapolítani *iti*, Marawa *isa* 'blood'

(23) *yawi* : Baré *nabi*, Achagua *yahe*, Piapoco *api* 'bone'

(24) *tiki* : Manao *teki*, Lokono *-dike* 'ear'

(25) *uti* : Baré *rati* 'earth'

(26) *ike* : Baniva, Piapoco *(h)ipe* 'earth'

(27) *he* : Waliperi *he*, Achagua *iha* 'eat'

(28) *ho* : Island Carib *háu* 'eat'

(29) *muku* : Manao *uku-* 'eye'

(30) *ite* : Lokono *itʰi* 'father'

(31) *huyu* : Achagua *ku-* 'fish'

(32) *isa* : general Northern Maipuran *isa* 'good'

(33) *penani* : general Northern Maipuran *-p/bi* 'with the hands : hand'

(34) *kuna* : Manao *küuna* 'head'

(35) *čito* : Piapoco, Catapolítani *iwita* 'head'

(36) *nu-* : Baré *nu-* 'know'

(37) *čofa* : Carútana *čupana* 'liver'

(38) *tapola* : Guaná *tsoporo*, Terena *soporo* 'maize'

(39) *ano* : general Northern Maipuran *ena-* 'man'

(40) *aku* : Baré *ki*, Yavitero *ke*, Lokono *kači*, Yamamadí *maxi* ('sun') 'moon'

(41) *wali* : Baniva *tali*, Layaná *bahalo* 'mouth'

(42) *hiwa* : Baré *hi·ya*, Goajiro *huyá* 'rain'

(43) *ene* : Machiguenga *nea* 'see'

(44) *yorowa* : Lokono *óri* 'snake'

(45) *čuwowo* : Piapoco, Baniva *-wi-* 'star'

(46) *yowo* : Achagua, Goajiro, Piapoco *iba*, Manao *ipa*, Baré *tiba* 'stone'

(47) *ela* : Achagua *eri*, Tariana, Piapoco *-eri* ('moon'), Amarizana *eri-* ('fire'), Arekena *ale*, Goakiro *-ali* 'sun/day'

(48) *api* : Tariana, Arekena, Carútana, Baré *-ip/bi* 'tail'

(49) *iwi(ne)* : Baré *uni*, Baniva-Yavitero, Maipuré *weni* 'water'

(50) *nia* : Baré, Tariana, Piapoco, Achagua, Baniva *ina-* 'woman'

It may be noted that there are three primary Arawakan subgroups to which Timucua lexemes show resemblances: (1) Non-Maipuran (Culino, Chamicuro, Paumarí, Yamamadí, Apolista), (2) Pre-Andine Maipuran (Canamarí, Ipuriná, Piro, Campa), and (3) Northern Maipuran (especially Baré, Piapoco, Baniva-Yavitero, Achagua, Carútana, Tariana—the Vaupés-Inírida-Guaviare branch of Northern Maipuran). The implications of this will be examined in greater detail later in the chapter.

Of the 151 Timucua forms showing resemblances to northern South American forms, fifteen show what may be called multiple-resemblance. That is, these forms show similarity to more than one stock or phylum. The greatest degree of similarity is with the Arawakan languages. Inasmuch, however, as all the Amazonian languages, regardless of stock or phylum affiliation, borrowed very heavily from one another beginning in very early times, it is difficult to assign a clear-cut origin to such putative loans into Timucua. The intense riverine trade of the entire Amazon region since time immemorial has tended to blur many language differences, grammatical as well as lexical, within and between phyla (Migliazza 1985:20), and it is accordingly nearly impossible to define with any degree of reliability the exact origin of most of the pan-Amazonian lexemes. In the list below, the Arawakan forms are from Noble (1965), Matteson (1972), or Taylor (1977); Proto-Tucanoan forms are from Waltz and Wheeler (1972); Warao forms are from Osborn (1967a, 1967b, 1968) and Barral (1957). Other forms, largely Macro-Chibchan, are from Loukotka (1968), Rodrigues (1985), and my own notes.

	Gloss	Timucua	Arawakan	Tucanoan	Warao	Other
1.	'alligator'	itori	*(iy)akare	*iSo(-ri)	[duru-]	yakare (Tupí)
2.	'blood'	isi	iti/isa	*zie		
3.	'drink'	uku	-ika ('eat')	*ūkū		
4.	'earth'	uti	-atu		hota	
5.	'eat'	ho	hau		ho-	
		he	he/ha			
6.	'eye'	muku	-uku		mu	
7.	'fire'	taka	tak-/tik-		[dokia]	
8.	'hand'	hue/we	we-/wa-	*wā		hua (Chocó)
9.	'heart'	kume	*tsomi		kobe	
10.	'maize'	tapola	tsoporo			pe (Chocó)
11.	'man'	wiro	-eri/-ali		arao	waro (Yanomama)
						oi (Yaruro)
12.	'moon'	aku	-axi		waniku	axo- (Chocó)
13.	'snake'	yorowa	óri		-hara-	
14.	'star'	čuwowo	-wi-			boé (Yaruro)
15.	'water'	iwi(ne)	weni/uni			wi (Yaruro)

It may be noted that Timucua resemblances to Arawakan, unlike those to Warao and the Macro-Chibchan languages, seem to cover at least two fairly specific semantic domains: (1) natural phenomena and animal forms; and (2) body parts.

One of the most obvious and striking characteristics of lexemes in the Arawakan languages and in many other Amazonian language groups is what Matteson (1972:164) refers to as a "clutter of grammatical markers," lexemes consisting of long strings of predominantly monosyllabic morphemes, many of which do not naturally occur alone with a clear denotative semantic content but which have clear semological connotative meaning (that is, a broad semantic "freight" and consistent grammatical function). Some of the most difficult to analyze of these bound-bases occur at the beginning of lexemes and, as Noble (1965:27–35) pointed out quite accurately, usually have the phonological form $t(a)$-, k-, $č$-, m-, n-, x- (= /h/), a-, i/y- and u-. He unfortunately referred to these forms as "class prefixes," immediately calling to mind a situation similar to that in the Bantu languages and others in which genuine class prefixes are a dominant grammatical fixture. This, one quickly finds, is distinctly not the case in Arawakan. In some cases such "prefixes" do not seem to be independent, separable morphemes at all but simply phonological components of free-base root morphemes. Even in cases in which we clearly *are* dealing with separable, prefixlike morphemes, they do not—in any instance of which I am aware—define clear-cut or even broad semantic or semological classes, as in the Bantu languages. It seems clearly more realistic, as Taylor and Hoff (1966:305) have pointed out, to consider such morphemes "petrified affix" components of frozen compounds in which the first element has become a nonproductive morpheme in the language. Such "petrified affixes" seem to occur not always lexeme-initial, as Noble implies, but also, in complete agreement with the norms of Arawakan lexeme structure, in varying lexeme-internal position (Matteson 1972:163), as morpheme *ha* 'liquid' in **yi-ha-ki-le* 'eye', **ka-ha-re* 'lake', **ha-po-e-ni-ha* 'river', **ka-si-ha* 'sap', **w/hini/i-ha* 'water', **pa-ka-hā-ka* 'wet', **po-piri-ha-ri* 'dry' (Matteson 1972: 176–85).

In my view, this in no way invalidates Noble's valuable work; it simply means that much more careful phonological, grammatical, and comparative work is needed before we will be able to iron out the problems of lexeme-initial "petrified" bound-morpheme definition versus ordinary lexeme-initial regular phonological correspondences. Certainly the wide use of morphemes such as *pi* 'rod-shaped object' in words such as "vine," "finger"; of *-pi* in words for "furry, fuzzy objects" such as "bat," "bird," "body hair," "feather"; of *tsa* 'cord' in words for "rope," "vine," "hair"; of *ke/ki* 'pole or sticklike objects' in words for "crocodile," "fish," "leg," "neck," "spine," "stick" (Matteson 1972:163–64) does seem to point to a former system of word-class definition similar to that of Bantu and many other language groups throughout the world. As Taylor and Hoff point out (1966:304), "In some cases at least, Noble is undoubtedly right as to the one-time morphemic status of some synchronically immovable segments." To decide which are and which are not "petrified affixes" and then to determine which, if any, of these affixes are indeed class-designating is the unresolved problem. In any event, such lexeme-initial "entities" also occur in Timucua, but only in those lexical items that show a similarity to one branch or another of Arawakan, such as Timucua *ta-pola* 'maize', Arawakan (Guaná) *tso-poro* 'maize', Arawakan (Terena) *so-poro* 'maize', quite possibly containing the Arawakan *tsa* 'cord' morpheme, widely used in words for "hair" and other objects with long or twisted fibers (such as corn silk?). The fact that there is a widely recurring *pe* 'maize' morpheme in many languages of Amazonia and the neighboring regions (Chocó *pe* 'maize', for example), perhaps related to or identical with the Arawakan *pi* 'rod-shaped object' cited above, reinforces the suggestion. The Timucua lexeme-final *-lo* is quite conceivably related to the Guaná and Terena *-ro*, probably the widely recurring Arawakan *-rV* "noun-combining form" morpheme.

Timucua also shows a small number of lexical similarities to the Muskogean languages of the southeastern United States. These can clearly be called loans. They can be derived from one of two sources: (A) Proto-Muskogean, as reconstructed by Mary Haas (1940, 1941, 1945, 1946, 1947, 1948, 1949, 1950, 1956, 1960), or (B) the historically known later Muskogean languages, particularly those of the western section of Eastern Muskogean—Alabama and Koasati.

(A) PROTO-MUSKOGEAN

(1) *kočo* : **kač-* 'cut'
(2) *puen/pon-* : **(xʷu/hu)pun-* 'go/come: go'
(3) *ikʷi* : **akʷi* 'kill'
(4) *ukʷa* : **ik-. . .-a* 'not'
(5) *hukʷe* : **umkʷa* 'rain'
(6) *neka* : **nuči-* 'sleep'

(B) LATER MUSKOGEAN

(1) *čulufi* : Koasati *kulu·si* 'bird'
(2) *kaya* : Alabama *aka·ka* 'chicken'
(3) *laka* : Alabama, Koasati *loča* 'black/dirty'
(4) *efa* : Koasati *ifa* 'dog' (cf. also Proto-Arawakan **ifè-* 'capybara')
(5) *ukučua* : Alabama, Koasati *okhiča* 'door'
(6) *ipa-ru* : Koasati *ipá* 'eat'

(7) *muku* : Choctaw *muču·(li)* 'eye'
(8) *neha* : Koasati *niha* 'fat'
(9) *taka* : Alabama, Koasati *tikba*,
     Creek *tó·tka* 'fire'
(10) *čeketa* : Alabama, Koasati *ošta·ka*
     'four'
(11) *oke/oka* : Alabama *ak-* 'this/that'
(12) *čupi* : Koasati, Hitchiti, Creek
     čokpi '100'
(13) *isa* : Koasati *iški* 'mother'
(14) *aya* : Choctaw *aiya* 'mountain'
(15) *nipita* : Choctaw *itopa* 'mouth'
(16) *-ti* : Alabama, Koasati *-ti* 'not'
(17) *eye* : Choctaw *ayi-* 'road'
(18) *api* : Alabama, Koasati, Choctaw
     hapi 'salt'
(19) *uwa* : Alabama, Koasati *opahk-*
     'swim'
(20) *aye* : Hitchiti *ahi* 'tree'
(21) *aliho-* : Koasati *čayahli* 'walk'
(22) *nali-sono* : Alabama, Koasati *la·na*,
     Creek *lá·n-i* 'yellow'
(23) *ho-či-e* : Choctaw *či/čia* 'you'

It should also be noted that the Timucua form *ilake* 'night', already com-
pared with Pre-Andine Piro *ilačinu* 'night', bears a strong resemblance to
Proto-Muskogean *niNaki 'night' (*N = Western Muskogean /n/, Eastern
Muskogean /ł/).

Finally, there are two Timucua items with resemblances to lexical
forms in non-Muskogean languages of the southeastern United States:
(1) *mike* : Atakapa *mo·k-* 'go'; and (2) *iyola* : Natchez *ula* 'snake'.

The resemblances discussed above, it should be borne in mind, account for only 8 percent of the surviving Timucua lexicon. The remaining
92 percent still resists any effort of comparative treatment.

Interpretation

Structural and lexical data, then, indicate that Timucua probably originated as a native language of northwestern Amazonia. While it does not
seem in a lexical sense genetically related to any of the languages of Greenberg's Andean-Equatorial or Macro-Chibchan phyla, its grammar is quite

clearly Waroid-based. We know from toponymic data that both Warao-proper as well as Warao-related languages were spoken from an indeterminate time in the past until at least the time of Spanish intervention all along the Caribbean littoral of northern South America, from somewhere to the west of Lake Maracaibo east to and including the Orinoco Delta (Wilbert 1957). Waroid toponyms occur with some frequency as far south in Colombia as the Meta, Caquetá, and Vaupés region and as far south in Venezuela as the northern banks of the Orinoco. The toponymic evidence pointing to a western origin for the Warao is reinforced by the nature of their cult practices, with startling Central and Meso-American parallels, and by their own oral traditions of such an origin (Wilbert 1972, 1973).

The presence in Timucua of Cuna-like noun- and verb-designating and deriving morphemes would argue for Timucua contact with these Chibchan peoples somewhere in the area of northwestern Colombia or the Colombia-Panama border region. The small number of root morphemes showing resemblances to both Cuna and Chocó, on the one hand, and Yaruro, on the other, would stretch the possible contact region from the Colombia-Panama border area southeastward to Yaruro lands in south-central Venezuela.

The presence of even the small number of resemblances to non-Maipuran Arawakan may argue for possible contact with pre-Maipuran Arawak speakers, perhaps as early as 3500 B.C., if we follow Noble and Lathrap (Noble 1965:111, Lathrap 1970:70–81). This would presumably have taken place somewhere along the upper reaches of the Rio Negro, near its confluence with the Amazon, prior to the time of the development of Maipuran innovations (Lathrap 1970:70–79).

That the Timucua remained in contact with Arawakan speakers for a long period of time in the Rio Negro region is attested by the number of lexical similarities to Pre-Andine Maipuran and later Northern Maipuran. The time level for the split of Maipuran from general Arawakan can be tentatively placed at about 2000–1500 B.C., perhaps earlier (Noble 1965: 111). Certainly, the Maipuran languages were themselves developing from Proto-Maipuran by 1800 B.C., and Proto-Maipuran had probably developed dialect variants leading ultimately to the present-day Maipuran languages by about 1700 B.C.

The remainder of the Arawakan-Timucua resemblances clearly indicate Northern Maipuran contacts. Owing, however, to the imperfect phonological fit with extant Northern Maipuran, it is evident that such putative Timucuan borrowings from these sources came not from the individual languages as they exist today, but from a period when Proto-Northern Maipuran was in its early developmental stages, a pre-Proto-Northern Maipuran. This would be approximately 1900–1700 B.C.

That is, Timucua speakers seem to have been in relatively close and constant contact with Arawak speakers from Proto-Arawakan times (ca. 3500 B.C.) until approximately 1700 B.C., the time by which the different Maipuran branches had developed essentially their present characteristics. The area of contact must have been the middle Rio Negro, Vaupés, middle Japurá-Caquetá region, shown circled on the map in Figure 2. The major possible Arawak donors to the Timucua lexicon are still today located in this region, though in much altered guise after the passage of so many years. The area in question is just on the southern and eastern edges of both Macro-Chibchan speech and the earliest distribution of Waroid speech. All the essential ingredients to explain Timucua lexical and grammatical peculiarities lie within this area.

Proto-Tucanoan similarities in Timucua reinforce the Arawakan evidence. Tucano is today the lingua franca of the Vaupés region (Sorensen 1967, 1985), and multilingualism along the middle and lower Vaupés is the norm among native speakers of Tucanoan and Arawakan languages, particularly the Tariana, Baré, and Baniva. Most of these peoples speak their own language as well as Tucano and the Tupí *lingoa gêral* Nheengatú, though the latter is less frequent in some parts of the region. The only exception are the Makú, of undetermined language affiliation (Migliazza 1985:52–54). This situation seems to have been in place since pre-European times, though its epicenter was likely the lower Vaupés in aboriginal times (Sorensen 1967).

Tribal/language exogamy is the norm in this region, and members of a given longhouse group grow up speaking a mother tongue, a father tongue, and two or more other Indian languages with equal fluency. Nheengatú and/or Spanish and/or Portuguese are usually added to this list. Each language is reserved for use under specific circumstances and with specific individuals for whom the language in question is a native tongue. Ease in language-learning is a cultural trait into which each new member of the society is born. Multilingual, polyglot circumstances are not viewed with the sense of awe (and peculiarity) they engender in Western European and Euro-American societies. Because the use of each language is carefully prescribed, there is little if any lexical or grammatical mixing by the users, and there is no indication of incipient creolization in any of the languages.

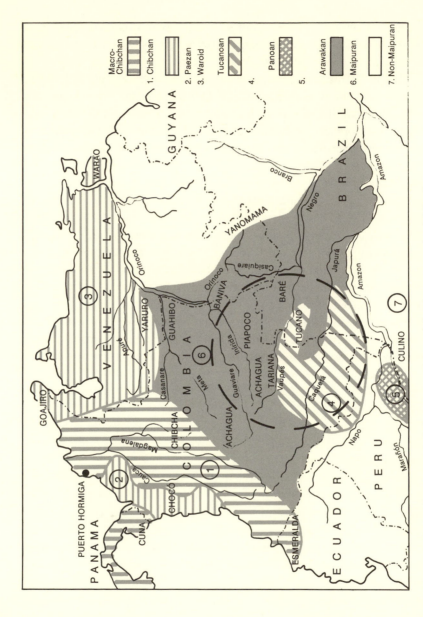

Figure 2. Probable epicenter of Timucuan origin and development and neighboring ethnolinguistic groups (ca. 2000 BC, epicenter circled).

Timucuan resemblances to Proto-Tucanoan rather than to some later form of the language indicates a Timucua presence in the critical area certainly by 2500 B.C.

With regard to the possibility that Timucua may have developed in a region in which multilingualism has been a dominant characteristic for millennia, it is of interest to note that there are many lexical pairs or triplets in Timucua in which one variant is of native origin (that is, origin unknown), one showing Waroid, Tucanoan, or Arawakan resemblance, and another of southeastern United States origin: (1) 'snake' (a) *elatuwasa*—origin unknown, (b) *yorowa* : Lokono *óri*, (c) *iyola* : Natchez *ula*; (2) 'strong' (a) *tari* : Warao *taera*, (b) *čokori* : Culina *kara-*; (3) 'eat' (a) *ho* : Warao *ho-*, (b) *he* : Waliperi *he*, (c) *ipa-ru* : Koasati *ipá*; (4) 'skin' (a) *kečela* : Proto-Tucanoan **kasero/katsero*, (b) *pek^{w}a*—origin unknown.

Multiple- and variant-lexical resemblances rarely occur under conditions of cultural contact in which one member is considered, for whatever reason, "lower" and the other dominant or "upper." The latter situation usually results in a considerable degree of relexification of the nondominant language, the dominant language remaining unscathed. We have in Timucua a situation most closely paralleling what Morris Goodman referred to as *linguistic interpenetration* in the case of the Mbugu language of Tanzania (Goodman 1971:252). It is the same phenomenon noted by Čestmír Loukotka years ago in his classification of native South American languages, one which he called simply "mixed languages" (Loukotka 1968:13). He found it very characteristic of South American languages in general and of Amazonian tongues in particular. Most professional linguists looked with something akin to horror on Loukotka's pedestrian term, but it is quite apt at a certain descriptive level. There is in Amazonia a very broad common lexical substratum running through all the languages of the equatorial region, regardless of family, stock, or even phylum. This is certainly the result of widespread trade, population movement (temporary or permanent), intermarriage (as in the Vaupés region's preferred language-exogamy), and other factors over an extremely long period of time. The lexical result is a very real "mixing" in which the grammars peculiar to given languages, stocks, and phyla remain surprisingly stable and enduring.

Mixing or *interpenetration,* as distinct from relexification, takes place as the result of particularly intense but peaceful long-term cultural contacts in which no single party is culturally dominant. In the development of pidgins and true, relexified creoles, it is universally the norm that morphological complexity is drastically reduced and irregularities are regularized. This is usually not so with "mixed" languages.

Timucua, while stemming from multiple sources, seems a case of mixing or interpenetration. The primary lexical parent(s), possibly an independent stock within Macro-Chibchan or Pano-Tacanan, perhaps not, has remained intact. If Timucua's closest genetic relatives are the Waroid languages, then its grammatical structure is also largely intact. If its grammatical structures were taken from Waroid neighbors, its own original structures must have been very close indeed to the borrowed ones— perhaps resulting from pan-areal structural similarities (cf. Migliazza 1985:20), though this does not seem to be the case. What relexification has taken place, if that is what it is, is so slight that it is questionable that the term should be used at all with regard to Timucua. A mere 8 percent of the lexicon was affected, and many of the "borrowings" were additions to, not replacements of, native terms.

It is difficult to assess the exact nature of the contact between the early Timucua, Tucano, Arawak, Macro-Chibchan, and Panoan peoples that could have led to the situation we see in seventeenth-century Timucua. We have nothing in the way of archaeological data from the Vaupés-Caquetá region to help us out and very little in the way of carefully done ethnographic descriptions or ethnohistorical documentation. We are, however, fortunate in having considerable valuable ethnohistorical and archaeological data from areas to the north, west, and, to a lesser extent, south of the Timucua epicenter. Of particular value are the data from the archaeologically defined *Intermediate Area,* encompassing Ecuador, Colombia from the Eastern Cordillera west and north to the Pacific and Caribbean, and most of Central America south of Guatemala.

This important crossroads region between North and South America has recently begun to receive the archaeological attention it deserves, and specialists now realize both the critical nature of its geographic position and the highly civilized energies of its aboriginal inhabitants. Feldman and Moseley have recently pointed out that the peoples and cultures of the Intermediate Area were frequently the donors, not just the half-way-point recipients, of some extremely important cultural innovations (Feldman and Moseley 1978:139–77). It is, however, of equal importance to realize that this region did serve as the point from which Middle American innovations spread into South America and from which South American innovations spread to Middle and North America.

The Intermediate Area is circumscribed by the Pacific on the west, Honduras to the northwest, the Caribbean on the north, and the Colombian Eastern Cordillera to the east. It is from the flanks of the latter that most of the rivers of eastern Colombia and western Venezuela arise, including the Apure, Casanare, Meta, Guaviare, Inírida, Vaupés, and Caequetá-Japurá, emptying their increasing torrents ultimately into the Orinoco, Rio Negro, and the Amazon itself. The rivers served, as they do today, as vast networks for commerce, linking rather than separating regions in northwestern South America and leading directly to the Goajira Peninsula coast in the northwest and the Orinoco Delta in the northeast as logical receiving points from outside and as transporting points to that outside.

It has long been known, from archaeological and ethnohistorical data, that movement of peoples in the northern third of the continent has been largely by water. Accounts from early European travelers support this contention. Archaeological data certainly substantiate the notion for Arawakan speakers from the earliest times (Lathrap 1973, Rouse 1986). We know that the distances traveled for trading purposes alone were incredibly vast—Wallace noted in the late 1800s that the Vaupés region peoples regularly traveled back and forth to the Upper Amazon to sell cassava graters (Wallace 1889 : 336), and Schomburgk, some forty years earlier, had noted that the Waika traveled regularly to Colombia and Brazil to barter for dogs (Schomburgk 1847 : 198). Journeys from the Guianas to and from southeastern Colombia were not exceptional (Roth 1924 : 632–37).

Feldman and Moseley point out that, at the time of Spanish intervention, there were four major trading networks in the northern third of South America (Feldman and Moseley 1978 : 142). Two of these were largely limited to the Andes region and moved goods in the north-south direction. The other two, however, centered in east-west movement of goods in Ecuador, Colombia, the southern Andes, and Amazonia. The early Spanish noted these systems, stating that they were largely run and organized by distinct hereditary groups of merchants referred to as *mindalaes* (Salomon 1977/78 : 236).

In the Colombian region, the *mindala* formed a group who stood apart from the usual community; they were exempt from taxation and tribute and were of high social rank—similar to the *pochteca* of Aztec Mexico (Feldman and Moseley 1978 : 143). The very term *mindala* is of interest, for it could readily be translated in Timucua as 'The Lords' or 'The Great

Ones' (*mine* 'lord, great' > *min-* + *-ta* 'durative time' = [da] by automatic allophonic change after /n/ + *-la* 'immediate time' = 'Those Who are Lords').

In Amazonia, the Shipibo of Peru traveled as far as 1,600 km downstream to obtain suitable wood for blowguns (Feldman and Moseley 1978:145; Lathrap 1973:171–72). Such trade networks were not only in effect on the river systems, but also involved sea voyages of considerable distances—certainly from Ecuador and Colombia as far as Peru to the south and Guatemala and Mexico to the north (Borhegyi 1959, Lathrap et al. 1975, Coe 1960, Edwards 1965). Lathrap (1973) feels that our data justify an antiquity for such sea-trading of at least 1500 B.C., and it is not impossible that it existed as early as 3500 B.C. (Zeidler 1977/78:26).

Trade of the nature described by the Spanish chroniclers and later European travelers, and substantiated by both archaeological data and oral tradition, is often accompanied by the development of special linguistic structures, such as Sabir (the lingua franca of the Mediterranean) or the many pidgins of the world. Normally such pidgins remain just that unless the contact is particularly intensive and long-lasting. In that case, a creolized speech-form usually develops, building on the grammar of the less dominant language with the vocabulary of the dominant one— relexification.

If, however, long-term, intensive trade is largely in the hands of a professional trading class, such as the *pochteca* or *mindala*, and neither the language of the buyers nor the sellers is considered dominant socially or politically, then the usual result is that phenomenon we have defined as *interpenetration*, Loukotka's "mixed languages." The classic example is, of course, Swahili: Bantu in grammar and largely Bantu in lexicon, but with large infusions of Arabic and Perso-Arabic lexicon as well. Swahili has also developed grammatical peculiarities atypical of Bantu proper, largely noun-class and concordance phenomena, which have resulted from the new, Arabic lexical material. While much of such new lexical material defines concepts new to the receiving culture (Swahili *kitabu* 'book'—from Arabic; *meza* 'table'—from Portuguese, for example), in many cases new, alternate lexemes for familiar concepts are added to account for the use of the concept in a new social situation (Swahili *amkia* '(to) greet'—native Bantu *salimu* '(to) greet'—from Arabic)—a familiar situation in Timucua, as we have seen.

It is our suggestion that Timucua, as we see it in the late sixteenth and early seventeenth centuries, is such a creolized language. Given the lack of full-scale relexification, the assumption would be that the language resulted from long-term development and use by a professional trading class, such as the Perso-Arabic traders or the *pochteca*. Its original genetic base was probably Macro-Chibchan-related, stemming from southeastern Colombia or southwestern Venezuela and far northwestern Brazil. This area could readily have supplied the Waroid, Tucano, Panoan, and Arawak lexical forms seen in Timucua. That the contact was long-lasting is clearly indicated by Proto-Tucanoan, Proto-Arawakan, and Pre-Andine Maipuran resemblances on the one hand (as early as ca. 3500–2500 B.C.) and by early Northern Maipuran resemblances on the other hand (from approximately 2000–1800 B.C.). The long history of multilingualism in the target areas substantiates the assumption. That Timucua was a traders' tongue seems verified by the similarities to Chibchan Cuna and Paezan Chocó, far removed from the original putative Timucua homeland, and by clear Proto-Muskogean loans from the southeastern United States.

If this picture is even partly valid, the trade network we are suggesting must have stretched from the Vaupés-Caquetá region along the river systems to the northwest, continuing along the Magdalena, Cauca, and Sinú Rivers, and culminating somewhere in or near Cuna-Chocó country. Archaeological evidence has indicated for some time now that the Caribbean coast of Colombia, centering around Barlovento and Puerto Hormiga, to the immediate west of the mouth of the Magdalena, was the focus of a trading nexus from at least 2500 B.C. It seems not unlikely that the Timucua trade network articulated with this from early times.

The late James Ford has brought together a considerable amount of cogent evidence to support the contention that the appearance of the first ceramic wares in North America, on the Florida-Georgia coast, was a result of direct trade from the Barlovento–Puerto Hormiga area of Colombia's Caribbean coast (Ford 1969). While there are many who will resist the idea, Timucua language data lend additional credence to it, for we know the Timucua ended up in Florida and Georgia, and the presence of Proto-Muskogean lexical loans in Timucua would date such an arrival, from whatever source, at approximately 2000–1500 B.C. This date is quite in keeping with the radiocarbon dates for fiber-tempered Stallings Island and Orange wares in Late Archaic sites in the Savannah and St. Johns River area of the American southeast.

The fact that these North American ceramic wares occur in sites whose other artifactual content is typical of the Late Archaic is, I think, an indication that Timucua movement to North America was not the large-scale movement of a people but, rather, the result of trading expeditions. The fact that the earliest Stallings Island radiocarbon dates are ca. 2515 B.C. (Rabbit Mount site, Lab. No. GX0-345) may well indicate that the Timucua were not the first traders from the Colombian coast. The early Northern Maipuran resemblances in Timucua would preclude Timucua arrival much before 1800 B.C. It is not impossible that the differences between Stallings Island wares and later Orange wares (ca. 1625 B.C., Turner site, Lab. No. G-598) are attributable to the entrance of the Timucua into this trans-Caribbean trade network. As Ford points out (1969 : 187), the stylistic changes in Orange ware mirror similar changes in Colombian wares, implying a continuation of such trade over a long period of time. Changes in the physical characteristics of the local southeastern population from the more usual Late Archaic dolicocephalic type to a decidedly brachycephalic type in Stallings Island sites also indicates the probable presence of a significant number of alien people (Claflin 1931 : 43–45).

Rouse (1986 : 121) erroneously attributes to me the hypothesis of "a migration of ancestral Warao speakers northward through the West Indies from Venezuela to Florida." This is a mistaken interpretation of my statement that Timucua has a large Waroid (not Warao) element in its grammar (Granberry 1971 : 607). In fact, it seemed clear then and even clearer now that the route of such a trade network, as Ford suggests, was through the Yucatán Channel, around western Cuba, through the Florida Straits, and northward by way of the Gulf Stream to the St. Johns and Savannah River areas (Ford 1969 : 185). Since there is no indication of Antillean-Timucua interaction, linguistically or archaeologically, from any time period, a West Indian route would be quite out of the question. It might, however, be noted that there are many Waroid toponyms throughout the Greater Antilles, with the heaviest concentration in Pinar del Rio and Habana provinces in western Cuba (Granberry 1987b). These, however, are attributable, it would seem from archaeological evidence, to physical Waroid population movement at a time level at least a thousand years earlier, likely associated with the Ortoiroid lithic expansion, which did enter the Antilles by way of Trinidad and the Windward Islands. It is not beyond possibility that the earlier familiarity with the Antilles by Macro-Chibchan speakers was what laid the groundwork for the subsequent Colombia-Florida trade nexus.

It may be noted that both Stallings Island and Orange sites are located away from the coast proper, generally on the shores of a river. This riverine niche is a salient characteristic of fiber-tempered ware sites and remains so until the advent of horticulture. This environment would, of course, have been the preferred one for the Timucua if our hypothesis of their riverine South American origins is correct. Inasmuch as the Floridian Mt. Taylor Late Archaic people also occupied such an environment, it should come as no surprise to find continuity from the Late Archaic into the ceramic-producing Early Formative in such Floridian locales nor to find Stallings Island sites, such as the Sapelo Island site, also in riverine locations. It might also be added that just as site location is similar on both the Florida/Georgia coast and the Colombian Caribbean coast, so the physical shape and nature of such sites is similar—large shell rings (Willey 1971:268–71).

With later ceramic wares in Florida and Georgia, the Deptford in particular, we find quite a different settlement pattern (Milanich 1973). Deptford sites are located either along coastal marshes, on both the Atlantic and Gulf coasts, or, if inland, not in exclusively riverine locales. With the beginning of horticulture, both coastal and riverine patterns begin to weaken, as inland settlement on better agricultural lands takes precedence. In early Deptford times, however, the then-remnant fiber-tempered cultures and the Deptford cultures complement each other rather than compete within the same ecological zones (Milanich 1973:53).

The implication is that the Deptford peoples, who show cultural continuity with the succeeding Wilmington and Savannah peoples, were likely Muskogean in both language and material culture. This seems substantiated by archaeological evidence indicating that the Guale (Apalachee *wayli* 'border'), of known Muskogean affiliation, were the end-product of the Wilmington-Savannah tradition (Milanich 1976, Larson 1978). It seems likely that the same can be said for the Gulf coast Deptford peoples, to judge from the long cultural continuity on that coast from the Late Archaic. Gulf coast fiber-tempered wares, such as that called Norwood (Phelps 1965), are distinctively different from both Orange and Stallings Island wares, giving the strong impression that their presence is due to the spread of an idea and a set of artifactual techniques rather than to the spread of a people. Primary cultural ties on the Gulf coast were always to the north and the south, along the coastal periphery, rather than to the east.

The two broadly defined linguistic-archaeological traditions, native Muskogean and intrusive Timucua, do blend in later times in Florida's geographical middle-ground, the Alachua Prairies and neighboring Columbia and Taylor counties, to produce the Alachua Tradition. The two heartlands—the St. Johns River valley and the Gulf coastal plain—remain Timucua and Muskogean, respectively, developing into the long St. Johns Tradition in the first and the Safety Harbor/Fort Walton/Leon-Jefferson Tradition in the second.

A final problem that remains is the interesting fact that the bulk of Muskogean loans in Timucua come from Alabama and Koasati, the westernmost of the Eastern Muskogean languages. One would expect Creek and Hitchiti, the more easterly of the Eastern Muskogean tongues, to have been the major contributors, but they are not. There are a few probable loans from Choctaw as well, and also the two possible loans from Natchez and Atakapa, indicating contact considerably farther west than Timucua heartland country.

There are two possible explanations for this phenomenon. First, at the time level we are referring to, circa 1800 to 1000 B.C., the Creek and Hitchiti may have been located farther to the north and west than in later times, perhaps on the Georgia-Tennessee border. At the same time, the ancestral Alabama-Koasati may have formed a "layer" of population south of the Creek and Hitchiti, spreading farther east than we now recognize. This possibility is raised by the use of the Apalachee name *Guale* (the English spelled it Wali), Apalachee *wayli(n)* 'border', to refer to this easternmost of the known Muskogean peoples. Apalachee has been shown to have been most closely related to Alabama and Koasati and to have fallen in what we know as the western branch of Eastern Muskogean (Haas 1949, Kimball 1987). If the unknown language of the Guale was indeed most closely related to Apalachee, Alabama, and Koasati, the problem would not be difficult to resolve, and it would be likely that the greatest bulk of Muskogean loans in Timucua had a Guale source. A grammar of Guale was written by Fr. Domingo Augustín between 1565 and 1585, but it has vanished in the maw of Spanish colonial bureaucratic records, either in the Consejo de Indias or perhaps the records of the Jesuit order (Swanton 1946:135).

Secondly, if we should find that Guale belonged in the eastern branch of Eastern Muskogean, with Creek and Hitchiti, then we are in trouble, for this would imply that the Timucua were primarily in long-term contact not with the Guale but with their Alabama and Koasati neighbors to the west. This, however, might not be quite as troublesome as it seems on first glance, given the interesting riverine dispersion of the Oconi and Tawasa. These two Timucua groups were distributed along the river systems

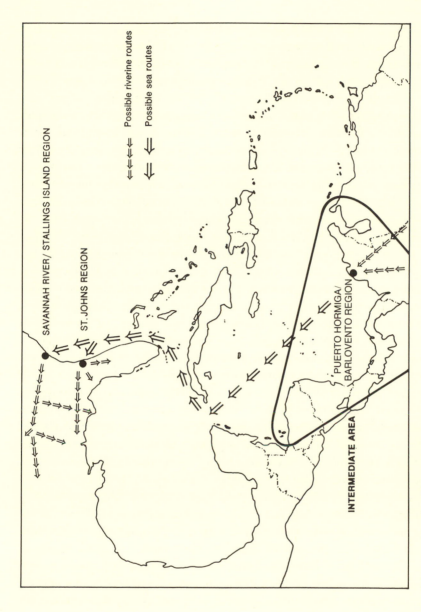

Figure 3. Possible Timucua trade routes (ca. 1800 BC).

penetrating later Alabama and Koasati lands, and it is not impossible to envision them as the forefront of a Timucua trading wedge into the southeastern heartland, even though their home base was along the Atlantic coast in the Savannah and St. Johns River regions.

Either hypothesis could be tested archaeologically, and the presence of fiber-tempered wares at both the undated Fourche Maline site-complex in eastern Oklahoma (Newkumet 1940) and the Bayou La Batre complex near Mobile Bay (Greenwell 1984), dating to around 500–1000 B.C., may be an indication that the second hypothesis is correct. Fiber-tempered wares at both complexes are remarkably similar to Floridian Orange wares, so similar that direct migrations of Orange ware makers have been suggested for the Fourche Maline area (Ford 1969:176).

It may in fact be the case that both explanations have some truth in them. The earliest fiber-tempered ware sites in the Savannah River region may have been central dispersion points from which riverine trading expeditions put out. We do not know what the major commodities traded were. One of them, however, may well have been salt—Timucua *api*, a term borrowed from the western Koasati, Alabama, or Choctaw /hapi/. This vital human commodity is abundant not only on the Atlantic seaboard as ocean salt, but also in extremely large deposits in the central Mississippi Valley region (Kentucky, southern Indiana, southeastern Illinois).

Salt was used not only as a food commodity but also increasingly as a vital temper ingredient in the production of good-quality ceramic wares from clays of poor workability (Stimmell, Heimann, and Hancock 1982: 219–26). We know that the gradual growth of ceramic industries in the Southeast led to a salt-trading system of considerable dimensions and sophistication by the Early Mississippian Period (ca. A.D. 500), stimulating development of the great Mississippian cultural centers, such as Cahokia and Angel, which in turn led to the widespread exchange of all types of cultural commodities between these centers and all parts of the Southeast (Stimmell, Heimann, and Hancock 1982:227).

It is not at all impossible that the Timucua became the leading salt-traders of the Mississippi-Southeast region at a very early date, taking their ceramic wares and ceramic-making techniques with them as they moved on their expeditions. This would certainly help explain the startling identities and similarities between Floridian Orange wares and the fiber-tempered wares of the Fourche Maline site-complex in southeastern Oklahoma. A closer examination of the artifactual inventory of all fiber-tempered sites is certainly called for, particularly in the Savannah and Tennessee River regions.

The present interpretation of Timucua language data, correlated with archaeological information, tends to support a Chibchan-related ultimate origin for the language and people somewhere in the Vaupés-Caquetá region of Colombia. The people seem to have been traders and to have participated in the north-south network between the northwestern Amazonian jungles and the northwestern Caribbean coast of Colombia. Eventually, they seem to have become one of the prime movers, if not the prime mover, of transoceanic trade between that coast and the southeastern United States. They seem to have established major trading stations on the Savannah and St. Johns Rivers and to have continued to build a Southeastern trading network along the same lines as in northwestern South America, oriented along major river systems of the region. The main trading commodities may have been salt and, to judge from the archaeological distribution of fiber-tempered wares, ceramic wares, or at least ceramic-making techniques. Such a trade network must have survived for a considerable period of time—at least until the advent of horticulture as the major form of livelihood and the creation of a more settled way of life.

A Note on Timucua Orthography and Phonology

It is, of course, difficult to impossible to reconstruct accurate phonetic and phonemic entities for a language for which one has only orthographic evidence. This is particularly the case if the orthography was devised by linguistically unsophisticated users. In the case of the surviving Timucua documents, we are unusually fortunate in that Fr. Pareja was an astute observer of the language. The orthographic system he devised for Timucua is based on sixteenth-century Spanish spelling conventions, with exceptions carefully noted and described (Adam and Vinson 1886). We are able to recover considerable phonetic detail from Pareja's descriptions, and the resulting phonemicization is therefore probably rather accurate. Pareja even provides us with lists of minimal pairs and considerable information on suprasegmental phenomena. For a more detailed description of Timucua reconstructed phonology see Granberry (1987a, 1990). The present description is essentially that given in an earlier article (Granberry 1956) except for the definition of vowel phonemes, which has been considerably altered here. The table will enable the reader to reconstruct the source orthography for the Timucua forms given in this paper:

Phoneme	Source spellings
/a/	a
/e/	e
/i/	i, y + consonant
/o/	o
/u/	u, v + consonant
/p/	p
/t/	t, (n)d ~ (n)t
/k/	c(a,o,u), q(e,i)
/kʷ/	qu
/č/	ch
/f/(= /ɸ/?)	f, h + vowel, b (rare)
/s/	s, c(e,i) (rare), ç (rare)
/h/	h, j (rare), g(e,i) (rare)
/m/	m
/n/	n
/l/	l
/r/	r
/w/	b, bu, g(a,o,u) (rare), gu(a,o), hu + vowel
/y/	y, vowel + i + vowel (rare)

REFERENCES

Adam, Lucien and Julien Vinson, eds.
    1886   "Arte de la lengva Timvquana, compvesto en 1614 por el Pᵉ Francisco Pareja, y publicado conforme al ejemplar original único." *Bibliothèque Linguistique américaine*, vol. II. Paris: Maisonneuve Frères et Ch. Leclerc, Éditeurs.

Barral, Basilio María de
    1957   *Diccionario Guarao-Español, Español-Guarao*. Monografías N°3. Caracas: Sociedad de ciencias naturales La Salle, Editorial Sucre.

Borhegyi, Stephen
    1959   "Pre-Colombian cultural connections between Meso-America and Ecuador." *Middle American Research Records* 2.6:141–55.

Brinton, Daniel Garrison
    1858   *Notes on the Floridian Peninsula*. Philadelphia.

Bullen, Ripley P.
    1978   "Tocobaga Indians and the Safety Harbor culture." In *Tacachale*, ed. Jerald Milanich and Samuel Proctor, pp. 50–58. Gainesville: University Presses of Florida.

Claflin, William H., Jr.
    1931   "The Stallings Island mound, Columbia County, Georgia." *Papers of the Peabody Museum of Archaeology and Ethnology* 14.1:1–47. Cambridge: Harvard University.

Coe, Michael
    1960   "Archaeological linkages with North and South America at La Victoria, Guatemala." *American Anthropologist* 62:363–93.

Conzemius, Eduard
    1929   "Notes on the Miskito and Sumu languages of eastern Nicaragua and Honduras." *International Journal of American Linguistics* 5:57–115.

Crawford, James M.
    1979   "Timucua and Yuchi: Two language isolates of the Southeast." In *The Languages of Native America,* ed. Lyle Campbell and Marianne Mithun, pp. 327–54. Austin: University of Texas Press.

Deagan, Kathleen A.
    1978   "Cultures in transition: Fusion and assimilation among the Eastern Timucua." In *Tacachale,* ed. Jerald Milanich and Samuel Proctor, pp. 89–119. Gainesville: University Presses of Florida.

Edwards, Clinton R.
    1965   "Aboriginal watercraft on the Pacific coast of South America." *Ibero-Americana* 47.

Feldman, Robert A. and Michael E. Moseley
    1978   "The northern Andes." In *Ancient South America,* ed. Jesse D. Jennings, pp. 139–77. San Francisco: W.H. Freeman and Company.

Ford, James A.
    1969   "A comparison of Formative cultures in the Americas: Diffusion or the psychic unity of man." *Smithsonian Contributions to Anthropology* 11. Washington, D.C.: Smithsonian Institution Press.

Gatschet, Albert Samuel
    1880   "The Timucua language." *Proceedings of the American Philosophical Society* 18:465–502. Philadelphia.

Goggin, John M.
    1953   "An introductory outline of Timucua archaeology." Laboratory of Anthropology, University of Florida, Gainesville. Paper presented to the 1952 Southeastern Archaeological Conference, 31 Oct–1 Nov. 1952, Macon, Georgia.

Goodman, Morris
    1971   "The strange case of Mbugu." In *Pidginization and Creolization of Languages,* ed. Dell Hymes, pp. 243–54. London: Cambridge University Press.

Granberry, Julian
    1956   "Timucua I: Prosodics and phonemics of the Mocama dialect." *International Journal of American Linguistics* 22.2:97–105.
    1971   "Final collation of texts, vocabulary lists, grammar of Timucua (Penrose Fund Grant No. 4633, 1967)." *Year Book of the American Philosophical Society, 1970,* pp. 606–7. Philadelphia.

1987a   "A grammar and dictionary of the Timucua language." *Anthropological Notes* 1, Horseshoe Beach, Florida.

1987b   "Antillean languages and the aboriginal settlement of the Bahamas: A working hypothesis." Paper presented to the Bahamas 1492 Conference, Freeport, Bahamas, 17 Nov. 1987.

1990   "A grammatical sketch of Timucua." *International Journal of American Linguistics* 56.1:60–101.

Greenberg, Joseph H.

1960   "The general classification of Central and South American languages." In *Men and Cultures,* 5th International Congress of Anthropological and Ethnological Sciences, ed. Anthony F. C. Wallace, pp. 791–94. Philadelphia: University of Pennsylvania Press.

Greenwell, Dale

1984   "The Mississippi Gulf coast." In *Perspectives on Gulf Coast Prehistory,* ed. Dave D. Davis, pp. 124–55. Gainesville: University Presses of Florida.

Haas, Mary R.

1940   "Ablaut and its function in Muskogee." *Language* 18:141–50.

1941   "The classification of the Muskogean languages." In *Language, Culture, and Personality,* ed. Leslie Spier, pp. 41–56. Menasha.

1945   "Dialects of the Muskogee language." *International Journal of American Linguistics* 11. 2:69–74.

1946   "A Proto-Muskogean paradigm." *Language* 22.4:326–32.

1947   "Development of Proto-Muskogean *k^w." *International Journal of American Linguistics* 13.3:135–37.

1948   "Classificatory verbs in Muskogee." *International Journal of American Linguistics* 14.4:244–46.

1949   "The position of Apalachee in the Muskogean family." *International Journal of American Linguistics* 15.2:121–27.

1950   "On the historical development of certain long vowels in Creek." *International Journal of American Linguistics* 16.3:122–25.

1956   "Natchez and the Muskogean languages." *Language* 32.1:61–72.

1960   "Some genetic affiliations of Algonkin." *Culture in History,* pp. 977–92. New York: Columbia University Press.

1975   "What is Mobilian?" *Studies in Southeastern Indian Languages,* ed. James M. Crawford, pp. 257–61. Athens: University of Georgia Press.

Holmer, Nils Magnus

1946   "Outline of Cuna grammar." *International Journal of American Linguistics* 12.4:185–97.

Key, Mary Ritchie

1968   *Comparative Tacanan Phonology: With Cavineña Phonology and Notes on Pano-Tacanan Relationship.* The Hague: Mouton.

Kimball, Geoffrey

1987   "A grammatical sketch of Apalachee." *International Journal of American Linguistics* 53.2:136–74.

Larson, Lewis H., Jr.
    1978   "Historic Guale Indians of the Georgia coast and the impact of the
            Spanish mission effort." In *Tacachale,* ed. Jerald Milanich and Samuel
            Proctor, pp. 120–40. Gainesville: University Presses of Florida.
Lathrap, Donald W.
    1970   *The Upper Amazon.* New York: Praeger.
    1973   "The antiquity and importance of long-distance trade relationships
            in the moist tropics of pre-Columbian South America." *World Ar-
            chaeology* 5.2:170–86.
Lathrap, Donald W., Donald Collier, and Helen Chandra
    1975   *Ancient Eduador: Culture, Clay and Creativity 3000–300 B.C.* Chicago:
            Field Museum of Natural History.
Le Moyne, Jacques
    1875   *Narrative of Le Moyne, An Artist Who Accompanied the French Expedi-
            tion to Florida under Laudonnière, 1564.* Translated from the Latin of
            De Bry. Boston: Osgood Company.
Loewen, Jacob A.
    1963   "Chocó II: Phonological problems." *International Journal of Ameri-
            can Linguistics* 29.4:357–71.
Lorant, Stefan, ed.
    1946   *The New World.* New York: Duell, Sloan, and Pearce.
Loukotka, Čestmír
    1968   *Classification of South American Indian Languages,* ed. Johannes Wil-
            bert. Latin American Center Reference Series, vol. 7. Los Angeles:
            University of California.
Matteson, Esther
    1972   "Proto Arawakan." In *Comparative Studies in Amerindian Languages,*
            ed. Esther Matteson, Alva Wheeler, Frances L. Jackson, Nathan
            Waltz, and Diana R. Christian, pp. 160–85. The Hague: Mouton.
Migliazza, Ernest C.
    1978   "Some evidences for Panoan-Yanomama genetic relationship." Paper
            presented at the Linguistic Society of America Summer Meeting,
            Urbana.
    1985   "Language of the Orinoco-Amazon region." In *South American In-
            dian Languages: Retrospect and Prospect,* ed. Harriet W. Manelis Klein
            and Louisa R. Stark, pp. 17–139. Austin: University of Texas Press.
Milanich, Jerald T.
    1973   "The Southeastern Deptford culture: A preliminary definition." Bu-
            reau of Historic Sites and Properties, *Bulletin* 3: pp. 51–63. Tallahas-
            see: Florida Department of State.
    1976   "Georgia origins of the Alachua tradition." Bureau of Historic Sites
            and Properties, *Bulletin* 5: pp. 47–56. Tallahassee: Florida Depart-
            ment of State.
    1978   "The western Timucua: Patterns of acculturation and change." In
            Tacachale, ed. Jerald Milanich and Samuel Proctor, pp. 59–88.
            Gainesville: University Presses of Florida.

Milanich, Jerald T. and Charles H. Fairbanks
   1980   *Florida Archaeology.* New York: Academic Press.
Milanich, Jerald T., and William C. Sturtevant
   1972   *Francisco Pareja's 1613* Confessionario: *A Documentary Source for Ti-mucuan Ethnography.* Tallahassee: Division of Archives, History, and Records Management, Florida Department of State.
Newkumet, Phil J.
   1940   "Preliminary report on excavation of the Williams Mound, Leflore County, Oklahoma." *Oklahoma State Archaeological Society* 3.2:1–9.
Noble, G. Kingsley
   1965   "Proto-Arawakan and its descendants." *International Journal of American Linguistics* 31.3 (July), part II:1–129 (also pub. 38, Indiana University Research Center in Anthropology, Folklore and Linguistics, Bloomington).
Osborn, Henry
   1967a   "Warao I: Phonology and morphophonemics." *International Journal of American Linguistics* 32.2:108–23.
   1967b   "Warao II: Nouns, relationals, and demonstratives." *International Journal of American Linguistics* 32.3:253–61.
   1968   "Warao III: Verbs and suffixes." *International Journal of American Linguistics* 33.1:46–64.
Pareja, Francisco
   1627   *Cathecismo, y examen para los que comvlgan, en lengua Castellana, y Timuquana.* Mexico.
Phelps, David S.
   1965   "The Norwood series of fiber-tempered ceramics." *Southeastern Archaeological Conference Bulletin* 2:65–69.
Prost, Gilbert R.
   1962   "Signaling of transitive and intransitive in Chacobo (Pano)." *International Journal of American Linguistics* 28.2:108–18.
Rodrigues, Aryon Dall'Igna
   1985   "Evidence for Tupi-Carib relationships." In *South American Indian Languages: Retrospect and Prospect,* ed. Harriet E. Manelis Klein and Louisa R. Stark, pp. 371–404. Austin: University of Texas Press.
Roth, Walter E.
   1924   "An introductory study of the arts, crafts, and customs of the Guiana Indians." *Thirty-eighth Annual Report of the Bureau of American Ethnology, 1916–17,* pp. 26–745. Washington, D.C.
Rouse, Irving
   1986   *Migrations in prehistory: Inferring Population Movement from Cultural Remains.* New Haven: Yale University Press.
Salomon, Frank
   1977/78   "Pochteca and mindala: A comparison of long-distance traders in Ecuador and Mesoamerica." *Journal of the Steward Anthropological Society* 9.1–2:231–46.

Schomburgk, Moritz Richard
    1847   *Reisen in Britisch-Guiana in den Jahren 1840–44.* 3 vols. Leipzig: Ver-
            lagsbuchhandlun von J.J. Weber.
Sorenson, Arthur P., Jr.
    1967   "Multilingualism in the northwest Amazon." *American Anthropologist*
            69:670–684.
    1985   "An emerging Tukanoan linguistic regionality: Policy pressures."
            In *South American Indian Languages: Retrospect and Prospect,* ed. Har-
            riet E. Manelis Klein and Louisa R. Stark, pp. 140–56. Austin: Uni-
            versity of Texas Press.
Stimmell, Carole, Robert B. Heimann, and R. G. V. Hancock
    1982   "Indian pottery from the Mississippi Valley: Coping with bad raw
            materials." In *Archaeological Ceramics,* ed. Jacqueline S. Olin and
            Alan D. Franklin, pp. 219–28. Washington, D.C.: Smithsonian Insti-
            tution Press.
Swadesh, Morris
    1964   "Linguistic overview." In *Prehistoric Man in the New World,* ed.
            Jesse D. Jennings and Edward Norbeck, pp. 527–56. Chicago: Uni-
            versity of Chicago Press.
Swanton, John R.
    1929   "The Tawasa language." *American Anthropologist* 31:435–53.
    1946   "The Indians of the Southeastern United States." Bureau of Ameri-
            can Ethnology, *Bulletin* 137. Washington, D.C.
Taylor, Douglas M.
    1977   *Languages of the West Indies.* Baltimore: The Johns Hopkins Univer-
            sity Press.
Taylor, Douglas M. and Berend Hoff
    1966   "'Proto-Arawakan and its descendants,' by G. Kingsley Noble: A re-
            view." *International Journal of American Linguistics* 32.3:303–8.
Wallace, Alfred Russel
    1889   *A Narrative of Travels on the Amazon and Rio Negro.* 2nd edition. Lon-
            don: Ward, Lock & Company.
Waltz, Nathan E. and Alva Wheeler
    1972   "Proto Tucanoan." In *Comparative Studies in Amerindian Langauges,*
            ed. Esther Matteson, Alva Wheeler, Frances L. Jackson, Nathan
            Waltz, and Diana R. Christian, pp. 119–149. The Hague: Mouton.
Wheeler, Alva
    1972   "Proto Chibchan." In *Comparative Studies in Amerindian Languages,*
            ed. Esther Matteson, Alva Wheeler, Frances L. Jackson, Nathan
            Waltz, and Diana R. Christian, pp. 93–108. The Hague: Mouton.
Wilbert, Johannes
    1957   "Prólogo." In *Diccionario Guarao-Español, Español-Guarao,* by Basílio
            María de Barral, pp. 7–18. Caracas: Sociedad de ciencias naturales La
            Salle, Editorial Sucre.
    1972   *Survivors of Eldorado.* New York: Praeger.

1973   "Eschatology in a participatory universe: Destinies of the soul among the Warao Indians of Venezuela." Paper presented to the Dumbarton Oaks Conference on Death and Afterlife in Pre-Columbian America, 27–28 October 1973.

Willey, Gordon R.
1971   *An Introduction to American Archaeology, Vol. 2: South America*. Englewood Cliffs, N.J.: Prentice-Hall.

Zeidler, James
1977/78   "Primitive exchange, prehistoric trade and the problem of Mesoamerican-South American connection." *Journal of the Steward Anthropological Society* 9.1–2:7–39.

Lila Wistrand-Robinson

Uto-Aztecan Affinities with Panoan of Peru I: Correspondences

Abstract

Allusions have been made to North and South American Indian linguistic relationships but no positive proof has been presented, aside from Ronald Olson's work on Chipaya and Maya, published in 1964–65, which reached only into Central America. I present here a preliminary chart of sound correspondences of Cashibo and Comanche, with corresponding Proto-Panoan, Proto-Uto-Aztecan, Proto-Numic, and Proto-Shoshonean. A list of tentative cognates is also given. Cashibo and Comanche are target living languages with which I have worked linguistically. These actual, present-day languages give more positive and accurate data for comparison than reconstructed artificial forms, which have an enormous timespan that date back to the proto languages. Inclusion of all members of each family group in the reconstructed forms obscures the relationships that are more unique to the older and more isolated Panoan and Shoshonean groups.

The purpose of this chapter is to present: (1) brief phonological sketches of Comanche and Cashibo;[1] (2) a standard 100-word list, including Proto-Uto-Aztecan (*UA), Comanche (Com), Hopi (Ho), *Panoan (*PN), Cashibo (Csh), and Shipibo-Conibo (SC); (3) charts of sound correspondences of *UA and *PN, Com and Csh; and (4) evidence of a tentative relationship between *UA and *PN, thus linking North and South American Indian language families at the proto level. Comanche and Cashibo are chosen as major representatives of the two language families since the author is acquainted with these through work on both languages. Occasionally, a few other representatives of the two language families are given in the comparative list: Mayo El Fuerte (Sinaloa) dialect (Ma); Mayo Jijiri (Sonora) dialect (My), *Numic (*NUM), Aztec (Az), and Papago-Pima (PaPi). The lexicostatistical method has been used to show tentative dates of separation from three 100-word lists and one 200-word list, though only one 100-word list is included here. The background for the above studies is also given.

The 100-word list by Rea was used, supplemented by the lists of Uto-Aztecan by Kenneth L. Hale (HAL: 1958); C. F. Voegelin, F. M. Voegelin, and Kenneth L. Hale (VVH: 1962); Lyle Campbell and Ronald W. Langacker (C and L: 1978); David E. Iannucci (IAN:1972); William Bright and Jane Hill (B&H: 1967); Andrés Lionnet (LIO: 1985); Burton W. Bascom (BAS: 1965); Wick R. Miller, Kevin J. Hegg, and Cindy High (MIL: 1987); and my work with James L. Armagost in Comanche (ROB: 1990). Hopi items are from *Hopi Domains,* by Voegelin and Voegelin (IJAL: 1957). Proto Panoan items are from Olive A. Shell (SHL: 1975),[2] and Shipibo-Conibo from James Loriot (LOR).[3] Miller's (1987) recent compendium of information, *Computerized Data Base for Uto-Aztecan Cognate Sets* (CDB), was a great help for checking all information collected prior to its publication and for adding some additional information. I have attempted to coordinate my information with these data to a certain extent. For this reason, the reader is referred to CDB introductory information for further background, which I will not repeat here.

The Swadesh method of glottochronology, used on three 100-word lists, resulted in 60 percent, 66 percent, and 72 percent cognates. The same method, used on a 200-word standard list, resulted in 58.5 percent cognates. The latter was chosen as most representative, implying a separation of Panoan from Uto-Aztecan approximately 1,650 years ago, or at A.D. 337, according to the following formula:

$$t = \frac{\log 58.5}{2 \log 85} = \frac{-.566}{2 \times -L.63} = 1{,}649 \text{ years ago, or A.D. } 337$$

One commonly sees Sanskrit, Latin, Greek, German, and English words compared as cognates, yet we know they span continents and have a common origin in *IE. Meillet (1924 [1967]:29) states that "the agreements are less striking and the rules of correspondences more difficult to determine if we observe languages separated by larger intervals of space and time." The number of phonological and grammatical correspondences are striking in my comparison of Comanche-Cashibo precisely because of the large intervals of space and time, possibly suggesting a migration independent of the fact that both Comanche and Cashibo were isolated for longer periods than their fellow tribesmen, at extreme ends of both language families. The Comanche were the last tribe in the United States to be subdued by government troops. The Cashibo were isolated due to their location in the foothills of the Andes, away from the more heavily traveled riverine area where contact with other tribes would have been made more easily. Because of their separation, these two tribes conserved some of the same older characteristics of their proposed common ancestor. A later article will present the proposed reconstructions to the ancestor of *UA and *PN.

We are faced here with the problem of vocabulary attrition due to the extremely long time span and with extremely differing ecological settings. The Comanche are located in a dry ecological area, lying in the rain shadow of the Wichita Mountains of Oklahoma in the United States in North America whereas the Cashibo are in the tropical rain forest of Central Peru, in the foothills of the Andes Mountains in South America.

Meillet has also stated (1924 [1967]:36) that morphology is "the most stable thing in language." My studies show grammatical correspondences and processes that are equally as important as the phonological ones as a result of movement of sets of morphemes in agglutinative languages, rather than individual phonemes. Though grammatically important morphemes are included with the phonological data, space does not permit treatment of the grammar in this chapter; that topic will be the focus of a future article.

Panoan

The Panoan (PN) languages are Amahuaca, Cashinahua, Capanahua, Sharanahua, Mayoruna, Yaminahua, Conibo-Shipibo, Cashibo, Cacataibo, Chacobo, and Marubo. These tribes are located in Peru, Brazil, Bolivia, and possibly also previously in Colombia.

*PN was reconstructed by Shell (1975 version, in Spanish) with augmented data to her 1965 dissertation. This work was added to or modified by Loriot (1965). (See also Key 1968, and Loos 1973a, b.) A reconstruction of Proto Tacanan (*TC) was published by Key (1968, for Tacanan, located only in Bolivia), but not dealt with here. It might be useful to do a parallel study of Tacanan and Aztec, as suggested by Key (1978, 1981b). Relationships of Panoan to Tacanan have been presented by Loriot (1965), Loos (1964), and Key (1968). The Summer Institute of Linguistics series *Estudios Panos,* written in Spanish, also gives detailed phonological and grammatical background information on the Panoan languages.

My work on the Cashibo language took place between 1957 and 1965. In 1978, I was given the opportunity to direct a National Endowment for the Humanities project with the goal of editing the late Elliott Canonge's card file of rough lexicon entries so that a dictionary and grammar description could be compiled.[4] As I checked entries for the dictionary, apparent cognates with Cashibo turned up. In addition to phonological correspondences, grammatical relationships also became evident. Experience with Cashibo gave insight into Comanche—a kind of depth that had not shown up in the bits and pieces of grammatical descriptions previously published on Comanche or Shoshone. In the years that have followed the initial grant work, Armagost's grammar studies and McLaughlin's (1982) phonological articles have added still more depth to Comanche linguistics.

Comanche Phonemes

Comanche phonemes are shown in Tables 1 and 2 in phonemic form of vowels and consonants respectively.[5] General stress falls on the first (C)V(C) syllable, with a general rule of alternating stress. Most pro-clitics follow the general stress rules; that is, they take on the initial stress, pulling it away from the main stem, for example: /háni-/ 'do'; /tíhani-/ 'cut up, butcher'; /wósa/ 'sack'; /ká:wosa/ 'coyote'. There are also non-stress-changing prefixes that

TABLE 1. PRELIMINARY CHART OF VOWEL CORRESPONDENCES

*UA	Com	Csh	*PN	Comanche	Cashibo	English
*i	/i i: I/	/i i:/	*i	-ʔi-	ʔi-	be, become
				púhi	píi	leaf
*ɨ	/ɨ ɨ: Ɨ/	/ɨ ɨ:/	*i	íri-	irín-	burn bright
				tíhani-	tíat-	cut, butcher
				tírah-	tirín-	erase, rub off
*u	/u u: U/	/o o:/	*o	hu-	o-	come
				túa	toá	son; child
				kùyuʔní:	kóŝo	turkey
*o	/o O/	/o/	*o	móha	móka	bitter
				sóni	ŝóbi	grass, weeds
*o	/o:~ɔ:]	/ɔ:/	*awa	to: [~tɔ:]	tɔ:	cane, stick
				-o:- [~ɔ:]	-ɔ:-	make, build
*a	/a a: A/	/a a:/	*a	ha-, -ʔa-	ʔa-	do, make
				ta-	ta-	of/with foot
				páka	páka	bamboo, reed
*ai	/e e:/	/e e:/	*aya	kúʔe	kʷé:	top, upper

TABLE 2. PRELIMINARY CHART OF CONSONANT CORRESPONDENCES

*UA	Com	Csh	*PN	Comanche	Cashibo	English
*p	/p/	/p/	*p	páka	páka	bamboo, reed
				pɨ́rA	pɨnyã́	arm
*ƀ	/ƀ/	/ƀ/	*ƀ	[nɨ]ƀúi	ƀíro	[my] eye
				[tái]ƀo	[kái]ƀo	people, group
				ƀá:ƀa	ƀábá	grandson, grandchild
*ƀ	/p/	/ƀ/	*b	pɨ:-	ƀɨ-	bring
*t	/t/	/t/	*t	ta-	ta-	of/with the foot
				túhu-, tu-	to-	black, dark
				tóki-	tó:[ki/ka]-	break in pieces
*r	/r/	/r/	*r	tírah-	tɨrín-	erase, rub off
*k	/k/	/k/	*k	nókima-	nóko-	come moving; arrive
				kúpIta?	kóki	light; torch
*k	/k/	/kʷ/	*k	kíma?	kʷɨƀí	lip, edge
				kímakwai	kʷícima	dull (edge)
*kʷ	/kʷ/	/k[o]/	*k	kʷí:[pɬ]	koí	smoke, cloud
*h	/h/	/?/	*?	háni	?áno	beaver; paca
	initial			híƀi-	?é:-	drink; swallow
	ø	/?/	*?	usú?uya?i-	?osãn-	laugh (at), smile
*h	/h/	ø	ø	tɨháni-	tía-	cut, butcher
	medial			púhi	pɨ́i	leaf
				náhnia-	ánɨ-	name (vb)
*w	/w/	/ƀ or w/	*w	[áta]ƀìci	ƀíci	other
*y	/y/	/i/	*i	núhya?	noí	snake; worm
*y	/y/	/ŝ/	*s	kùyu?[ní:]	kóŝo	turkey
				tóyopI	tíŝá	neck
*c	/c/	/c/	*c	ícɨ[?itɬ]	máci	[be] cold
				-ci	-co	little (dimin.)
*s	/s/	/s/	*s/	tísu?i-	?ísɨ-	advise, counsel
				usu?u[yá?i-]	?osãn-	laugh, smile
				sí:petɬ	sapãN	level
*s	/[?]s/	/c/	*c	[tá]?si:tO	[on]cís	claw, [toe]nail
*s	/s/	/ŝ/	*s	túsika-	túŝu-	expectorate, spit
				sámohpɨ?	ŝáno	sibling; woman
*m	/m/	/m/	*m	móha ~ múhka	múka	bitter
				ma-	mɨ-	hand (pref.)
*n	/n/	/n/	*n	nókima-	nóko-	come moving; arrive
				háni	?áno	beaver; paca
*n	/n/	/ñ~y/	*y	kíno?i-	kíño ~ kɨyo-	finish, kill
				háni	áño ~ áyo	what(ever)

leave the stress on the appropriate stem syllable, for example: /ciwá:'i-/ 'feel around with something sharp" [ci + wa:'i-]. These rules also hold for Cashibo. There is contrast between long and short vowels, even under stress (' = primary stress on the preceding vowel), for example: /ka:'wosA/ 'fox, coyote'; /ku'pIta?/ 'light', with the stress overtly marked on both initial vowels (these are not generally marked since they follow the phonemic rule); /usu'?uya'i-/ 'laugh (at)' (' = secondary stress on the preceding vowel.) In compounds, the noun retains main stress, while the bound modifier has secondary stress, for example: /k'yu?ni'i/ 'turkey'.

Comanche consonants group as stops, affricate, fricatives, nasals, flap, resonant, and semivowels.

Stops are /p/, /t/, /k/, and /kʷ/, all nonvoiced, nonaspirated, and nonglottalized. /p/ becomes [ƀ] or phonetic variant [v] from English influence, and /t/ becomes flap [r] in unstressed syllables word-medially. Although this rule holds rather firmly, the /ƀ/ and /r/ are here treated as separate phonemes, since these are in a state of flux. /k/ has a backed allophone [q] preceding back vowels /u/ and /o/. The labialized velar stop /kw/ has the allophone [gw] word-medially when it occurs in unstressed syllables, varying in different dialects of Comanche, for example, /kwahi/ 'back', /kɨmakwai/ [kɨmagwai] 'dull edge'.

The unaspirated voiceless affricate /c/ is at times difficult to distinguish from /?s/ within a verb, for example: /cih-/ 'fill full'; /cahpi?e-/ 'pull out, fish'.

The grooved fricative is /s/ with [š] only as a pejorative, borrowed variation of /s/ in certain words, for example: /tɨsu?irɨ/ 'counsel'; /pisuni'i?/ [pisuni'i?/pišuni'i?] 'skunk'. The use of [š] adds intensification.

Nasals are /m/ and /n/, for example, /múhka/ 'bitter'; /kíma?/ 'lip, edge'; /nókima-/ 'arrive, come moving'; /táni?yɨki-/ 'make sound of footsteps running.'

Semivowels are /y/, /w/, /h/, and /?/, for example: /kuyu?ni'i-/ 'turkey'; /núhya?/ 'worm'; /wóƀi-/ 'wood'; /ká:wosA/ 'fox'; /cíwa:i-/ 'feel around with something sharp'; /háni/ 'beaver'; /kwáhi/ 'back (body part)'; /húhci, hú:ci/ 'grandmother'.

Comanche vowels consist of two sets of three-way contrasts: high vowels /i, ɨ, u/, and mid-to-low vowels /e, a, o/. The vowel in an isolated syllable has two morae of time by phonemic rule, for example: /kí/ [ki:] 'corner'; /á/ [a:] 'animal horn'; /nó/ [no:] 'sure, definite'; /pá/ [pa:] 'water'; /má/ [ma:] 'him, her, it'; /mí/ [mi:] 'your (second-pers. pl.)'. There is no contrast of short and long vowels on single-syllable words in isolation.

This same rule holds for the Cashibo. Double morae has either mid or high falling tone.

Under stress, the vowel has some phonetic length, whether under primary or secondary stress, for example, /amakwo:ˀa pa/ 'cider, apple juice'; /ana:ˀ/ 'ouch!'; /kahuˀu/ 'mouse'. As mentioned above, under phonemic first-syllable basic stress, length versus nonlength shows contrast, for example: /tɨ́:pe/ 'lips, mouth'; /tɨ́ranA/ 'long bones of leg', with the first-syllable vowels under stress, also seen in the following: /túaˀ/ 'son', /tú:meˀsO/ 'young catfish'.

Unstressed vowels following voiceless consonants or in word-final position are voiceless; for example, /hábi-kɨnoˀ/ 'cradle-board, day cradle'; /ká:wosA/ 'fox, jackal'; /nácahkweniitɨ/ 'hung up, hanging'; /tacɨ́:tO/ 'toe-nail'.

High vowels are shown in various positions in the following words:

i: /hínanahìmiti/ 'to exchange'; /háni/ 'beaver'

ɨ: /ɨ́rɨ-/ 'light a fire'; /másɨatɨ/ 'to tend by hand'

u: /hú-/ 'come'; /kúˀe/ 'top, upper part'

      /húhci, hú:ci/ 'grandmother'

Mid vowels [e] and [o] are historically diphthongs, as corresponding Shoshoni /ai/ and /au/ reveal. Mid back-rounded vowel /o/ has a morphophonemic variant [ɔ:] which has developed from the combination of [o] and [a], lowering the [o] and moving it slightly forward, with length to account for the two morae. The [o:] and [ɔ:] are in free variation when the combination has been stem-forming, but usually occurs as [ɔ:] in the morphophonemic post-position,

o: /páro/ 'swollen river'; /wóbi/ 'wood'; /to:/ 'cane'

e: /éka-eˀre/ 'swamp rabbit'; /é:bi/ 'blue color'

a: /háni/ 'beaver'; /núhyaˀ/ 'woman'; /á/ 'horn'

Canonge interpreted the voiceless preconsonantal nonglottal consonant as [h] in all cases. Actually, preceding nasals it is phonetically [M] preceding /m/, [N] preceding /n/, parallel to Miller's geminate clusters /mm/ and /nn/. Even so, the phonemic status of /h/ requires its maintenance as a separate morpheme meaning "made, but belonging to," for example: /húhmaraˀ/ 'falcon'; /hu-pihná/ 'syrup, molasses'.

The glottal stop is phonemic, with both phonological and grammatical functions. It occurs word-medially between reduplicated identical vowels, for example /usúˀuyaˀi-/ 'laugh at'. It also occurs between nonidentical nondiphthongal vowels, for example, /kuˀe/ 'top, upper part', and word-finally as nominalizer for verb stems, for example, /táci:ˀ/ 'louse egg'.

Cashibo Phonemes

Cashibo (or Uni, as speakers call it) consists of four main dialects: (1) Cacataibo (Cac), spoken on the San Alejandro River; (2) Shambuyacu (Cshl), of the Lower Aguaytia River; (3) Pindayo (Csh2), of the Upper Aguaytia River; and (4) Sungaroyacu (Sun), spoken on the Sungaro-yacu River. Shell (1950) used a taxonomic approach, basing her description on the Shambuyacu dialect (Cshl). In a later article, following the transformational-generative phonology (Robinson 1976), I dealt with the Pindayo (Csh2) as possibly basic for all.

Cashibo (Csh) includes a system of five voiceless stops /p/, /t/, /k/, /kw/ and /ʔ/; two affricates /c/ and /č/; four fricatives /ƀ/, /s/, /š/, and /ŝ/; three nasals /m/, /n/, and /ñ/; one resonant flap /r/; and six vowels, three high /i/, /ɨ/, and /o/, and three mid to low /e/, /a/, and /ɔ/. Intrinsic stress falls on the first syllable, with a basic alternate syllable stress system. Length may also occur on any vowel. Single syllables in isolation always have phonemic-lengthened vowels. Examples of the vowels are:

i: /mi/ 'you'; /ʔíca/ 'many'
ɨ: /ʔɨ/ 'I'; /ɨma/ 'village, cluster of houses'
o: /o/ 'he, she, it (distal)'; /ói/ 'who'
a: /a/ 'that, he, she, it (over there)'; /ána/ 'tongue'
e: /me/ 'earth, land'; /ʔé:ti/ 'to swallow'
ɔ: /ƀɔ/ 'parrot'; /ƀími5/ 'rubber tree'

The two vowels /e/ and /ɔ/ have a history of origin similar to those of Comanche, and involve the collapse of clusters of sounds from /*aya/ and /*awa/ respectively, while sister languages have kept the /ai/ and /au/, as in Shipibo-Conibo. All vowels may be either nasalized or lengthened.

Stops are all voiceless and unaspirated syllable-initially. Only /n/, /s/, /š/, /ŝ/, and /ʔ/ occur syllable-finally as interpreted by Shell (1975) and using the work of Loos (1973b) and my work with Comanche, I now see that the syllable-final glottal stop and nasal reflect the Numic geminate consonants discussed by Miller for Shoshoni. Loos also pointed out for the Panoan languages the fact that in such words as Cashibo /kakíti/ 'to be on top of' the stem is /kakít-/ plus the suffix /-ti/ 'to be', which is actually a remnant of the geminate consonants as found in the Uto-Aztecan family, specifically seen in Shoshoni, as analyzed by Miller (1973). Cashibo noun suffix /-ŝ/ is a morpheme signifying the subject of an intransitive verb, as /á:ŝ/ 'he, she, it (subject of vi)'; /iníŝ/ 'this (subject of vi)'. As verb suffix, it signifies the subordinate verb link to an intransitive principal verb, as in /kwaánŝ/ 'having gone'; /míkamaŝ/ 'having stolen'.

Obstruent /p/ and its fricative counterpart /ƀ/ have been labialized preceding central high vowel /ɨ/ in the speech of Cashibo individuals of advanced age, but this feature is being lost in most of the speech of younger members of the community, as /píti/ [pwíti, píti] 'to undress'; /ƀíci/ [ƀwíci, ƀíci] 'other'.

Although Comanche /ƀ/ and /r/ cannot occur word-initially and could be considered word-medial submembers of /p/ and /t/, the /ƀ/ and /r/ of Cashibo are separate phonemes from the /p/ and /t/ and occur freely word-initially, for example, /ƀaƀa/ 'grandchild'; /ƀari/ 'sun, year'; /rani/ 'body hair'.

Voiceless affricates /c/ and /č/ occur in word-initial and word-medial positions, but never syllable-final, for example, /cáca/ 'fish'; /čiči/ 'grandmother'. Cashibo developed the /č/ whereas many of the other Panoan languages still have only /c/ as in Comanche.

Nasals occur in three-way contrast m, n, and ñ in the Cashibo-Shambuyaca dialect, but in two-way m and n in all others, as /mápa/ 'Dioscoreaceae'; /nía/ 'pale-winged trumpeter'; /ñápa/ 'dorado fish'; /ʔáno/ 'paca'. Older speakers tend to labialize /m/ before central high vowel /ɨ/, though this is being lost by the younger generations, for example, /mɨú/ [mwɨú, mɨú] 'inside, in the middle'. A bilabial stop release that occurs in the speech of older persons is also being lost by younger generations, for example, /mɨínkoma/ [mƀwɨínkoma, mɨíŋkoma] 'small crab'. The syllable-final preconsonantal nasal archiphoneme N has allophones assimilating to the point of articulation of the following stop, but to the Cashibo it is phonemically /n/, as a psychological reality, for example, /kánti/ 'bow'; /šánpa/ [šámpa] 'gourd'; /ñónkɨ/ [ñoŋkɨ] 'kind of lizard'.

Cashibo grooved fricatives are voiceless in a three-way contrast: alveolar /s/, palatal /š/, and retroflex /ŝ/. These have occasional voiced variants /z/, [ž], and [ẑ] in Csh1 and Csh2, regularized in Cac. In the Cac dialect /š/ is lost altogether word-initially or has the allophone [y], for example, /masi/ [masi, mazi] 'sand'; /ší:pi/ [ší:pi, í:pi] 'marmoset monkey'; /šápo/ [šápo, ẑápo] 'cotton'.

The Comparative List

A few explanatory remarks regarding the comparative list are necessary.

Comanche and Cashibo phonemic elements are summarized as follows:

COMANCHE	p	t	c	k	kw			i	ɨ	u
	b	s							e		o
	m	n							a	
	w	r	y	h	?			Length /:/		

CASHIBO	p	t	c	k	kw	?		i	ɨ	o
	b	s	š	ŝ				e	ɔ	
	m	n	ñ					a		
	r							Length /:/		

A hyphen following a single syllable usually indicates a prefix, though the morpheme may also be a single-syllable verb root if the meaning so indicates. Verb roots or stems are generally followed by hyphens.

In a few cases, the Shipibo-Conibo (SC) has been left out if it was either identical to the Cashibo or not a cognate at all. The SC has been given to provide a means of showing some other aspects of, and depth for, Panoan, and also to show that SC has /h/ whereas Cashibo does not. Panoan also has /ai/ and /au/ whereas Cashibo has gone to /e:/ and /ɔ:/. Unfortunately, Capanahua is not given, which would have shown the V?V of medial vowels: in Cashibo, simply VV. The V?V occurs in Capanahua and other Panoan languages.

To save space, the main given meaning of the heading has sometimes been abbreviated by its first letter in the listings in cases where the meaning has been modified in some way; for example, "seed" = "s".

Subscript sounds from VVH and others have been capitalized (see a more complete explanation in CDB).

Length has in most cases been standardized to V; in Cashibo, this practice ignores some of the aspects of tone glide, for the glide may be stressed either on the first mora or the second. Cashibo has inherited remnants of tone from its oriental ancestors. For the purposes of this chapter, ignoring the finer points of tone does not affect the comparative aspects.

Finally, unmarked meanings have the same sense as the heading.

My first wish was to publish a long list of all the words that I consider cognates, but I realized that it would not have a good reception. Thus this standard list, limited in the number of cognates, is presented with the hope that in the future a longer enumeration of the words I consider cognates may be published for the study of other interested linguists.

100-WORD UTO-AZTECAN AND PANOAN COMPARATIVE LIST

(1) Eng: all, entirely
    Span: todo
    *UA
    Ho VV   só:sok(-t)
    Com   ʔóyetɫ
    *PN SHL-52   *ati
    Csh ROB   kámaƀi
    SC LOR   hatíƀi

(2) Eng: ashes
    Span: ceniza
    *UA BAS-147   *matai
    Com ROB   ʔétɫsipɫ
    *PN SHL-126   *čiʔi mapo
    Csh ROB   čí:mapo
    SC LOR   čímapo

(3) Eng: bark of tree
    Span: corteza
    *UA MIL-21   *ko
    BAS-105a   *ʼkómi
    Ho VV   cí:pɨ
    Com   póʔa
    *PN SHL-395   *šakata 'bark, skin'
    Csh ROB   šáka, ƀíči póʔa 'potato with barklike skin'

(4) Eng: belly, abdomen, stomach
    Span: panza
    *UA MIL-417   *to
    Ma   tóppa
    Ho VV   póno
    Com ROB   sápɫ
    *PN SHL-341   *poko
    Csh, SC   póko

(5) Eng: big, large
    Span: grande
    *UA VVH-100   *wɨ-
    LIO-127   *kʷíru
    Ho VV   wí:pa 'tall'
    Com ROB   píapɫ
    *PN SHL-12   *ʔɨwa
    Csh ROB   ʔiɔ; čá:
    SC LOR   áni

(6) Eng: bird
   Span: ave
   *UA BAS-333   *ʔuʔu'higi 'birds'
      IAN-261   *(hu[i][h])ci
      Com ROB   (huh)cú:ʔ
      Ho VV   síkaci 'canarylike'
   *PN SHL-16   *ʔiʔsaka
      Csh ROB   ʔisá
      SC LOR   isá

(7) Eng: bite, grit teeth
   Span: morder
   *UA VVH-43   *kɨU(ʔi), *kɨU(ʔi)
      Ho VV   kí:ki
      Com ROB   kíhcia-,
                  kíhkarɨʔi-
   *PN
      Csh ROB   kɨrúŝka-; natíŝ-
      SC LOR   náka, yíns

(8) Eng: black, dark
   Span: negro, oscuro
   *UA IAN-224   *tu(h)
      VVH-23   *tuU(ku)
      MIL-45a   *tu, *tunu
      BAS-232   *tuku
      Ho VV   tóho, tó:ki
      Com ROB   túhu, tu-
   *PN SHL-464   *tonān
      Csh ROB   tonã́:, to-

(9) Eng: blood
   Span: sangre
   *UA MIL-47a,b   *ʔet, *ʔew
      LIO-13
      Ho VV   ʔíŋʷa
      Com ROB   pí:hpI
   *PN SHL-141   *imi
      Csh ROB   ími
      SC LOR   hími

(10) Eng: bone
   Span: hueso
   *UA VVH-61   *ʔoho
      MIL-52   *ʔo, *ʔoho
      IAN-260   *cuhni
      Com ROB   cúhni[pɨ]
   *PN SHL-398   *ŝao
      Csh   ŝáo

(11) Eng: burn, hot
Span: quemar
*UA
  Ho VV   ʔíti
  Com ROB   ʔíriʔi
*PN SHL-17   *ʔicisa 'hot'
*PN SHL-136   *iri- 'burn'
  Csh ROB   irín- 'burn'
                   ʔicís 'hot'

(12) Eng: cloud(s), smoke
Span: nube(s), humo
*UA HAL-19   *kʷi:ci
    VVH-35   *kʷiSci
  Ho VV   kí:hi
  Com ROB   tómo 'cloud'
                   kʷí: 'smoke'
*PN SHL-187   *koʔini
  Csh ROB   koï
  SC LOR   koïn

(13) Eng: cold
Span: frío
*UA VVH-11   *siU(pi)
    IAN-262   *-ci, *si, *sih-
  Com ROB   íciʔi-
*NUM   *ʔici
  Az   mačí
*PN SHL-205   *maci
  Csh, SC   máci

(14) Eng: come
Span: venir
*UA VVH-159   *kiUma
    MIL-96   *kim
    IAN-71   *kihma
  Com ROB   kíma-, hú-
  PaPi   dáiw
*PN SHL-296   *o
  Csh ROB   ó- ~ ái-
  SC LOR   hó-

(15) Eng: die
Span: morir
*UA HAL-23   *muki
    MIL-128d   *mek, *me
  Co ROB   kó:i-, tiyá:i-
  Ho VV   mó:ki
*PN SHL-233   *mawa-

Csh ROB   ɓáma-
SC LOR   mawá-

(16) Eng: dog
      Span: perro
      *UA VVH-46   *puNku 'dog, pet'
         MIL-135   *puku, -137 *cu
         LIO-78   *kawasi 'fox'
         Com ROB   sá:ri, pú:kU
      *PN SHL-20   *ʔinaka
         Csh ROB   kamó, ʔočíti
         SC LOR   ʔočíti

(17) Eng: drink
      Span: tomar, tragar
      *UA VVH-77   *hiS-
         IAN-40   *hipi
      Ho VV   hí:ko
      Com ROB   híɓi-
      *PN SHL-405   *ŝiʔa-
      Csh ROB   ŝía- 'drink'
                           ʔé;- 'swallow'

(18) Eng: dry
      Span: seco
      *UA VVH-99   *waki
         LIO-325   *wakɨ, wak-i 'secarse'
      Com ROB   pásapI
      *PN
      Csh ROB   í:ski-, totóān-
                           pacá- 'wash'
      SC LOR   manŝán-

(19) Eng: ear
      Span: oreja, oído
      *UA VVH-47   *naNka
         MIL-148   *naka
      HO VV   náqvɨ
      Com ROB   náki
      *PN SHL-310   *paɓiki
      Csh ROB   paɓí
      SC LOR   paɓíki

(20) Eng: earth, ground
      Span: tierra
      *UA MIL-151   *kʷi-
         VVH-112   *kʷiya
         IAN   *soko
         Com ROB   sokó:ɓI, sóko-

*PN SHL-208	*mai, *mawi
SC LOR	mái
Csh ROB	mé: [cf. koī 'dust, smoke']

(21) Eng: eat
Span: comer

*UA VVH-88	*kuUmi, *kuUma
Com ROB	tíhka-, tɨki-
Ho VV	sówa, pi(kɨyi) 'nurse, suckle'
*PN SHL-326	*pi
Csh ROB	pí-,
	koáŝka- 'drink'
SC LOR	pí-

(22) Eng: egg
Span: huevo, blanquillo

*UA MIL-156	*kawa
Com ROB	nóʔi, nóoyo
PaPi	nóhnaa
My	kábba
*PN SHL-64	*ɓásci
Csh ROB	ɓáci ~ waci
SC LOR	ɓáči

(23) Eng: eye
Span: ojo

*UA VVH-5	*puNsi
IAN-155	*puʔi(h)
Ho VV	pó:si
Com ROB	púi(h)
*PN SHL-80a	*ɓiro
Csh, SC	ɓíro

(24) Eng: fat, grease
Span: grasa

*UA VVH-102	*wi-
Com ROB	yúhU
Ho VV	wíhɨ
PaPi	nóhna:
*PN SHL-412	*ŝíni
*Csh ROB	ŝíni
	yúʔa- 'render'

(25) Eng: feather, down
Span: pluma(s)

*UA MIL-168	*pi'
*NUM	*pɨhɨ
Com ROB	píhɨ
*PN SHL-325	*piʔi

Csh ROB   píči
SC LOR   píi, namán

(26) Eng: fire, by means of fire
      Span: fuego
      *UA MIL-170a   *ku, *ko?
         IAN-64   *kuh-
         HO VV   köyöhi, ko-
         Com ROB   kóhto:pI, ku-
      *PN ROB   *ko-
         Csh ROB   ko-, kóki
                        koƀín- 'boil'

(27) Eng: fish
      Span: pez
      *UA IAN-146   *peŋkʷi, *paŋkʷi
         LIO103-   *kucu
         Com ROB   pé:kʷi
         Ho VV   pá:kiw(t)
      *PN SHL-111   *caca
         Csh ROB   cáca 'generic f.'
                        páki, ƀái, 'f. types'
         SC LOR   yápa 'small f.'

(28) Eng: fly, make fly
      Span: volar
      *UA MIL-183   *hini
         HO VV   póoka, piɨyala
         Com ROB   yóri-
      *PN SHL-295   *no(ya)
         Csh ROB   noán-
         SC LOR   nóya-

(29) Eng: foot
      Span: pie, pata
      *UA MIL-187   *ta, *to
         VVH-28   *tala
         Com ROB   ta(h)-
                        tásum 'toes'
      *PN SHL-436   *ta?ɨ, *ta-
         Csh, SC   táɨ, ta-

(30) Eng: give; exchange; sell
      Span: dar; vender
      *UA VVH-83   *maSka
         Com ROB   máka-, ?utU-;
                        hínanahimi- 'exchange'
      *PN SHL-21   *?ina; *?inanan-

```
       *PN ROB          *maro- 'sell'
        Csh ROB          ʔinán- 'give'
                         ʔinánan- 'exchange'
                         máro- 'sell, buy'
        SC LOR           míni- 'give'
                         máro- 'exchange'
```

(31) Eng: good
      Span: bueno
      *UA MIL-200   *cam
       Com ROB   cá:
       Ho VV   hopí
      *PN SHL-383   *šara
      *PN ROB   *opi
       Csh ROB   opí
       SC LOR   hakón

(32) Eng: green
      Span: verde
      *UA
       Com ROB   ʔébɨ
       Ho VV   móki
      *PN SHL-320   *paŝa 'v., crudo'
       Csh ROB   páŝa
       SC LOR   yankón

(33) Eng: hair of head
      Span: pelo
      *UA MIL-212b   *po 'body hair'
         CL-240   *ku:pa
       Ho VV   hó:mi
       Com ROB   papI
       My   bówwa 'body h.'
      *PN SHL-106   *ɓo:
       Csh ROB   ɓó:
       SC LOR   ɓo:

(34) Eng: hand
      Span: mano
      *UA MIL-215   *ma, *moʔ
         CL-78   *ma:(y)(V)-
         CL-242   *ma:
       Com ROB   ma(h)-, moʔO
       Za   máay
      *PN SHL-240   *mɨkɨnɨ, *mɨɓi
       Csh, SC   mɨkī, mɨ-

(35) Eng: head
Span: cabeza
*UA IAN-138   *pampi
    VVH-134   *moʔo
    MIL-219a   *co
Com ROB   pá:pI
*PN SHL-221   *mapo, *ƀoskata
Csh ROB   maŝká, mápoŝɔ
SC LOR   mápo

(36) Eng: hear, understand
Span: oír, entender
*UA VVH-126   *kahi, *kaha
    BAS-98a   *kaɨ
Com ROB   (na)ka
Ho VV   návota
*PN SHL-148   *nɨka- 'hear'
                     *kʷáʔɨ- 'understand'
Csh ROB   kʷá-
SC LOR   nínka-

(37) Eng: heart
Span: corazon
*UA VVH-98   *sula
HO VV   ʔínaŋwa
Com ROB   pIcámU, pici
*PN SHL-301   *oiti
Csh ROB   nóito 'heart'
                    oín- 'breathe'
SC LOR   hoínti

(38) Eng: I
Span: yo
*UA IAN-118   *nɨ
    BAS-295   *ʔa:nɨʔi~ɨ
Com ROB   níʔ, níʔu
*PN SHL-11   *ʔɨ
Csh ROB   ʔí:
SC LOR   ʔía

(39) Eng: kill
Span: matar
*UA VVH-45   *koya (pl.)
                     *me
Com ROB   péhka-
Ho VV   mó:ki
*PN SHL-1   *ʔa- 'do, kill'
Csh ROB   ʔá-, rí-
SC LOR   rítɨ

(40) Eng: know
Span: saber
*UA VVH-25 *mati
            *supanaʔi-
Com ROB   súabetai-,
            másuabetai-
Ho VV   nanápta
*PN SHL-36 *ʔonā- 'k., learn'
Csh ROB   ʔonán-

(41) Eng: leaf
Span: hoja
*UA VVH-64 *sawa
B&H   *pala-
ROB   *pɨhɨ
*NUM   *pɨhɨ
Com ROB   púhi
*PN SHL-325 *piʔi
Csh ROB   píi
SC LOR   píi

(42) Eng: lie, lie down
Span: acostar(se)
*UA VVH-130 *poʔi, *poʔo
Com   há:bI, hábi-
Ho VV   qá:ci-
*PN SHL-356 *raka-
Csh ROB   (ra)kát-
SC LOR   raká-

(43) Eng: liver
Span: hígado
*UA VVH-89 *nɨSma
Ho VV   níɨma
Com ROB   táni
*PN SHL-438 *takʷa
Csh ROB   tákʷa
SC LOR   táka

(44) Eng: long
Span: largo
*UA LIO-294 *tɨpɨ
Com ROB   páʔatɬ
Ho VV   wíɨko, wíɨyavo
*PN
Csh ROB   ámpako, časkí
SC LOR   ninkí 'long flat'
            kɨyá 'long/tall'

(45) Eng: louse
       Span: piojo
       *UA ROB   *pusIʔa 'l. of head'
           VVH-24   *ʔatɨ 'l of body'
       Ho VV   ʔátɨ 'l of body'
       Com   sá:bebusía 'l. of body'
                            yúpusia 'l. of head'

       *PN SHL-344   *ʔia 'l. of head'
       Csh ROB   ʔía 'l. of head'
                            ʔupús 'chigoe'

(46) Eng: man/male
       Span: hombre, macho
       *UA BAS 57a   *haʔduni 'm. relative'
           LIO-24   *ʔowi 'male, macho'
       Com ROB   ténahpɨʔ
       Ho VV   táaqa
       *PN SHL-303   *oni
       Csh ROB   óni ~ ónᵈi 'man, male relative'

(47) Eng: many
       Span: mucho(s)
       *UA ROB   *so
       Ho VV   so:-wɨɨhaq-hiita 'lots of things'
       *PN SHL-28   *ʔišca
       Csh ROB   ʔíca
       SC LOR   ʔíca

(48) Eng: meat, flesh
       Span: carne
       *UA VVH-22   *tuUku
       Com ROB   túhkU, tíhkapɨ
       *PN SHL-258   *nami
       Csh, SC   námi

(49) Eng: mountain, hill
       Span: montaña
       *UA MIL-289a,b   *kawi, *kai
           IAN-49
           VVH   *touno
       Com ROB   toyá:bI
       *PN ROB   *baši
       Csh ROB   báši ~ wáši
       SC LOR   manã

(50) Eng: mouth
       Span: boca
       *UA MIL-293   *teni
           VVH-19   *tɨUni

Ho VV	mó?a
Com ROB	tí:pE
*PN SHL-455	*tíšo 'throat, neck'
Csh ROB	tíro 'throat'
	tišá 'neck'
	kʷiɓí 'lips, mouth'

(51) Eng: name
Span: nombre

*UA IAN-117	*ni(C)a, *nih-
Com ROB	náhni(a)-
Ho VV	tíŋʷa
*PN SHL-49	*aní
Csh ROB	ání
SC LOR	háni

(52) Eng: neck
Span: nuca

*UA VVH-154	*kuSta
Ho VV	kʷá:pi
Ho VV	tóna 'voice, throat'
Com ROB	tóyopɫ, tóyo-
*PN SHL-455	*tišo
	tiro 'throat'
Csh ROB	tišá
SC LOR	tíšo 'neck, trachea, throat'

(53) Eng: new
Span: nuevo

*UA IAN-173	*piti(h) 'n., recent'
Ho VV	píihi
Com ROB	íki
*PN ROB	*iɔ́
*PN SHL-72	*ɓi?ná 'young man'
Csh ROB	iɔ́
SC LOR	ɓiná

(54) Eng: night
Span: noche

*UA VVH-144	*tuSki~a
IAN-228	*tuka
Ho VV	míhi,
	tóoki 'last night'
Com ROB	túka(ni)
*PN SHL-57	*ɓa?kiši
Csh ROB	imí,
	topíɓoki 'sundown, evening'

(55) Eng: nose
    Span: nariz
    *UA VVH-110   *yaSka
        MIL-308   *yaka
    Ho VV   yáqa
    Com ROB   mú:pI, múɓi-
    *PN ROB   *rɨkini
    Csh ROB   rɨkɨ́

(56) Eng: no, not
    Span: no
    *UA VVH-136   *ka
        MIL-306   *ka, *kai
    Ho VV   qá
    Com ROB   ké
    *PN SHL-493   *(-ya)ma
    Csh ROB   -ma
    SC LOR   yáma, má

(57) Eng: one
    Span: uno
    *UA HAL-33   *se
    *NUM   *sɨɨnʷi
    Com ROB   símɨʔ, sɨ́ɨ
    *PN SHL-480   *wɨstita
    Csh ROB   ačóši
    SC LOR   huistióra, hábičo

(58) Eng: person, Indian
    Span: persona
    *UA IAN-122   *nɨ(h)mɨ
    Ho VV   síno
    Com ROB   ní:mɨ
                  -ɓu 'people, persons'
    *PN ROB   *honi 'p., man'
    *PN ROB   *-ɓo 'tribe'
    Csh ROB   óni 'man, persons, people'
                  nó: 'enemies'
                  -ɓo 'tribe, peo.'

(59) Eng: rain
    Span: lluvia
    *UA LIO-62   *horo (vb)
        HAL-25   *yuki
    *NUM   *ʔɨma
    Com ROB   íma(h)-
    Ho VV   yó:ki
    *PN SHL-33   *ʔoi

Csh ROB   ʔóñe, ʔíbe
SC LOR   ʔói

(60) Eng: red
     Span: rojo
     *UA VVH-32   *sɨta
        MIL-343   *set
     Ho VV   pála
     Com ROB   éka-, pási-
     *PN SHL-319   *pašini

(61) Eng: road, path
     Span: camino
     *UA VVH-4   *po
     Com ROB   púʔE
     *PN SHL-56   *ɓaʔi, *ɓai
     Csh ROB   ɓái ~ wái
     SC LOR   ɓái

(62) Eng: root
     Span: raíz
     *UA VVH-151   *ŋa
     Ho VV   ná:pi
     Com ROB   tɨrahna, kʷítA
     *PN SHL-444   *tapono
     Csh ROB   tapṍ
     SC LOR   tapṍ

(63) Eng: sand
     Span: arena
     *UA IAN-194   *(pa)siwa(h)
     Ho VV   písa 'fine sand'
     Com ROB   pá:si(wapi)
     *PN SHL-226   *massi
     Csh ROB   mási
     SC LOR   máši

(64) Eng: say, tell
     Span: decir
     *UA BAS-94   *kaiti 'to say'
        MIL-434   *te 'to tell'
        IAN-82   *-kʷi(i)
     Ho VV   kíta 'say'
                       lávayi- 'word'
     Com ROB   ní-, yíkʷi- 'say'
                       pánaʔai 'praise'
     *PN SHL-62   *ɓana- 'talk, say'
     *PN ROB   *ki- 'say'; *ka- 'tell'
     Csh ROB   kí- 'say'; ká- 'tell'
                       ɓána- 'talk'

(65) Eng: see
     Span: ver
     *UA IAN-159   *puni, *puh-
     Ho VV   yóri
     Com ROB   púniʔ, -ɂúni
     *PN SHL-33   *ʔoi-; *is-
     Csh ROB   ís-
     SC LOR   oí

(66) Eng: seed
     Span: semilla
     *UA IAN-155   *puʔi(h) 's., eye'
     Ho VV   pósɨmi, pó:si
     Com ROB   péhe
     *PN SHL-137   *ɨ̂ŝɨ
     *PN SHL-80   *bíro 'eye, s.'
     Csh ROB   bíro, ɨ́nŝɨ
     SC LOR   bíro, híŝɨ

(67) Eng: sit
     Span: sentar
     *UA VVH-42   *kaStɨ,
        VVH-76   *yaNsa
     Com ROB   há:ɂI, hábɨ-
     Ho VV   qátɨ; có:va- 'live together, mate'
     *PN SHL-110   *caʔo-
     Csh ROB   có:t- 'sit, live'
     SC LOR   yáka (sg.);
                          sítí (pl.)

(68) Eng: skin
     Span: piel
     *UA CL-149   *kʷɨtaš- 'skin, leather'
     Ho VV   cí:pɨ
     Com ROB   póʔaʔ (n.)
                          cáhkweʔya- (v.)
     *PN SHL-395   *ŝakata
     Csh ROB   ŝáka, ɂíči
     *PN SHL-89   *biči

(69) Eng: sleep
     Span: dormir
     *UA VVH-34   *koSci, *koSco
        MIL-129b   *koci, -386 *ku
        LIO-91   *koco, *koc-i
     Com ROB   ʔáhpi:, íhpɨi
                          ísuaki- 'snore'
     Ho VV   tó:ka

*PN SHL-39   *ʔoŝa-
Csh ROB   ʔóŝ-

(70) Eng: small, little
Span: pequeño
*UA VVH-117   *tɨma
    IAN-235   *tɨ(e)(h)
    Com ROB   tíe-
            -(h)ci 'diminu.'
*PN SHL-336   *pi(s)t(i)a

(71) Eng: smoke
Span: humo
*UA VVH-35   *kʷiSci
    MIL-392a   *kʷi, *kuhi
    MIL-329b   *kʷici
    Ho VV   kʷí:ci(ŋʷɨ)
    Com ROB   kʷí:pɫ
*PN SHL-187   *koʔini
Csh ROB   koɨ́

(72) Eng: stand (up)
Span: parar, levantar(se)
*UA VVH-161   *wɨlɨ
    MIL-412   *ke
    BAS-132   *kɨ'kiva/i
    Ho VV   wíni-
    Com ROB   wínɨ-
*PN SHL-273   *ni-
Csh ROB   ní(ro)-
SC LOR   ní-, wɨní-

(73) Eng: star
Span: estrella
*UA VVH-71   *su
    Az VVH-71   sí:(tali:n)
    Com   tásinùpɫ, tácinùpi
*PN SHL-489   *wištima
Csh ROB   ʔíspa
SC LOR   wísti

(74) Eng: stone
Span: piedra
*UA VVH-169   *tɨUpa
    BAS-69   *ho'dai
    Ho VV   ʔówa
    Com ROB   tí:pI
*PN SHL-227   *maŝáŝ
Csh ROB   maŝáŝ
SC LOR   makán

(75) Eng: sun
    Span: sol
    *UA VVH-27   *taUca, *toŋa-la
    *NUM   *taƀe
     Com ROB   tá:ƀE
     Ho VV   tóŋ-va
    *PN SHL-63   *ƀari
     Csh ROB   ƀári ~ wári
     SC LOR   ƀári

(76) Eng: swim
    Span: nadar
    *UA IAN-131   *pahapi
     Com ROB   páhaƀi-
     Ho VV   mómori-
    *PN SHL-291,2   *nona~o-
     SC LOR   nóno
     Csh ROB   míño-

(77) Eng: tail
    Span: cola, rabo
    *UA VVH-51   *kʷaUsi
       HAL-28   *kʷasi
       BAS-22   *bahi
     Com ROB   kʷásI,
                      ínapɨ 'jerky'
    *PN SHL-142   *ina
     Csh ROB   ína 'tail, jerky'
     SC LOR   hína

(78) Eng: that (distal)
    Span: ese, aquel
    *UA IAN-18   *u(sɨ[N])
    *NUM   *ʔósɨ
     Com ROB   ʔósɨ
    *PN ROB   *o 'far'; *a 'near'
     Csh ROB   ó: 'far'; a: 'near'
     SC LOR   há 'near'
                      ʔóri 'far'

(79) Eng: this
    Span: este (prox.)
    *UA VVH-116   *ʔi
       BAS-306   *ʔi'da, ʔi'diʔi
     Com ROB   íni, ʔísɨ
    *PN ROB   *ɨnɨ
     Csh ROB   ínɨ

(80) Eng: thou, you
      Span: usted, tú
      *UA BH   *ʔi̧ [cf. *PN*ʔi̧ 'I']
         IAN-22   *ih
      Com ROB   ʔí (sg.),
                        míi (pl.)
      *PN SHL-246   *mi
      Csh ROB   mí
      SC LOR   mía

(81) Eng: tongue
      Span: lengua
      *UA VVH-94   *liŋi
         MIL-441a   *neni
         HAL-50   *nɛn
      Com ROB   é:kO
      Coa HAL-50   nánu
      *PN SHL-47   *ana
      Csh ROB   ána,
                        ʔé:- 'swallow'
      SC LOR   hána

(82) Eng: tooth
      Span: diente
      *UA VVH-29   *taSma
         MIL-442   *tam
      Com ROB   tá:mA, táma-
      *PN SHL-414   *ŝita
      Csh ROB   ŝíta
      SC LOR   ŝíta

(83) Eng: tree, wood
      Span: árbol
      *UA VVH-78   *hu
         MIL-9, 474   *hu
      Com ROB   hú:hpI, hú:-
      Ho VV   hímɨcki, hóhɨ
      *PN SHL-147   *iwi
      Csh ROB   í:,
                        ʔó- 'of trees'
      SC LOR   híwi

(84) Eng: two
      Span: dos
      *UA VVH-103   *wo-
      *NUM   *wa:haiʔi
      Com ROB   wáha(h)-
      *PN SHL-352   *rabɨta
      Csh ROB   rabɨ́

(85) Eng: walk
     Span: caminar, andar
     *UA IAN-101   *miʔa-, 'go, walk'
      Com ROB   míʔa-, kʷá- 'go'
      Ho VV   níma- 'go'
     *PN SHL-273   *ni- 'walk, go'
      Csh ROB   ní- ~ níc;
                        kʷān- 'go'
                        -biã-~kiã- 'going'

(86) Eng: warm, hot
     Span: caliente
     *UA IAN-26   *ɨtɨ(h)-'be h.'
      Com ROB   ʔɨrɨʔi- 'be h.'
      Ho VV   ʔɨtɨ 'h. weather'
     *PN SHL-17   *ʔicisa
      Csh ROB   ʔicís,
                        irín- 'burn, light fire'

(87) Eng: water
     Span: agua
     *UA VVH-123   *pa
         IAN-127   *pa:, *pa-
      Com ROB   pá:
     *PN SHL-37   *(ʔom)pašа
      Csh ROB   (ʔom)páš,
                        pa-~ ɫa-
      SC LOR   (ʔom)páš 'w. in a container'

(88) Eng: we
     Span: nosotros
     *UA BAS-297   *ʔa:tɨʔi ~
                        *ʔa:tɨʔi
         ROB   *nɨm
      Com ROB   nímɨ
     *PN SHL-283   *no(-)
      Csh ROB   nó:
      SC LOR   nóa

(89) Eng: what
     Span: que
     *UA VVH-37   *ha- 'what, who'
         VVH-138   *ha(ki)
         IAN-30   *hake
      Com ROB   há
     *PN SHL-43   *a:
      Csh ROB   á:

(90) Eng: white
    Span: blanco
    *UA VVH-31   *toUsa
      MIL-458   *tosa
      IAN-220   *tosa
      Com ROB   tósa
    *PN SHL-306   *oso
      Csh ROB   ʔóŝo(a)
      SC LOR   hóŝo

(91) Eng: who
    Span: quien
    *UA VVH-138   *ha(ki)
      IAN-30   *hake
      Com ROB   há-, hákarɨ
    *PN SHL-116   *co(a)
      Csh ROB   á:, ói
      SC LOR   cóa

(92) Eng: woman
    Span: mujer
    *UA VVH-79   *huSpi
      BAS-319   *ʔoʔkisi 'w., girl'
      MIL-472a,b   *nawi, *na
      Com ROB   sámohpɬ 'sister'
    *PN SHL-397   *ŝano
      Csh ROB   ŝáno
      SC LOR   ʔaínɓo

(93) Eng: yellow
    Span: amarillo
    *UA VVH-62   *ʔoha
      Com ROB   óhapI
    *UA BAS-327   *uama
    *PN SHL-319   *pašini
    *PN SHL-199   *koro 'tan, gray'
      Csh ROB   kóro, panšíá
      SC LOR   pánši

(94) Eng: breast
    Span: pecho, chichi(s)
    *UA VVH-6   *pi
      MIL-420   *cun 'suck'
      Ho VV   pí:hɨ
      Com ROB   pIcámU, píci
    *PN SHL-429   *ŝoma
      Csh ROB   ŝóma

(95) Eng: claw, (toe/finger) nail
      Span: uña
      *UA VVH-26   *suUtu, *siUtu
        IAN-193   *situN
        MIL-298   *sut
      *NUM   *cito
        Com ROB   (ta)sí:tO
      *PN SHL-298   *ocisi
        Csh ROB   ʔõncís

(96) Eng: full
      Span: lleno
      *UA
        Com ROB   tíhpeʔ-
        Ho VV   ʔó:pokiwta
      *PN
        Csh ROB   b̵oákak̵i
                          póro- 'fill'

(97) Eng: horn, antlers
      Span: cuerno
      *UA VVH-104   *ʔawa
        MIL-235   *ʔawa
        Ho VV   ʔá:la, -ʔála
        Com   ʔá:
      *PN SHL-207   *máča(n/mV)
      *PN SHL-8   *ʔawara 'tapir'
        Csh ROB   mánča,
                          ʔó: 'tapir'

        SC LOR   ʔáwa 'tapir'

(98) Eng: knee
      Span: rodilla
      *UA VVH-30   *toŋo
        IAN-108   *taŋa
      *NUM   *tanapɫ
        Com ROB   tánapɫ, tanáʔ
      *PN SHL-359   *ra-, *-toko
        SC LOR   rãntõnko
        Csh ROB   ráb̵o(ŝoo)

(99) Eng: moon, month
      Span: luna
      *UA MIL-286a,b   *mea, *meca
        IAN-102   *miʔa(h),
                          *mɨha(h)
        Com ROB   mía
        Ho VV   mɨ́ɨya-wɨ

```
*PN SHL-40        *ʔosi̭
 Csh ROB          ʔósi̭
```

(100) Eng: round, circular
      Span: redondo
```
      *UA VVH-148        *cikuri, cikori 'circular'
       Com ROB           tóponi 'round'
      *PN ROB            *toro-
       Csh ROB           tóroa 'round'
                         tóroki̭ 'circular'
                         topõn- 'count, beat of dance in a cir.'
```

NOTES

1. My fieldwork with the Cashibo was done under the auspices of the Summer Institute of Linguistics, Peru Branch, of which I was a member from 1954 to 1971. The Cashibo/Cacataibo, who call themselves *oni* 'men, people,' are located in the foothills of the Andes mountains of central Peru, on the Aguaytia, San Alejandro, and Sungaroyacu rivers and their smaller tributaries.

2. This work was published in Spanish in 'Las lenguas pano y su reconstrucción" (Spanish translation by Ezequiel Romero Sanchez-Concha). The Proto Panoan cited here is generally from her listings, though I have used i instead of her ü.

3. I acknowledge professional courtesies from James Loriot, though all mistakes are my own. His list of Shipibo-Conibo was relayed by correspondence.

4. This work was accomplished under National Endowment for the Humanities Research Grant number 2520-8-6006, Project 1366. Permission for working with Canonge's materials was granted by Viola Canonge Frew, SIL Center, Espanola, New Mexico, in 1977.

5. A more detailed discussion of Comanche phonemes is included in Wistrand and Armagost (1990).

REFERENCES

Armagost, James L.
    1982   "The temporal relationship between telling and happening in Comanche narrative." *Anthropological Linguistics* 24:193–200.
    1983   "Comanche narrative: some general features and a selected text." *Kansas Working Papers in Linguistics* 8.2:1–29.
    1984   "The grammar of personal pronouns in Comanche." *Mid-America Linguistics Conference Proceedings,* ed. David S. Rood, pp. 25–35. Boulder: University of Colorado.
Bascom, Burton William, Jr.
    1965   Proto-Tepiman (Tepehuan-Piman). Ph.D. dissertation, University of Washington.
Bright, William and Jane Hill
    1967   "The linguistic history of Cupeño." *Studies in Southwestern Ethnolinguistics,* ed. Dell H. Hymes with William E. Bittle, pp. 351–71. The Hague: Mouton

Campbell, Lyle and Ronald W. Langacker
    1978   "Proto-Aztecan vowels." *International Journal of American Linguistics* 44:85–102; 197–210; 262–79. [In three parts; last part has the reconstructions.]
Canonge, Elliott
    1958   *Comanche Texts.* Norman, Okla.: Summer Institute of Linguistics.
    [1974]
Freeze, Ray and David E. Iannucci
    1979   "Internal classification of the Numic languages of Uto-Aztecan." *Amerindia* 4:77–92.
Hale, Kenneth
    1958   "Internal diversity in Uto-Aztecan I." *International Journal of American Linguistics* 24.2:101–07.
    1959   "Internal Diversity in Uto-Aztecan II." *International Journal of American Linguistics* 25.2:114–21.
Heath, Jeffrey
    1975   "Major sub-groups in Uto-Aztecan." Paper read at American Anthropological Association meetings, San Francisco, December 3, 1975.
Iannucci, David E.
    1972   Numic Historical Phonology. Ph.D. dissertation, Cornell University.
Kensinger, Kenneth
    1981   "Recent publications in Panoan linguistics." *International Journal of American Linguistics* 47.1 (January 1981):68–75.
    1985   "Panoan linguistic, folkloristic and ethnographic research: retrospect and prospect." *South American Indian Languages: Retrospect and Prospect,* ed. Harriet E. Manelis Klein and Louisa R. Stark, pp. 224–85. Austin: University of Texas Press.
Key, Mary Ritchie
    1968   *Comparative Tacanan Phonology: With Cavineña Phonology and Notes on Pano-Tacanan Relationship.* The Hague: Mouton.
    1978   "Araucanian genetic relationships." *International Journal of American Linguistics* 44.4 (October):280–93.
    1979   *The Grouping of South American Indian Languages.* Ars Linguistica, 2. Tubingen: Gunter Narr.
    1981a   "Intercontinental linguistic connections." Irvine, Ca: Humanities Inaugural Lecture Series, University of California, Irvine.
    1981b   "North and South American linguistic connections." *La Linguistique* 17.1:3–18.
    1983   "Comparative methodology for distant relationships in North and South American languages." *Language Sciences* 5.2 (October):133–54.
Kroeber, Alfred L.
    1907   *Shoshonean Dialects of California.* Berkeley: University of California Press.
Langacker, Ronald W., ed.
    1977   *Studies in Uto-Aztecan Grammar Vol. 1. An Overview of Uto-Aztecan Grammar.* Dallas: Summer Institute of Linguistics and University of Texas at Arlington.

Lehmann, Winfred P.
    1962   *Historical Linguistics: An Introduction*. New York: Holt, Rinehart, and Winston. (Rea one-hundred-word list appears on pp. 112–13.)
Lionnet, Andrés
    1985   "Relaciones internas de la rama sonorense." *Amerindia* 10:25–58.
Loos, Eugene E.
    1964   "Maps of Panoan languages." Unpublished dialect maps showing movement of Panoan languages northward into Peru from Bolivia.
    1973a   "La señal de transitividad del sustantivo en los idiomas panos." *Estudios Panos I*, Serie Lingüística Peruana 10, 133–84. Yarinacocha, Peru: Instituto Lingüístico de Verano.
    1973b   "Algunas implicaciones de la reconstrucción de un fragmento de la gramática del Proto-Pano." *Estudios Panos II*, Serie Lingüística Peruana 11, 263–82. Yarinacocha, Peru: Instituto Lingüístico de Verano.
    1976   *Verbos Performativos*. Yarinacocha, Peru: Instituto Lingüístico de Verano. Chapter 4: "Datos comparativos de otros idiomas panos," pp. 137–215.
Loriot, James
    1965   "Shipibo Cognates with Tacanan." Field Notes No. 224, Microfilm Roll 10. Yarinacocha, Peru: Instituto Lingüístico de Verano, 16.
McLaughlin, John E.
    1982   "From aspect to tense, or, what's -nuh in Comanche." *1982 Mid-America Linguistics Conference Proceedings*, pp. 412–26. Lawrence, Kan.: University of Kansas.
    1983   "Gemination and morphologization in Central Numic." Paper read at XXII Conference on American Indian Languages, American Anthropological Association, Chicago, 18 November.
Meillet, Antoine
    1924   *La méthode comparative en linguistique historique*. Oslo: Aschehoug.
    [1967]   Translated by G. B. Ford as *The Comparative Method in Historical Linguistics*. Paris: Champion.
Miller, Wick R.
    1972   *Newe Natekwinappeh: Shoshoni Stories and Dictionary*. Salt Lake City: University of Utah Press.
    1973   "Some problems in Comanche historical phonology." Paper presented at Linguistic Society of America meetings, San Diego, December 1973.
Miller, Wick R., Kevin J. Hegg, and Cindy High
    1987   *Computerized DataBase for Uto-Aztecan Cognate Sets*. Salt Lake City: University of Utah.
Rea, John A.
    1958   "Concerning the validity of lexico-statistics." *International Journal of American Linguistics* 24:145–50.
Robinson, Dow Frederick
    1966   *Aztec Studies II: Sierra Nahuat Word Structure*. Norman, Okla.: Summer Institute of Linguistics.

Shell, Olive A.
    1950   "Cashibo I: Phonemes." *International Journal of American Linguistics*
            16.4 : 198—202.
    1975   "Las lenguas pano y su reconstrucción." *Estudios Panos III*, Serie Lin-
            güística Peruana 12. Yarinacocha, Peru: Instituto Lingüístico de
            Verano.
Swadesh, Morris
    1954   "Perspectives and problems of Amerindian comparative linguistics."
            Word 10.2—3 : 306—32.
Voegelin, Charles F. and Florence M. Voegelin
    1957   "Hopi Domains." *International Journal of American Linguistics* 23.2
            (supplement).
Voegelin, Charles F., Florence M. Voegelin, and Kenneth L. Hale
    1962   "Typological and Comparative Grammar of Uto-Aztecan: I (Pho-
            nology)." Indiana University Publications in Anthropology and Lin-
            guistics. Memoir 17. *International Journal of American Linguistics*
            28.1 : 1—144 (supplement).
Wistrand [Robinson], Lila
    1969   Folkloric and Linguistic Analyses of Cashibo Narrative Prose. Ph.D.
            dissertation, University of Texas at Austin.
Wistrand-Robinson, Lila
    1976   "Some generative solutions to problems in Cashibo Phonology."
            In *A. A. Hill Festschrift*, Vol. I, 287—95. The Hague: McRitter
            Publishers.
    1983   "Sample cognate list and preliminary sound correspondences toward
            a North and South American Indian language relationship." Paper
            read at Southeastern Conference on Linguistics XXVIII, University
            of Maryland at College Park, 8 April 1983.
    1985   "Bi-directional movement in historical change Shoshone: Comanche."
            Paper read at 1985 Annual Meetings, American Anthropological As-
            sociation, Washington, D.C.
Wistrand-Robinson, Lila and James Armagost
    1990   *Comanche Dictionary and Grammar*. Dallas: Summer Institute of Lin-
            guistics, University of Texas at Arlington. Manuscript produced in
            1979 by N.E.H. Grant #2520-8-6006, Project 1366, Kansas State
            University.

Appendix: Language Families

The references cited here are found in the Bibliography, and in chapters of this volume. See Loriot (1964) and Hoijer, Hamp, and Bright (1965) for further references. References marked with asterisks appear in this volume.

Aguaruna
> Gnerre, Larson

Arawakan
> Derbyshire, Gnerre, Heitzman, Matteson, Mosonyi, Noble, Payne (David L.), Shafer, Wise

Aruakan
> Shafer

Cariban
> Derbyshire, Durbin, Durbin and Seijas, Edwards, Rodrigues, Villalón

Chibchan
> Constenla, González de Pérez, Lévi-Strauss, Levinsohn, Moore, Wheeler

Chipaya
> Olson, Stark

Chocó
> Pardo

Chorote
> Gerzenstein

Cinta Larga
> Crowell

Cunza (= Kunza = Atacama)
> Lehnert, Rodríguez

Djuka
> Huttar

Gavião
> Crowell

Guahiban
> Christian and Matteson, Kondo, Queixalós

Guaycuru/Toba
    Bruno and Najlis
Jê/Ge
    Boswood, Davis, Hamp, Wilbert
Juma
    Pease
Mapuche (= Araucanian)
    Fernández Garay*, Salas*
Mataco
    Gerzenstein, Najlis
Mataguayan
    Najlis
Mundurucu
    Crofts, Rodrigues
Nambiquara
    Lévi-Strauss, Price
Panoan
    Key, Loos, Migliazza, Shell, Suárez, Wistrand-Robinson*
Parintintín
    Pease
Quechuan
    Cerrón-Palomino, Levinsohn*, Mannheim*, Orr, Orr and Long-
    acre, Parker, Proulx, Stark, Torero
Tacanan
    Key, Suárez
Toba
    Bruno and Najlis, Klein
Tucanoan
    Ardila, Barnes, Gómez-Imbert, Mountain, Waltz and Wheeler
Tupi
    Boswood
Tupi-Guaraní
    Dietrich, Jensen (Allen A.), Jensen (Cheryl), Lemle, Priest, Ro-
    drigues, Soares and Leite*
Yagua
    Payne (Doris L.)
Yanomama
    Migliazza

Bibliography of Comparative Studies

Ardila, Olga
    1988   "La sub-familia lingüística Tucano-Oriental: Estado actual y perspectivas de investigación." Seminario-Taller: Estado actual de la clasificación de las lenguas indígenas colombianas. Yerbabuena, Colombia, February 1988.

Barnes, Janet
    1980   "La reconstrucción de algunas formas del proto Tucano-Barasano-Tuyuca." *Artículos en Lingüística y Campos Afines* 8:37–66.

Boswood, Joan
    1971   "Phonology and morphology of Rikbaktsa and a tentative comparison with languages of the Tupí and Jê families." Arquivo Lingüístico No. 086. Brasília: Summer Institute of Linguistics.

Bruno, Lidia N. and Elena L. Najlis
    1965   *Estudio comparativo de vocabularios Tobas y Pilagas*. Buenos Aires: Universidad de Buenos Aires.

Cerrón-Palomino, Rodolfo
    1987   "La flexión de persona y número en el Proto Quechua." In *Comparative Linguistics of South American Indian Languages*. Special Issue: *Language Sciences* 9.1:77–89.

Christian, Diana R. and Esther Matteson
    1972   "Proto Guahiban." In *Comparative Studies in Amerindian Languages*, ed. Esther Matteson et al., pp. 150–59. The Hague: Mouton.

Constenla Umaña, Adolfo
    1981   Comparative Chibchan Phonology. Ph.D. dissertation, University of Pennsylvania.
    1985   "Clasificación lexicoestadística de las lenguas de la familia Chibcha." *Estudios de Lingüística Chibcha* 4:1–189.
    1988   "Familia lingüística Chibcha." Seminario-Taller: Estado actual de la clasificación de las lenguas indígenas colombianas. Yerbabuena, Colombia, February 1988.

Constenla, Umaña Adolfo, director and editor
    1983–1986   *Estudios de Lingüística Chibcha*, Universidad de Costa Rica, San José, Costa Rica. (Contains many articles on comparative problems.)

Crofts, Marjorie
    1967   "Notas sôbre dois dialetos do Munduruku." *Atas do Simpósio sôbre a Biota Amazônica* 2:85–91.

Crowell, Tom
    1976   "Comparison of Cinta Larga and Gavião." Arquivo Lingüístico, No. 024. Brasília: Summer Institute of Linguistics.

Davis, Irvine
  1966   "Comparative Jê phonology." *Estudos Lingüísticos* 1.2:10–24.
  1968   "Some Macro-Jê relationships." *International Journal of American Linguistics* 34.1:42–47.
Derbyshire, Desmond
  1961   "Notas comparativas sôbre três dialectos Karíbe." *Antropológica* 14, Boletim do Museu Paraense Emílio Goeldi, Belem, pp. 1–10.
  1986   "Comparative survey of morphology and syntax in Brazilian Arawakan." In *Handbook of Amazonian languages:* Vol. 1, ed. Desmond C. Derbyshire and Geoffrey K. Pullum, pp. 469–566. Berlin: Mouton de Gruyter.
Derbyshire, Desmond C. and Geoffrey K. Pullum, eds.
  1986   *Handbook of Amazonian Languages,* vol. 1. Berlin: Mouton de Gruyter.
  1990   *Handbook of Amazonian Languages,* vol. 2. Berlin: Mouton de Gruyter.
Dietrich, Wolf
  1988   "More evidence for an internal classification of Tupi-Guarani." Manuscript.
Durbin, Marshall
  1977   "A survey of the Carib language family." In *Carib-Speaking Indians: Culture, Society and Language,* ed. Ellen B. Basso, pp. 23–38. Tucson: University of Arizona Press.
Durbin, Marshall and Haydée Seijas
  1972   "The phonological structure of the Western Carib languages of the Şierra de Perijá." *Atti del XL Congresso Internazionale degli Americanisti* (Estratto):69–77.
  1973   "Proto-Hianacoto: Guaque-Carijona-Hianacoto-Umaua." *International Journal of American Linguistics* 39.1:22–31.
Edwards, Walter F.
  1978   "Some synchronic and diachronic aspects of Akawaio phonology." *Anthropological Linguistics* 20.2:77–84.
Gerzenstein, Ana
  1987   "The Chorote language: Three examples of internal reconstruction." *Comparative Linguistics of South American Indian Languages.* Special Issue: *Language Sciences* 9.1 (April):11–15.
Gnerre, Maurizio
  1988   "Jivaroan and Maipure-Arawakan." Paper presented at the 46th International Congress of Americanists, Amsterdam.
Gómez-Imbert, Elsa
  1988   "Problemas en torno a la comparación de las lenguas Tukano-Orientales." Seminario-Taller: Estado actual de la clasificación de las lenguas indígenas colombianas. Yerbabuena, Colombia, February 1988.
González de Pérez, María Stella
  1980   *Trayectoria de los estudios sobre la lengua Chibcha o Muisca.* Bogotá: Instituto Caro y Cuervo, Series Minor XXII.
Greenberg, Joseph H.
  1987   *Language in the Americas.* Stanford, Calif.: Stanford University Press.

Hamp, Eric P.
1969   "On Maxakalí, Karajá, and Macro-Jê." *International Journal of American Linguistics* 35.3:268–70.

Heitzman, Allene
1975   "Correspondencias entre ciertos grupos de fonemas en varios dialectos Campa." *Actas del 39 Congreso Internacional de Americanistas* 5:165–79. Lima.

Hoijer, Harry, Eric P. Hamp, and William Bright
1965   "Contributions to a bibliography of comparative Amerindian." *International Journal of American Linguistics* 31.4 (October): 346–53.

Huttar, George L.
1972   "A comparative word list for Djuka." In *Languages of the Guianas,* ed. Joseph E. Grimes, pp. 12–21. Norman, Okla.: University of Oklahoma Summer Institute of Linguistics.

Jakway, Martha
1975   "Listas comparativas de palabras usuales en idiomas vernáculas de la selva." Lima: Instituto Lingüístico de Verano. Datos etnolingüísticos, Microfiche 4.

Jensen, Allen A.
1979   "Comparação preliminar das línguas Emerillon e Oiampí no seu desenvolvimento do Proto Tupi-Guaraní." Arquivo Lingüístico No. 135. Brasilia,: Summer Institute of Linguistics and UNICAMP.

Jensen, Cheryl
1987   "Object-prefix incorporation in Proto Tupí-Guaraní verbs." *Comparative Linguistics of South American Indian Languages.* Special Issue: *Language Sciences* 9.1:45–55.

Key, Mary Ritchie
1968   *Comparative Tacanan Phonology: With Cavineña Phonology and Notes on Pano-Tacanan Relationship.* The Hague: Mouton.
1988   "Situación actual, tareas y problemas de la clasificación de las lenguas indígenas en suramérica." Seminario-Taller: Estado actual de las clasificación de las lenguas indígenas colombianas. Yerbabuena, Columbia, February 1988.

Key, Mary Ritchie, ed.
1987   *Comparative Linguistics of South American Indian Languages.* Special Issue: *Language Sciences* 9.1.

Klein, Harriet E. Manelis
1979   "Comparative Toba-Kadiweu: semantics and morpho/syntax." Paper presented at the Linguistic Society of America, December.

Klein, Harriet E. Manelis, and Louisa R. Stark, eds.
1985   *South American Indian Languages: Retrospect and Prospect.* Austin: University of Texas Press.

Kondo, Riena W.
1982   "La familia lingüística Guahibo." *Artículos en Lingüística y Campos Afines* 11:37–75.

Larson, Mildred L.
1957   "Comparación de los vocabularios Aguaruna y Huambisa." *Tradición: Revista Peruana de Cultura* 7.19–20:147–68. Cuzco, Peru.
Lehnert, Roberto
1987   "En torno a la lengua Kunza." *Comparative Linguistics of South American Indian Languages.* Special Issue: *Language Sciences* 9.1:103–12.
Lemle, Miriam
1971   "Internal classification of the Tupi-Guarani linguistic family." *Tupi Studies I,* ed. David Bendor-Samuel, pp. 107–29. Norman, Okla.: Summer Institute of Linguistics.
Lévi-Strauss, Claude
1948   "Sur certaines similarités structurales des langues Chibcha et Nambikwara." *Proceedings of the International Congress of Americanists* 28: 185–92.
Levinsohn, Stephen H.
1975   "El Bokotá, el Guaymí, y el Teribe respecto al proto-Chibcha." *Lenguas de Panamá* II. Panama City: Instituto Lingüístico de Verano and Instituto Nacional de Cultura, pp. 3–18.
Loos, Eugene
1973   "Algunas implicaciones de la reconstrucción de un fragmento de la gramática del Proto-Pano." *Estudios Panos* II, Serie Lingüística Peruana 11, 263–82. Yarinacocha, Peru: Instituto Lingüístico de Verano.
Loriot, James
1964   "A selected bibliography of comparative American Indian linguistics." *International Journal of American Linguistics* 30.1 (January): 62–80.
Mannheim, Bruce
1983   "Structural change and the structure of change: the linguistic history of Cuzco Quechua in relation to its social history." Ph.D. dissertation, University of Chicago.
1988   "On the sibilants of Colonial Southern Peruvian Quechua." *International Journal of American Linguistics* 54.2:168–208.
Matteson, Esther
1964   "Algunas afiliaciones de la familia Arawak." *Actas del 35 Congreso Internacional de Americanistas, 1962,* 2:519–25. Mexico, D.F.
1972   "Proto Arawakan." In *Comparative Studies in Amerindian Languages,* ed. Esther Matteson et al., pp. 160–242. The Hague: Mouton.
Matteson, Esther, Alva Wheeler, Frances L. Jackson, Nathan E. Waltz, Diana R. Christian
1972   *Comparative Studies in Amerindian Languages.* The Hague: Mouton.
Migliazza, Ernest C.
1978   "The position of Yanomama and Panoan in South America." Paper presented at the Linguistic Society of America Summer Meeting, Urbana.
1983   "Lenguas de la región del Orinoco-Amazonas: Estado actual." *América Indígena* 43.4:703–84.

Moore, Bruce R.
    1962   "Correspondences in South Barbacoan Chibcha." In *Studies in Ecuadorian Indian Languages: I,* ed. Benjamin Elson, pp. 270–89. Norman, Okla.: Summer Institute of Linguistics.
Mosonyi, Esteban Emilio
    1988   "Familia lingüística Arawak: Colombia-Venezuela." Seminar-Taller: Estado actual de la clasificación de las lenguas indígenas colombianas. Yerbabuena, Colombia, February 1988.
Mountain, Kathy
    1978   "Lista de palabras Swadesh y Rowe." *Artículos en Lingüística y Campos Afines* 4:1–57.
Najlis, Elena L.
    1968   "Dialectos del Mataco." Anales No. 4, Universidad del Salvador, Buenos Aires, pp. 232–41.
    1971   "Premataco phonology." *International Journal of American Linguistics* 37.2:128–30.
    1984   *Fonología de la protolengua Mataguaya. Cuadernos de Lingüística Indígena* 9, Buenos Aires: Universidad de Buenos Aires, Facultad de Filosofía y Letras, Instituto de Lingüística.
Noble, G. Kingsley
    1965   "Proto-Arawakan and its descendants." *International Journal of American Linguistics* 31.3 (July), part II:1–129 (also pub. 38, Indiana University Research Center in Anthropology, Folklore and Linguistics, Bloomington).
Olson, Ronald D.
    1964   "Mayan affinities with Chipaya of Bolivia I: Correspondences." *International Journal of American Linguistics* 30.4:313–24.
    1965   "Mayan affinities with Chipaya of Bolivia II: Cognates." *International Journal of American Linguistics* 31.1:29–38.
    1980   "Algunas relaciones del Chipaya de Bolivia con las lenguas Mayanses." *Notas Lingüísticas de Bolivia* 11, Instituto Lingüístico de Verano.
Orr, Carolina D.
    1978   "Dialectos Quichuas del Ecuador: Con respecto a lectores principiantes." *Cuadernos Etnolingüísticos* 2. Quito, Ecuador: Instituto Lingüístico de Verano.
Orr, Carolyn and Robert E. Longacre
    1968   "Proto-Quechumaran." *Language* 44.3 (September):528–55.
Pardo, Mauricio
    1988   "Grupo Chocó." Seminario-Taller: Estado actual de la clasificación de las lenguas indígenas colombianas." Yerbabuena, Colombia, February 1988.
Parker, Gary J.
    1969–71   "Comparative Quechua phonology and grammar" *University of Hawaii Working Papers in Linguistics* I: 1.1:65–88; II: 1.2:123–47; III: 1.4:1–61; IV: 1.9:149–204; V: 3.3:45–109.

Payne, David L.
    1987   "Some morphological elements of Maipuran Arawakan: Agreement
            affixes and the genitive construction." *Comparative Linguistics of South
            American Indian Languages,* Special Issue: *Language Sciences* 9.1:
            57–75.
    1988   "Una vision panorámica de la familia lingüística Arawak." Seminario-
            Taller: Estado actual de la clasificación de las lenguas indígenas co-
            lombianas. Yerbabuena, Colombia, February 1988.
Payne, Doris L.
    1984   "Evidence for a Yaguan-Zaparoan connection." Workpapers of the
            Summer Institute of Linguistics, University of North Dakota, pp.
            131–56.
    1987   "Noun classification in the Western Amazon." *Comparative Linguis-
            tics of South American Indian Languages,* Special Issue: *Language Sci-
            ences* 9.1:21–44.
Pease, Helen
    1977   "Juma-Parintintín similarities." *Arquivo Lingüístico,* No. 038. Brasília,
            D. F.: Summer Institute of Linguistics.
Pottier, Bernard
    1988   "Tipología de las lenguas indígenas de América." Seminario-Taller:
            Estado actual de la clasificación de las lenguas indígenas colombianas.
            Yerbabuena, Colombia, February 1988.
Price, P. David
    1976   "Southern Nambiquara phonology." *International Journal of Ameri-
            can Linguistics* 42.4:338–48.
    1978   "The Nambiquara linguistic family." *Anthropological Linguistics* 20.1:
            14–37.
Priest, Perry N.
    1987   "A contribution to comparative studies in the Guaraní linguistic
            family." *Comparative Linguistics of South American Indian Languages,*
            Special Issue: *Language Sciences* 9.1:17–20.
Proulx, Paul
    1987   "Quechua and Aymara." *Comparative Linguistics of South American
            Indian Languages,* Special Issue: *Language Sciences* 9.1:91–102.
Queixalós, Francisco
    1988   "La familia Guahibo." Seminario-Taller: Estado actual de la clasifica-
            ción de las lenguas indígenas colombianas. Yerbabuena, February 1988.
Rodrigues, Aryon Dall'Igna
    1980   "Tupi-Guarani e Munduruku: Evidencias lexicais e fonológicas de
            parentesco genético." *Estudos Lingüísticos* III, pp. 194–209. Arara-
            quara, Universidade Estadual Paulista.
    1985   "Evidence for Tupi-Carib relationships." In *South American Indian
            Languages: Retrospect and Prospect,* ed. Harriet E. Manelis Klein and
            Louisa R. Stark, pp. 371–404. Austin: University of Texas Press.
Rodríguez de Montes, María Luisa, ed.
    In press *Memorias del seminario: estado actuel de la clasificacion de lenguas
            indígenas Colombianas.* Bogotá: Instituto Caro y Cuervo.

Ruhlen, Merritt
    1987   *A Guide to the World's Languages, Vol. 1: Classification.* Stanford, Calif.: Stanford University Press.

Shafer, Robert
    1959   "Algumas equações fonéticas em Arawakan." *Anthropos* 54.3−4: 542−62.
    1962   "Aruakan (not Arawakan)." *Anthropological Linguistics* 4.4:31−40.

Shell, Olive Alexandra
    1965   Pano Reconstruction. Ph.D. dissertation, University of Pennsylvania. University Microfilms 66-4648.

Stark, Louisa R.
    1972   "Maya-Yunga-Chipayan: A new linguistic alignment." *International Journal of American Linguistics* 38.2:119−35.
    1975   "A reconsideration of proto-Quechua phonology." *Actas del 39 Congreso Internacional de Americanistas* 5:209−19. Lima.

Suárez, Jorge A.
    1969   "Moseten and Pano-Tacanan." *Anthropological Linguistics* 11.9 (December): 255−66.
    1973   "Macro-Panoan-Tacanan." *International Journal of American Linguistics* 39.3 (July): 137−54.

Torero Fernández de Cordova, Alfredo
    1964   "Los dialectos Quechuas." *Anales Científicos de la Universidad Agraria* 2:446−78.

Waltz, Nathan E. and Alva Wheeler
    1972   "Proto Tucanoan." In *Comparative Studies in Amerindian Languages,* ed. Esther Matteson et al., pp. 119−49. The Hague: Mouton.

Wheeler, Alva
    1972   "Proto-Chibchan." In *Comparative Studies in Amerindian Languages,* ed. Esther Matteson et al., pp. 93−108. The Hague: Mouton.

Wilbert, Johannes
    1962   "A preliminary glottochronology of Ge." *Anthropological Linguistics* 4.2:17−25.

Wise, Mary Ruth
    1986   "Grammatical characteristics of Preandine Arawakan languages of Peru." In *Handbook of Amazonian languages, Vol. I,* eds. Desmond C. Derbyshire and Geoffrey K. Pullum, pp. 567−642. Berlin: Mouton de Gruyter.

Contributors

ANA FERNÁNDEZ GARAY is Assistant Researcher at the Consejo Nacional de Investigaciones Científicas y Técnicas (CONICET), Buenos Aires. She earned the degree "Diplôme d'Etudes Approfondies de Linguistique," Paris V, France. Her publications include "Formación de temas verbales araucanos" (1979); "Rogativas Mapuche" (1982); and *Relevamiento lingüístico de hablantes mapuches en la Provincia de La Pampa* (1988).

JULIAN GRANBERRY is a staff linguist and archaeologist with The Bahamas Archaeological Team, Nassau. His research and published work in these fields has been concentrated on the southeastern United tor for the ongoing Caribbean Handbook Series, published by the Phileas Society (Detroit/Ft. Lauderdale), and volume editor for the *Handbook of Caribbean Peoples* and *Handbook of Caribbean Languages* in that series.

MARY RITCHIE KEY is Professor of Linguistics at the University of California, Irvine. She has published linguistic studies in comparative American Indian languages, sociolinguistics, phonology, and nonverbal behavior. Most recently she has edited *General and Amerindian Ethnolinguistics: In Remembrance of Stanley Newman* (1989), with Henry M. Hoenigswald.

YONNE DE FREITAS LEITE is Associate Professor, Department of Anthropology, Museu Nacional (Federal University of Rio de Janeiro), with a Ph.D. from the University of Texas. Her specialties are Brazilian Indian languages (Tupi-Guarani) and Portuguese phonology. Her publications include "Lingüística e Antropologia" (1975); *Aspectos da fonologia e morfofonologia Tapirapé* (1977); "A classificação do Tapirapé na família Tupi-Guarani" (1982); and "As vogais pretônicas na fala carioca " (in collaboration with Dinah Callou).

STEPHEN H. LEVINSOHN has worked with the Inga people since 1968 and presently is a linguistic consultant to the Inga organization Musu Runacuna. He is an international linguistic consultant with the Summer Institute of Linguistics. His recent work includes *Textual Con-*

nections in Acts (1987), and the editing of *Thematic Continuity and Development in Languages of Malaysia.*

BRUCE MANNHEIM, PH.D. in anthropology and linguistics from the University of Chicago, has taught at Cornell University, the University of Arizona, and the University of Michigan. He is author of *The Language of the Inka Since the European Invasion* and numerous articles on Quechua language, culture, and history. He is currently completing a book on verbal art and cultural transmission.

AURORE MONOD-BECQUELIN is a Director of Research at the Centre National de la Recherche Scientifique, Laboratoire d'Ethnologie et de Sociologie Comparative, Université Paris X. Her main fields of research are Mayan linguistics, South American Indian languages and rituals, and oral tradition (rhetorical structures and ethnopoetics). She is the author of *La pratique linguistique des Indiens Trumai* and numerous articles.

GUSTAVO RODRÍGUEZ is Associate Professor, Institute of Hispanic Philology, Universidad Austral, Valdivia, Chile. His specializations are Hispanic dialectology and general and applied linguistics. His publications include "Linguistic Features of Atacameñan Spanish" (1980–81); "Substratum Effects in Atacameñan Spanish" (1980–81); and *Mother Tongue Methodology* (1983).

ADALBERTO SALAS is Profesor de Lingüística, Universidad de Concepción, Chile, and holds a Ph.D. in linguistics/ethnolinguistics from the State University of New York. His specialties include phonological and morphosyntactical studies on the Chilean languages: Aymara, Rapa Nui (Easter Island), Yamana or Yahgan (Tierra del Fuego), and, especially, Mapuche or Araucanian.

MARILIA FACÓ SOARES is Professor of Linguistics, Department of Anthropology, Museu Nacional (Federal University of Rio de Janeiro). She has studied Guajajara, Asurini, Kokama, Kayabi, and Tapirapé of the Guarani family, in addition to the unclassified Tikuna, which is the subject of her most important publications.

MARÍA EUGENIA VILLALÓN, Ph.D. candidate, University of California, Berkeley, has worked on several anthropology projects for government agencies in Venezuela. She has authored *Aspectos de la Organización social y la terminología de parentesco E'ñapa* and "Network Organization in E'ñapa Society," and is currently researching Panare narrative. She currently teaches in the Department of Anthropology at the Universidad Central de Venezuela, Caracas.

Lila Wistrand-Robinson is Professor of Language/Social Sciences, Southern Baptist College, Arkansas, and holds a Ph.D. in linguistics and anthropology/folklore from the University of Texas. She did fieldwork with the Shapra, Aguaruna, Cashibo (1954–65); and with the Iowa-Otoe (Siouan) of Kansas and Oklahoma (1972–74). She has taught at Kansas State University and Liberty University. Her numerous publications include "A Mandarin Grammar Sketch" (with Ling-Mei Lee-Liang et al.) and *Comanche Dictionary and Grammar* (with James Armagost).

Index

This book has been set in Linotron Galliard. Galliard was designed for Mergenthaler in 1978 by Matthew Carter. Galliard retains many of the features of a sixteenth century typeface cut by Robert Granjon but has some modifications which gives it a more contemporary look.

Printed on acid-free paper.